Combining Rug Hooking & Braiding

Basics, Borders & Beyond

Kris McDermet, Christine Manges, Dianne Tobias

Schiffer Publishing Ltd

4880 Lower Valley Road • Atglen, PA 19310

Dedication

The authors dedicate this book to their families and friends
for the extraordinary support they provided during the writing
of the book and to each other for sustained friendship.

Other Schiffer Books on Related Subjects:
Braiding with Barbara™ /Wool Rug Braiding with a Contemporary Flair.
Barbara A. Fisher. ISBN: 9780764334580. $19.99
Hooked on Rugs: Outstanding Contemporary Designs. Jessie Turbayne.
ISBN: 0764325027. $39.95
Modern Hooked Rugs. Linda Rae Coughlin. ISBN: 9780764326318.
$29.95
Punch Needle Rug Hooking: Techniques and Designs. Amy Oxford.
ISBN: 0764316893. $24.95

Designed by John P. Cheek
Cover design by Bruce Waters

Type set in University Roman Bd BT/New Baskerville BT

ISBN: 978-0-7643-3789-5
Printed in China

Schiffer Books are available at special discounts for bulk
purchases for sales promotions or premiums. Special editions,
including personalized covers, corporate imprints, and excerpts
can be created in large quantities for special needs. For more
information contact the publisher:

Published by Schiffer Publishing Ltd.
4880 Lower Valley Road
Atglen, PA 19310
Phone: (610) 593-1777; Fax: (610) 593-2002
E-mail: Info@schifferbooks.com

For the largest selection of fine reference books on
this and related subjects, please visit our website at
www.schifferbooks.com
We are always looking for people to write books on
new and related subjects. If you have an idea for a
book please contact us at the above address.

This book may be purchased from the
publisher.
Include $5.00 for shipping.
Please try your bookstore first.
You may write for a free catalog.

In Europe, Schiffer books are distributed
by
Bushwood Books
6 Marksbury Ave.
Kew Gardens
Surrey TW9 4JF England
Phone: 44 (0) 20 8392 8585; Fax: 44 (0)
20 8392 9876
E-mail: info@bushwoodbooks.co.uk
Website: www.bushwoodbooks.co.uk

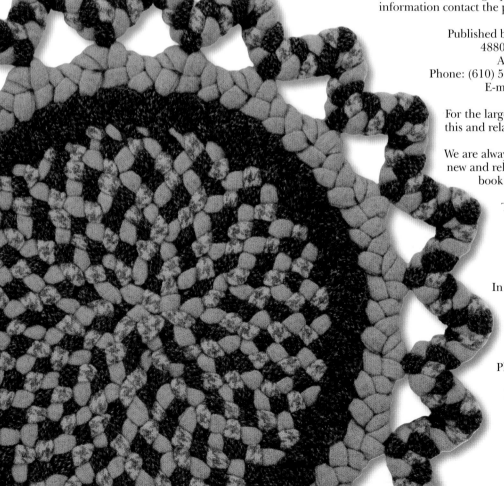

Contents

Acknowledgments

The authors acknowledge the many rug hookers and braiders who have come before us, many of whom are named in this book, with affection and gratitude for keeping these art forms vibrant and rewarding for us and for those who will come next.

1 Introduction

Objectives

The objectives of this book are to:

• Introduce rug hooking and braiding artists to the integration of both art forms, by exploring the creation of combination pieces, using both braiding and hooking as centers and as borders. Combination pieces have both art forms integrated throughout.

• Encourage the use of the hooking and braiding art forms to create pieces other than rugs. Techniques for baskets, wall hangings, table mats, trivets, and bags are discussed and specific projects are described with instructions. "Off the floor" projects invite both the use of a variety of fabrics and the addition of embellishments to create unique pieces.

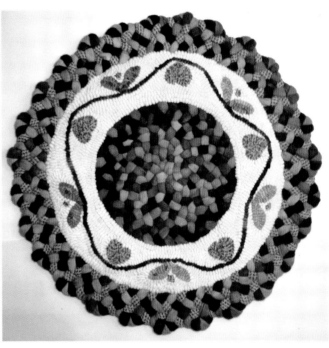

Blue Bonnet Wreath, Kris McDermet. 16" diameter. 2010.
Photographed by Laurie Indenbaum
Note integration of braiding and hooking.

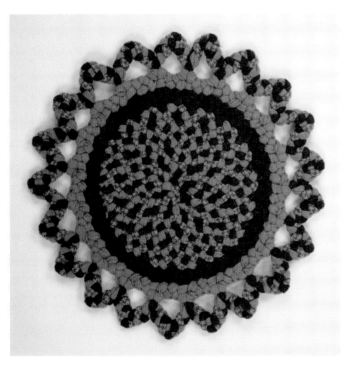

Sage and Shadows, Christine Manges. 16" diameter. 2010.
Note use of fabric and color to set off fancy borders.

Turquoise Bag with Hooked Pocket, Dianne Tobias and Kris McDermet. 16.5" x 12". 2010.
Note integration of braiding and hooking and embellishment of pocket.

5

Historically, when the simplest combination rugs were made, they were hooked pieces with surrounding braids. The braided edges were added to protect the hooking from wear, and to provide a decorative frame.

The two techniques both use wool as their preferred fabric, so they have similar wear characteristics. The same fabric can be used in the hooked and braided portions of the rugs, which further unites the look. Visual interest is created by combining the small loops of hooking with the large loops of braids.

The simplest way to design a combination rug or project is to plan a hooked or braided center, and then add a hooked or braided border. The most basic design presented in this book places a border of straight braids around a hooked center. More elaborate "fancy" borders can be added, in which straight braiding is altered to create a decorative edge. When open spaces are created between the borders and the main piece or rug, these borders are called "openwork." There are many photo examples and instruction for these "fancy borders."

Patterned borders are formed by arranging the dark and light strands of the braids to create designs such as diamonds and rick rack. A number of designs are described with instructions for incorporating them into braided rugs, baskets, and borders.

Multi-strand borders incorporate more than three strands of braiding and can provide an interesting border to hooked or braided centers. Several photographed examples of multi-strand borders are shown.

Hooked borders can be created as well, and then further surrounded by more braids, if desired. The alternation between hooking and braiding can expand the creative possibilities beyond each art form alone. Visit the Gallery, Chapter 14, for fascinating examples of pieces that incorporate braiding, hooking, and fancy braided borders.

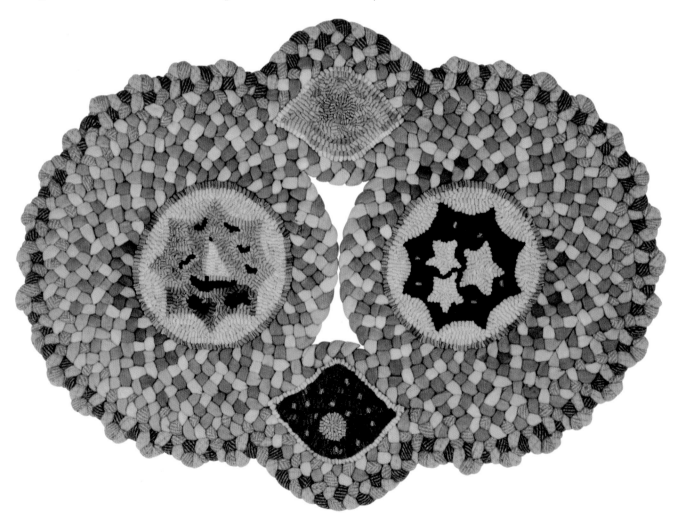

Starry Nights/Sunny Days, Kris McDermet. 24" x 18". 2009.
Photographed by Laurie Indenbaum
Good example of a combination piece, using both hooked and braided techniques with a fancy border.

Blues Heart, Christine Manges.
30" X 33". 2008.
Multi-strand border surrounds
triple-cornered heart.

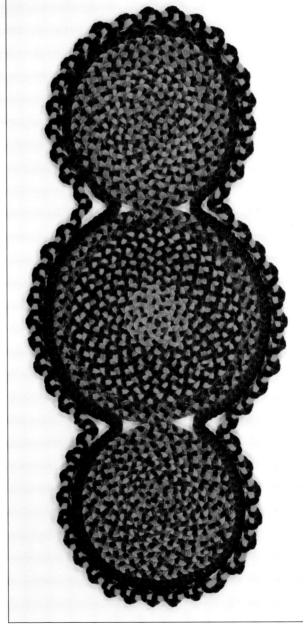

Velvet Table Runner, Dianne Tobias. 38" x 17". 2010.
Use of non traditional fabric to create an "Off the Floor" piece,
using tiny braids and a fancy border.

Organization of the Book

This book is organized into centers and borders and describes how combination pieces can be made with these building blocks. Both hooking and braiding can be used as centers or borders. Rugs and wall hangings can include a combination of centers and borders, either hooked or braided. Borders can be layered, so that a piece of textile art is created by shifting back and forth between techniques.

The beginning portion of this book describes the basics of both hooking and braiding, discussing techniques, terminology, and supplies. Instructions are given for making both hooked and braided centers. Simple centers of various shapes are presented, which can become combination pieces by adding borders.

The latter portion of the book covers more advanced skills, as the techniques for creating both hooked and braided borders are shown. Toward the end of the book, the reader will learn about embellishments and "off the floor" pieces, in which both hooking and braiding are combined to make bags, trivets, table mats and runners, and baskets from wool and other fabrics.

Information about suppliers, hooking and braiding guilds and camps are included at the end.

This book is not intended to provide exhaustive instruction on either braiding or hooking. References for more complete resources are given in the Appendix.

As with many art forms, the skills of both braiding and hooking can be approached in several ways to achieve most of the techniques, depending on instructor and personal preference. In most cases the authors have chosen only one technique to describe an instructional step, and refer the reader to the resource section for other options. The methods shown are not the only ways to effectively braid or hook; however, they have been chosen to most efficiently present the book's objectives.

Some assumptions are made:

• For braiding instruction, only left-opening braiding is presented.
• Only continuous braiding is used to make the braided centers. The one exception is the 9-Loop Center, which is described separately.
• The braided borders are butted, meaning that each row is a complete ring with the end connected to the beginning. Instruction is presented for a butting technique that works well with fancy, openwork borders.
• All hooked centers and hooked borders are finished so that a braided border can be attached.

The combination pieces in this book are mainly composed of hooking and braiding, but other fiber arts such as needlepoint, cross stitch, or wool appliqué can be incorporated. Consider a penny rug with macramé fringe, or a cross-stitched center with an edge of wool tongues. Explore the possibilities!

Historical Perspective

Since about the 1820s, North American women have turned leftover fabric into rugs. With the crafts of weaving, embroidery, quilting, shirring, tufting, hooking, braiding … and others, rug makers used precious scraps of fabric to make rugs for their drafty floors.

It is the essence of human nature to try to create beauty in our surroundings. Even with meager scraps of fabric, early rug makers sought to put colors together in pleasing combinations, to create pictures of personal meaning or significance, or to combine geometric patterns in visually interesting ways. The rug makers used what little they had to make useful and beautiful items.

Small House with Tulips, Helen Jeffrey. 12" x 12.5". 2010.
Photographed by Penelope Athey
Integrated hooking, braiding, and wool appliqué.

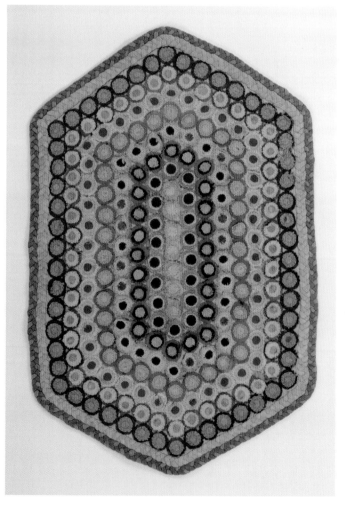

Antique Penny Rug, Artist and Date Unknown.
Owned by the authors.
Note two rows of braided border.

The desire for beautiful surroundings encouraged innovation. For early American women, trained since childhood in the essential skills of needlework, it was easy to combine different crafts to create fancier items. They created crocheted collars with beaded edgings, crazy quilts that not only combined scraps of fabric but also showed off exquisite embroidery, and appliquéd pillows with lacework borders. A needlepoint purse might have had a knotted or beaded fringe or an embroidered pincushion might have had a ruffled edge.

Notice that in the examples given, it was often the border or edging that was a focus for the decoration. Borders, as the frame or setting of a piece, visually define the edges but also evoke the style or importance of the work. As in an art gallery, the viewer is often cued to the apparent importance of the painting by the degree of gilding and scrolled plasterwork on the frame. Paintings, whatever their perceived quality, are enhanced by the perfect frame.

This same principle of a border giving importance and embellishment applies to rugs. Since at least the mid-1800s, edgings have been used to enhance the beauty of simple scrap rugs. These edgings were sometimes made with a craft different from that used in the rug's center. A quote from Stella Hay Rex describes an example, "There is also a quaint and altogether charming old-fashioned custom of sewing rows of braiding around a hooked center."[1]

And later, describing a hooked rug with a braided border made by Mrs. Caroline Erickson, "By using 2 strands of grays from the background … Mrs. Erickson has created such a sense of unity in her rug that the outer part seems but an extension of the center."[2]

In this instance, the braids served as a decorative element to define the border. The braided border also added stability to the hooked edge, which was often the site of the worst fraying due to wear.

SHAKERS

The Shakers are the group most associated with combining borders from other fiber crafts. This interesting group of people, also known as the United Society of Believers in Christ's Second Appearing, practiced communal living and celibacy. They attracted new members by conversion, and by adoption of orphaned children. The men of this group are perhaps best known for their crafting of Shaker furniture, which in its comfort and simplicity has made the original antique pieces quite expensive and often copied. But the women's needlework was also quite famous at the time.

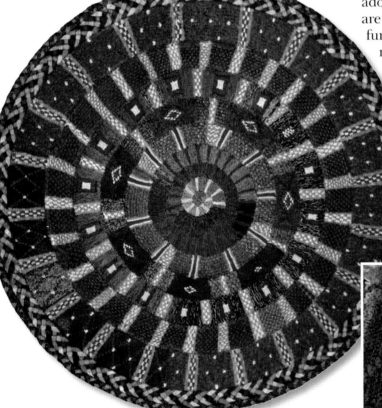

Shaker Knitted and Braided Rug, Elvira (**C**) Hulett (1805-1895). 43" diameter. Hancock, MA, ca. 1893. *Courtesy of Shaker Museum and Library, Old Chatham, NY.*
Vibrant knitted design; multi-strand braided border; final single row of straight braid; denim backing.

Shaker Knitted and Braided Rug, Knitted Border, detail, Elvira (**C**) Hulett. *Courtesy of Shaker Museum and Library, Old Chatham, NY* Intricate detail of a braided and knitted border surrounding a knitted center.

Many different techniques were used by the Shaker women for making rugs during their time of prominence in the 1840s to 1860s. They made knitted, crocheted, woven, hooked, shirred, penny, and braided rugs. In a comprehensive review of Shaker textiles, Beverly Gordon notes when describing a few Shaker knitted rugs, "Like so many other Shaker rugs, they are completed with braided edging."[3]

Sometimes there were borders stacked on borders, creating a level of complexity that was visually fascinating. A famous horse rug at Pleasant Hill Shaker community is described:

> ...the horse itself is in a rectangle defined by encircling scallops ... contained inside nine distinct border rows, eight of which are made of dollars folded in fourths. ... The last border row is a 7-strand braid.[4]

This combination of techniques within one rug was not unusual for Shaker women. "It is common to use one technique in the main part of the rug and a second and possibly third technique in the border."[5]

Shaker Hooked, Knitted, and Braided Rug, Artist Unknown, Hancock, M(A) 46.5" x 33.5". Late 19th Century.
Courtesy of Shaker Museum and Library, Old Chatham, NY
Note three fiber arts are used in this piece. Hooked floral and scroll center; knitted border of a chevron design; and final single row of straight braid.

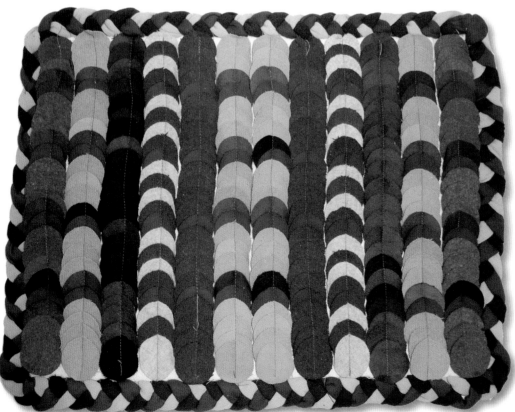

Shaker Dollar Mat, Sister Jennie Wells, Hancock, M(A) 16.5" x 12.5". 1952.
Courtesy of Shaker Museum and Library, Old Chatham, NY
Circles of silver dollar-sized wool attached to a background and sewn like falling dominos with a final braided row.

PENNSYLVANIA GERMANS

Other groups also combined techniques for centers and borders. Early Pennsylvania Germans are known for their beautiful fraktur designs on furniture and hex signs, but they decorated many other day-to-day items. Often when one thinks of Pennsylvania Germans, the Amish come to mind, with their emphasis on living a "plain" life, a life devoid of unnecessary decoration. The Amish, however, were only one of the many groups of Pennsylvania Germans immigrating in the 1600, 1700, and 1800s, and not all of these groups practiced being plain as did the Amish. Other "fancy" sects obviously delighted in the embellishment of everyday items, and have left us their illuminated manuscripts, ornate ceramics, and magnificently carved butter molds. Their rugs, similarly, were as fancy as could be made from scraps.

... after they had acquired the skill to produce a rug, women of a creative bent, not content to go on turning out simple braided ovals and circles, devised variations of the basic idea. On a loosely woven textile base, they arranged braided rondels in patterns. These were combined with hooked-in sections, creating a new type of hand-made rug.[6]

In describing rugs from Berks County in southeastern Pennsylvania, Helene von Rosenstiel notes in *American Rugs and Carpets* that, "Sometimes crochet was combined with knitting, or with knitting and embroidery to create a decorative rug."[7]

Other rugs from Intercourse, Pennsylvania, from the authors' collection, show knitted borders around braided or multi-strand braided rugs. This addition of knitted borders occurred at least as early as the beginning of the twentieth century. These rugs demonstrate the incorporation of multiple techniques into rugs that can be found in this historically immigrant German area.

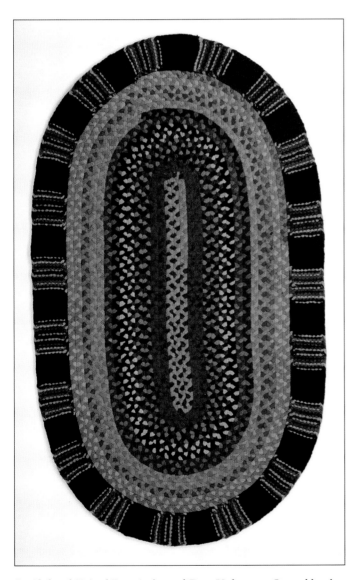

Braided and Knitted Rug, Artist and Date Unknown. Owned by the authors, purchased at an estate sale in Pennsylvania.
Note the use of a black knitted border around the braided center.

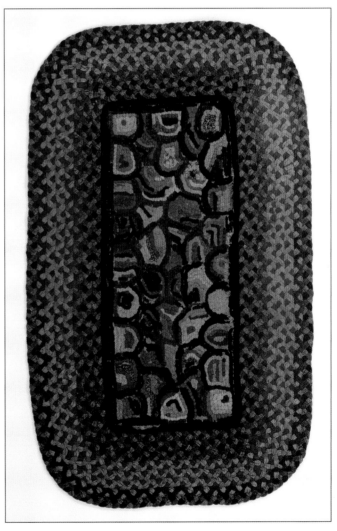

Hooked and Braided Rug, Artist and date unknown. Owned by Vicki Simpson. Found in Winter Harbor, Maine.
Early use of a braided border on a hooked rectangular center.

FORMAL INSTRUCTION BEGINS

The rugs mentioned so far were from distinct communities, in which rug making was taught mother to daughter or friend to friend. In the early 1900s, printed material started to appear that specifically encouraged the combining of techniques, especially in borders. In an undated, early 1900s booklet published by Diamond Dyes, "Practical Directions for Making Sixty-five Mats and Rugs" are given. This fascinating and colloquial little booklet describes techniques for making several combination rugs. A knitted center adds a crocheted border. A braided circle adds a border of tiny braided circles around the outside. One mat combines a crocheted circle with a fringed edge, another mixes braids of 3, 4, and 5 strands. A penny rug has a border of scallops. Another mat is described below:

> Duchess mat—This is a braided silk mat. Make it of very heavy and stiff pieces of ribbon and silk that are too badly spotted and creased to use for any other purpose. Use only strong pieces. The silk strips need not be cut very wide, as they should be folded over old pieces of print or other soft cotton goods. Make quite a fine braid, and sew the same as any braided mat…. Sew deep scallops or points around the mat. Cut these out of some thick cloth,

and make a star in each one with bright colored wool or cotton yarn.[8]

Other authors gave instruction on combination technique rugs as well. A text from 1929 by Lydia LeBaron Walker describes combining hooking and braiding:

> The trefoil or clover-leaf rug is one in which the shape of the rug is of special interest. It is made by joining three round (braided) rugs so that the edge of each touches that of the other two. The space that comes in the center can be filled in with braid sewed to fit the curved opening, or the space may be filled in with hooked-rug work. If the spaces are small, sew hemmed burlap under them and cover with hooked work…[9]

These same general instructions for a trefoil rug were repeated several times in later magazine articles, as well. It is thought that one of these descriptions may have inspired the rug pictured from the authors' collection, which is a rug of six braided circles with hooking in between. A later book by Dorothy Lawless[10] also describes combination hooked and braided rugs, although her book simply details the addition of straight braids around hooked items.

Antique Combination Hooked and Braided Rug, Artist and date unknown. Owned by the authors.
Beautiful use of hooking fills the open spaces between the braided circles.

DEVALUATION

In the late 1800s, American industry had made available machine-made rugs for families to purchase. In the fickle way of human nature, suddenly these rugs were of much greater value than those made by hand. Handmade rugs were considered a "rural" and "country" craft, often associated with poverty and traditionalism rather than innovation and refinement. Whether hooked, braided, hand-woven, or other, these handmade rugs were devalued.

REVALUATION AND ADULT EDUCATION

A variety of factors led to the resurgence of interest in handmade rugs in the first part of the 1900s. First, the Arts and Crafts movement, late 1870s to about 1915 in the United States, renewed the interest in handcrafted items. Second, the deprivation associated with the Great Depression, 1929 to about 1940, made thrift a necessity. Third, two Acts were passed by the U.S. government: the Cooperative Extension Act, and the Work Progress Act.

The Cooperative Extension Act of May 8, 1914, was passed to require funding for State Colleges to provide adult education, by teaching the best techniques in farming and home economics to rural counties throughout the United States. State Colleges were sites for research, distribution of materials, and demonstration of these topics. The Extension Agent traveled to counties throughout the states offering demonstrations.

In the area of Home Economics, there was a revitalization of interest in making rugs at home. Although sometimes the teaching booklets were shared with adjacent states, the agents often created Extension booklets with recommendations specific to their own state, its fashions, and resources. These booklets and the demonstrations of techniques were helpful in keeping rug making alive during the time period from 1914 to about 1960, although each technique was presented singly, with limited suggestions for a mixing of needlework techniques or styles.

Another influential Act was the Works Progress Administration (WPA), which passed April 8, 1935, and was designed to provide jobs and income to millions of Americans living in poverty during the Depression. The WPA projects familiar to most people are the roads, bridges, dams, and airports built by the mostly male workers, but women who headed households were also employed by the WPA. These women were taught to use sewing machines and make bedding, draperies, clothing, etc., for orphanages and other state facilities. In some states, the women became part of rug making projects, and learned skills that they continued to use later. The WPA projects were dissolved in 1943, when World War II eliminated the need to finance the unemployed: men now went to war or worked in war industries, and women filled the former positions of the new soldiers.

The societal and governmental factors listed above that promoted rug making in the first half of the 1900s slowly became less important to the larger populace. Although handmade rugs continued to be made in the second half of the 1900s, they less often used a combination of techniques. As women became a larger and larger portion of the work force, and as inexpensive imports became more widely available, fewer rugs were made by hand.

Early instructional booklets about hooked and braided rugs.

TODAY

Currently, hooked and braided objects are less frequently made because of necessity; if a simple rug is desired, it can be purchased at a local department store, discount store or online. Instead, the techniques of hooking and braiding have ventured into the realm of "Craft" or "Art." Crafters and artists are hooking and braiding because they enjoy fiber and using the traditional skills of yesteryear. Some enjoy learning new techniques that can create a useful object. Some enjoy giving beautiful, hand-crafted gifts, or filling their homes with textile art that complements their antiques.

Although there is historical documentation of combination rugs, as described above, it has been unusual recently to find many rugs that combine techniques. When learning to make a rug today, typically only one technique is learned. The rug maker is a hooking artist, or a braiding artist, or engages in other arts, but these techniques are approached singly. Rug hooking and braiding are not usually combined in one piece.

Recently, there has been a resurgence of interest in rugs that combine techniques. The designs of Kris McDermet are exquisite. Her integration of braids in hooking, and hooking into braids, goes beyond the simple addition of borders. Her combination pieces portray a truly unique enhancement and unify each technique in their beauty. Note the integration of hooking and braiding in *Tear of Sadness / Hearts of Peace*: a braided heart center, then a wide hooked border incorporating many of the same wool colors in a simple yet beautiful design, and ending with several rows of braided borders, both straight and fancy. Christine Manges specializes in creating fancy braided borders for hooked and braided pieces. Building off some of the earliest braided border designs, her decorative edges twist and turn to create fanciful flourishes as the borders to hooked or braided centers. Dianne Tobias' specialty is in adapting braiding and hooking techniques for finer wool and non-wool fabrics. Her pieces are more frequently for "off the floor" locations such as baskets, runners, mats, and trivets, and are often braided with tiny braids, bordered with fancy edgings, and embellished with hooked pockets or decorative beadwork.

Join the authors as we explore the art forms of hooking and braiding, which are beautiful whether used singly… or in combination.

Hopscotch, Kris McDermet. 29" x 34". 2007.
Photographed by Laurie Indenbaum
Geometric design integrating hooking and braiding throughout.

Tear of Sadness / Hearts of Peace, Kris McDermet. 30" x 34". 2010.
Good example of a combination rug, hooking is surrounded by braided center and final border.

1. Rex, Stella Hay. *Choice Hooked Rugs*. New York, New York: Prentice-Hall, Inc, 1953, 91.
2. Ibid., 92.
3. Gordon, Beverly. *Shaker Textile Arts*. Hanover, New Hampshire: University Press of New England, 1980, 111.
4. Ibid., 121.
5. Ibid., 121.
6. Lichten, Frances. *Folk Art of Rural Pennsylvania*. New York, New York: Charles Scribner's Sons, 1946, 184-185.
7. von Rosenstiel, Helene. *American Rugs and Carpets*. New York, New York: William Morrow & Company, Inc., 1978, 34.
8. Nay, Miss A.L. *Mats and Rugs: Art Work, Fancy Work*. Diamond Dyes, undated, estimate 1890-1920. Publisher not stated, 16.
9. Walker, Lydia LeBaron. *Homecraft Rugs*, New York City, New York: Frederick A. Stokes Company, 1929, 50.
10. Lawless, Dorothy. *Hooked and Braided Rugs for Pleasure and Profit*. New York City, New York: Funk & Wagnalls, 1976, 192-195.

Fabric Choices

Overview

Both hooking and braiding started as scrap crafts in America. The fabrics used were simply the remnants of worn clothing, or discarded cuttings from the textile industry. Early rug makers used wool, cotton, linen, or whatever was available, and mixed the fabrics indiscriminately. Velvets, rayon, and corduroy, as well as novelty fabrics have been used in both techniques for rug making. Some beautiful dresser scarves were braided from pieces of silk, and even discarded nylons were used in hooking and braiding.

The rugs that are most likely to have survived from early times are those made from wool. In this chapter, the favorable characteristics of wool for rug making are described, followed by a discussion of other fabric options.

Why Wool?

Wool is the desired fabric for both braiding and hooking. The array of solid colors, tweeds, plaids, etc. provides a rich palette for the braiding and hooking artist. Since wool accepts acid dyes, the color possibilities are endless. Wool wears especially well, and a braided or hooked rug made from wool will give years of use before showing wear. Wool rugs resist soiling and are easy to vacuum and spot clean. Braided rugs are reversible, which adds years to their useful life.

Hooking artists primarily use wool for making rugs, although some are experimenting with other kinds of fabrics and embellishments described later in the book. The richness of wool tweeds, plaids, and hand-dyed designs help to create the desired texture in the finished wall hanging or floor rug. Using the same wool for both the hooked and braided portions of a combination rug or hanging can be very interesting, because each technique retains its own character within the project while providing a blending and unifying effect. This feature is especially true of hand-dyed wool.

Example of hand-dyed wool that can be used in both hooking and braiding. Wool dyed by Nancy Jewett.

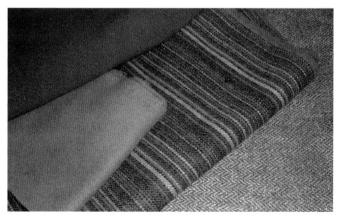

Example of bolt and remnant wool, e.g., solid flannels, stripes, herringbone, etc.

Although wool is the preferred fabric, it has become more challenging to find wool in the quantity, variety, and value desired, especially for large braided rugs. With the advent of synthetic fabrics, 100% wool has become harder to find. Online suppliers have expanded the possibilities, and mills in South America are new sources for wool. A list of current sources of wool for online purchasing is available in the Supplier section of the Appendix.

Wool blends have become more plentiful. If the fabric weight is sufficient and compatible with the other fabrics in the rug design, wool blends with at least 70% wool are considered satisfactory for braiders, although hooking artists still prefer 100% wool. Bolt wool or recycled wool from garments can be identified with the wool trademark, but remnants are usually unmarked as to content. For this discussion, the term wool includes both 100% wool and satisfactory wool blends. Wool weight is measured in ounces/yard but the buyer rarely has this data when buying wool. More often wool is categorized as heavy (coat weight), medium (skirt weight) or light (shirt weight).

Recycled Garments

Although braiding artists find it easier to work with long yardage of 60" wide wool, it is often not possible to find unlimited supply, colors and weaves at a reasonable price for a large project. Recycled garments offer both hooking and braiding artists more variety in wool. Early rug braiders incorporated used garments, often from family members. Recycled wool can be dyed or over-dyed for either hooking or braiding. Stocking some recycled garments in the fabric supply or "stash" can provide a variety of colors and thicknesses of fabric. It is nice to honor the memory of a friend by including a piece of fabric from them in a project. One of the authors strives to use one recycled garment in each of her projects.

Recycled garments should be examined carefully for wear before using and in most cases, washed. If the garment wool is very worn, the final project, especially a rug, may wear unevenly. Braiding strips that are pieced together from recycled garments have many more seams than from remnant or bolt wool. This is not as much of an issue in hooking, where shorter strips are used. Woolen coats, trousers, women's long skirts, especially wrap-around and hip-stitched pleated skirts, yield the best lengths of fabric, especially for braiding. If braiding with heavier wool, recycled blankets can provide long lengths of wool.

Dyeing

An exhaustive description of dyeing is beyond the scope of this book and the reader is referred to the Supplier and Resource sections of the Appendix for good references for basic dyeing.

One related technique is over-dyeing, which is a simple method to tone down strong colors and plaids. A small amount of dark colored fabric, e.g., black, purple, navy, is covered in water and "simmered" in a large pot on the stove until the water becomes intensely colored, usually within thirty minutes. The length of time to keep the darker fabric in the pot depends on the intensity of the colored water and desired change to the lighter wool. The dark fabric is removed and a small sample of the wool to be over-dyed is placed in the water for several minutes until fully wetted, and then compared with the original fabric. If the result is favorable, the remaining fabric can be added to the water until the desired color is achieved. Both the "new" fabric and the fabric that was used to color the water should be simmered in boiling water for thirty minutes to an hour, with about 1/2 cup white vinegar added at the end to set the colors.

Using Other Fabrics

FLEECE

Some braiders have used high quality fleece to make rugs. There is a wide array of colors and patterns available to create a striking rug. An advantage of using fleece is that fleece rugs are washable. Fleece is categorized by weight; it is best to use a mid- to heavy-weight fleece for rugs for durability. Thinner fleece can be used in projects other than rugs, e.g., baskets.

Braiding with fleece uses the same techniques as braiding with wool, but care must be taken in cutting the fleece. There is a stretchy side and a non-stretch side. Cut on the non-stretch side. Fleece stretches more easily with cross-grain cuts (from selvedge to selvedge) than with lengthwise cuts. Because the raw edges naturally fold inward, it makes fleece an easy fabric to fold and braid. A cloth cutter can be used to cut the fabric, although the fiber will dull the cutter faster than wool. A rotary cutter on a plastic quilting mat may also be used successfully.

COTTONS: DENIM, TOWELING

It is possible to braid rugs with cotton, using the techniques described in this book. With thinner cottons, often the fabric is doubled to plump the braid. Although cotton braids up nicely, its stain-resistance is poor and durability is not nearly as good as wool. If used in a high-traffic area, the frequent washings required will wear a cotton rug out within only a few years.

Interesting results can occur by using the wide variety of the vivid blue colors that are available in denim garments or bolt fabric. If recycled denim garments are used, pants and overalls yield the longest fabric strips. A disadvantage of denim is that it is rough and hard on the hands.

New or recycled towels can be cut, folded, and braided into washable rugs. The toweling is soft and fun to braid with, but the amount of debris generated by cutting strips can be unpleasant.

VELVET

Velvet is not ideal for making rugs, but can be braided into interesting table mats and baskets. A cloth cutter or rotary cutter is preferred to tearing because velvet frays extensively, and cutting with the velvet pile down on the cutter is recommended. The shimmering characteristic of velvet—by itself or braided with fine wool—is a special look, especially when braided in narrow strips to make tiny braids.

HOOKING WITH OTHER FABRICS

Hooking artists are pulling loops with all types of fabric, yarns, threads, fleece, denim, plastic, metallic wool-backed fabric, and silk, to mention just a few. If it can be cut in a strip and pulled up through the holes in rug backing, it can be hooked. As with braiding, many fabrics can be hooked successfully, but may not be suitable for a floor rug because they do not wear well with foot traffic.

3 Hooking Basics

Overview

The technique of hooking to produce rugs in America seems to have been common after the 1830s.[1] Although hooked rug historian William Kent initially believed that rug hooking had been introduced from Britain, the British rugs were not apparently made with a hook and were therefore from a different technique.[2] Whatever the origin, rug hooking found its creative birthplace in the New England states and eastern Canadian provinces. Hooking enabled rug makers to transform scraps into creative images with unlimited design potential. Hooked rugs depicted primitive farm life scenes, geometric designs, and images of personal significance, as well as copied the expensive Oriental carpets that were fashionable in the early 1800s.

Interestingly, the popularity of rug hooking was in part due to the 1840s discovery that the burlap obtained from India that was used to wrap imported goods was an excellent backing for rug hooking.[3] After finding a suitable backing, the craft flourished.

Although initially the rug maker was dependent upon her or his own drawing ability to make the rug designs, in the 1860s a woman named Philena Moxley began using copper-inlaid stamping blocks to print rug patterns.[4] Similarly, Edward Sands Frost made stencils for rug hooking patterns out of scrap metal in the late 1860s and 1870s, and sold them both locally and in popular magazines and newspapers of the time.[5] While some view these patterns as a welcome advancement in the beauty and complexity of design that could be achieved in rug hooking, others view the patterns as dampening the rug maker's own creativity and unique vision. Whatever one's opinion regarding patterns, their popularity has continued.

Rug hooking has remained one of the favorite techniques for hand crafted rugs in America. Today rug hooking is practiced as a gracious and lovely art form throughout the United States and Canada, and other countries as well.

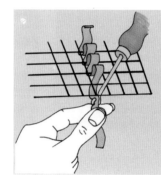

Techniques Discussed in this Chapter

- Hooking Supplies
- Patterns
- Cutting Strips
- Color Planning
- Pulling Loops

Hooking Supplies

The essential supplies for hooking are wool or other fabric, rug backing, a hook, bent handled scissors, a cloth cutter or straight scissors, and a rug hooking frame or hoop. These items may be purchased new or used from hooking and braiding suppliers, online, or at Hook-In auctions or sales.

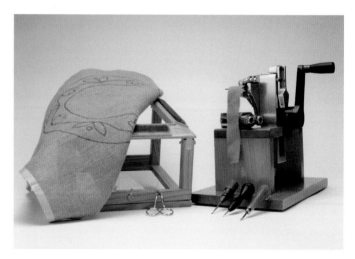

Basic Rug Hooking Supplies. Beginning with upper left corner and going clockwise: rug backing with design drawn with black marker; hooking frame with grippers; Townsend cloth cutter; various hooks; and bent handled scissors.

FABRIC

Wool is the most desirable fabric for rug hooking. Other fabrics may be used especially if the piece is not intended for the floor where durability is important. The wool should be soft and pliable. Open-weave wool can be hooked nicely if cut carefully, but wool that is slightly felted is preferred. Wool may be purchased new from the manufacturer, hand dyed, or recycled from garments. Other fabrics can be used as embellishments.

CLOTH CUTTER

Cloth cutters have interchangeable cutter heads that produce uniform strips ranging from 3/32" to 1/2" in width. Popular brands include Beeline-Townsend, Fraser, and Rigby. If a cloth cutter is not available, hooking strips can be cut by hand with scissors.

RUG BACKING

Hooked strips are pulled through a rug backing. Popular backings include linen, rug warp, monks cloth, Scottish burlap, and hemp because they provide durability and strength.

HOOKS

Hooks are available in a variety of sizes and shapes, with handles made of wood or metal. Handles can be straight, ergonomically bent, or made in a teardrop shape. Hooks are chosen by hand size and comfort. The width of the wool strip for a particular project may also dictate the hook to use, as some hooks are better suited for working with thinner or wider strips. A thicker shank on a hook also opens the rug backing threads wider, making it easier to pull a loop up through the backing.

BENT HANDLED SCISSORS

These special scissors are used to cut off the start and end tails of the hooked strips, so that they are equal in height with the pulled loops.

HOOKING FRAME

There are a variety of hooking frames available, including adjustable floor frames, collapsible frames for travel, swivel, lap or table top frames. Most have gripper strips around the frame to hold the rug backing taut while hooking. A padded cloth bonnet is often used to cover the sharp grippers when not in use. Rug backing may also be tacked to a frame or put in a large wooden hoop.

CHOOSING A PATTERN

Designs are drawn on the rug backing by the hooking artist or they are purchased commercially from a vendor at a rug show, rug hooking store, or from another artist. Designs may be drawn on the rug backing with a black waterproof marking pen. Simple designs such as hooking patterns made from cookie cutters or pictures in children's books can provide an easy design for a first project. It is against copyright regulation to copy another artist's design without permission.

After purchasing or drawing the design, the raw edges of the rug backing are finished to prevent unraveling. The raw edges of the backing are either sewn with a zigzag stitch or bound with a 1" piece of masking tape. Leave a 4" border of rug backing around the outside border of the design edge. This allowance of rug backing is pulled onto the gripper strips of a rug frame or in a hoop.

CUTTING STRIPS

Hooking Cut Widths

Cut	Width (in inches)
3	3/32
4	1/8
5	5/32
6	3/16
7	7/32
8	1/4
9	3/8

Strips are cut to the desired width by hand using sharp scissors, or with a mechanical cloth cutter. Width is determined by personal preference and size of the design. A good width to start with is a #6 strip, which is 3/16" in width. Cut enough strips to start the design but not enough for the entire project, as color choices may change as more hooking is completed.

RUG BACKING ON A HOOP OR FRAME

Place the rug backing design side facing up in the hoop or onto the gripper strips of the frame. It must be stretched moderately tightly to open the holes in the rug backing, making it easier to pull the wool loops up through the holes.

COLOR PLANNING

Color planning is important. Tweeds, plaids, and other textured fabrics help to create an interesting look when paired with hand dyed or solid wool. Complementary colors or dramatic, contrasting colors can be used for equally interesting effects. If a braided border is planned for a hooked center, both the hooked and braided portions should be made with similar or complementary wool.

READY TO HOOK

The design is on the rug backing and ready to hook.

WHERE TO START

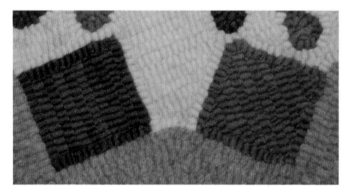

Where to start hooking on the backing and how to proceed are based on personal preference as there is no "one way" to hook rugs. A common approach is to outline a design just inside the black pattern line, then fill in the background of that design. Note here, the blue and green squares have first been outlined and then filled in, using the same colors. The blue square was filled in vertically and the green square diagonally.

A heart is a good example of how to hook a design. It is important not to make the design bigger than printed on the rug backing. Remember to hook inside of the black pattern/design lines.

This photo and the diagram of hearts show a variety of directions that the hooking can take to fill in design elements.

PULLING LOOPS

1. Hold the wool strip in the left hand underneath the rug backing between the thumb and index fingertips.

2. Slide the hook through one of the holes that is to the inside of the black pattern line, moving from the front to the back of the rug backing. Grab the strip with the hook.

3. Pull the beginning end of the strip up through a backing hole and leave this end in place, higher than the desired loops.

4. Slide the hook in an adjoining or nearby hole, and pull a loop up and away from you. Avoid twisting the strip. Repeat these steps.

For more detailed instruction, see rug hooking references in the Resource section of the Appendix.

Once a strip length has been hooked or another color is needed, pull the finish end up above the loops. Cut the beginning and finish ends off at the same height as the loop height, using bent handled scissors.

Hooking is a series of beginning strip ends, loops, and finish ends. The pressure of the loops against each other helps to keep the loops from coming out, which is especially important if the piece will be walked on. Generally the height of the loop is based on personal style; however, loops are often pulled to the same height as the strip width.

Pull the loops up through the hole in the rug backing towards the direction of the last loop hooked if using the same piece of wool. If the loop is pulled away from the last hooked loop, it may pull out. The loops should be moderately packed but it is important that the hooking does not look like a series of mountains and valleys. This could be caused by over hooking or under hooking an area. Even tension helps to keep the hooked loops in place. As with braiding, maintaining even tension comes with practice. The background can be hooked horizontally, vertically, or in a more free form, random design. Some find they can hook in all directions without moving the frame, but others may need to move the frame to hook in another direction. Both are correct.

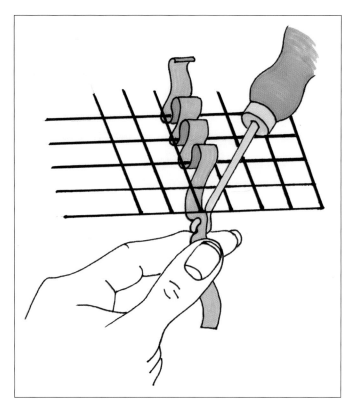

Pulling Loops

HOOKING THE BACKGROUND

One common approach is to outline all of the hooked designs with the background color and then fill in the spaces of the background left between the outlining. Here the heart has been outlined with the beige and white as have the inside and outside borders of the hooking closest to the braid.

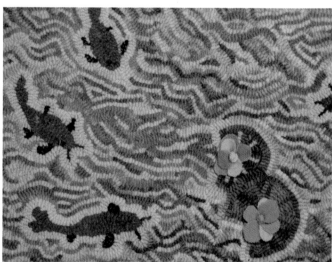

Background hooked directions may be vertical or horizontal, or may be random to simulate moving water, rays of the sun, or the swirling of the wind.
In this photo note the multi-colored blue green water surrounding the fish.

The light background hooked strips follow the outline of the hooked leaf and 9-Loop Center designs.

1. *The Needle Arts: a Social History of American Needlework.* Time Life Books, Alexandria, Virginia, 1990, p. 121
2. Ibid., p. 121
3. Von Rosenstiel, Helene. *American Rugs and Carpets: From the Seventeenth Century to Modern Times.* William Morrow and Company, Inc., New York City, New York, 1978, p. 41.
4. Ibid., p. 42.
5. Ibid., p. 43.

4 *Hooked Centers*

Overview

This chapter provides instruction for making hooked centers, which can become the centers of chair pads, table mats, wall hangings, or floor rugs. Although traditionally hooked rugs were primarily oval or rectangular in shape, hooked centers can be made in any size or shape. They can be made as small as coasters, and as large as room-sized rugs; they can be made shaped as diamonds, circles, stars, or flowers.

In the 1800s, if hooked centers were surrounded by braids, they were usually surrounded simply by one row of straight braid. Occasional examples exist of several rows of braided edging, but these are uncommon. The single braid was typically added only to stabilize the edges of the hooking, and not with any particular artistic plan.

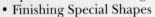

Techniques Discussed in this Chapter

- Blocking the Hooked Center
- Padding and Lining the Hooked Center
- Finishing the Edges in Preparation for Attaching Braids
- Finishing Special Shapes

Lamb Chair Pad, Kris McDermet.
15" diameter. 2006.
Photographed by Laurie Indenbaum
Note that the edge of the hooked center uses the same wool as in braided border. One strand of white in the border complements the hooked center.

In present times, hooked centers are being combined with braids in ways that go beyond simple straight braid borders. Hooked centers can be surrounded by braids in repeating patterns. Hooked round centers with braided borders can be linked to form a table runner, or hooked squares can be made in a grid alternating between hooked and braided squares. Hooked centers do not need to be the classic shapes described above. They can be shaped as irregularly as leaves or coastlines, and still be finished in such a way that more braids or other borders can be attached. Multiple small hooked shapes can also be made, and attached to each other to form a larger center, or spaced around a center as a border.

All of the hooked centers described in this chapter are hooked using the techniques and instructions described in Chapter 3, Hooking Basics. This chapter reviews how to finish the hooked centers in preparation for attaching braids as borders. The hooking must be padded and lined to achieve the same height as the surrounding braids because braids are "taller" than most hooked loops.

Since one of the goals of this book is to encourage experimentation with combining the techniques of hooking and braiding, traditional methods for finishing a hooked piece *without* attaching braids are not presented in this book. For those finishing techniques, see Rug Hooking Resources in the Appendix.

Sea Foam, Kris McDermet. 39" x 48". 2004.
Photographed by Laurie Indenbaum
Hooked centers and hooked triangles fill in the open spaces created by the joined braided circles.

Designing a Hooked Center

Before specific instructions are given for hooked centers, think about the following approaches to design.

A hooked center can be any shape. It must be finished with at least one row of braid to cover the edges of the hooking, padding, and lining. Once a row of braid has been attached, a variety of smaller hooked shapes can be made to surround the center motif. These smaller hooked shapes also need to have at least one row of braid attached before lacing them onto the larger hooked center.

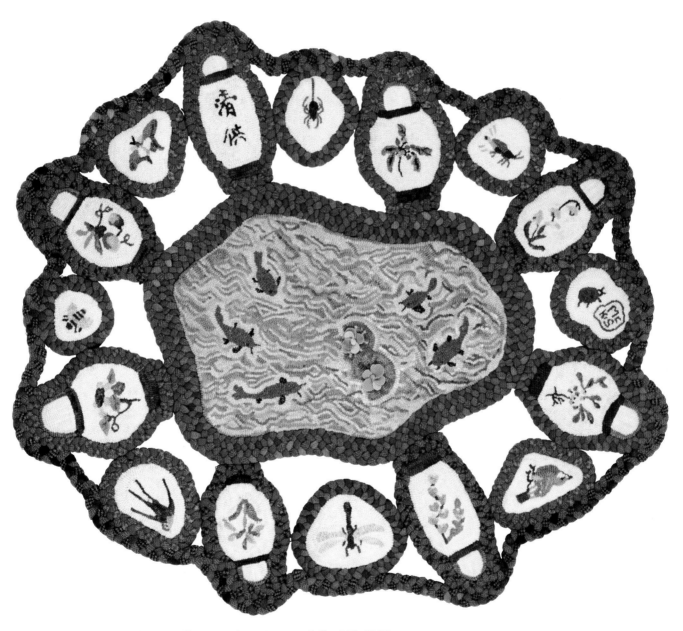

Peaceful and Quiet Offerings, Kris McDermet. 34" x 39". 2006.
Note multiple shaped hooked centers, each surrounded and interlaced by braid. *Photographed by Laurie Indenbaum; Designs used with permission, Chinese Brush Painting Studio by Pauline Cherretts, 1997, Barnes & Noble.*

Experiment with designs and colors. To help in the design process, use colored paper to make cut-outs of the shape envisioned for the center, and then try cutting out different shapes to go around this center. Use either the same motif as the center, or try different motifs. For instance, experiment with hearts spaced around the center, or maybe a combination of hearts, diamonds, and triangles. The smaller hooked designs might tell a story about the center, or they might just be complimentary shapes.

Use some of the ideas below to explore designs for your hooked centers.

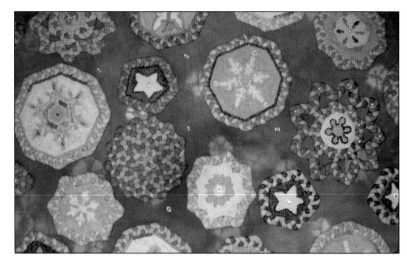

Small hooked or braided centers, surrounded by one row of braid, can be sewn onto a piece of background fabric to simulate falling snow.

Lettering, such as the word February, can be hooked into the center, to become part of the story. Decide on the style of letters, leave enough space between the letters for the background hooking, and hook the letters.

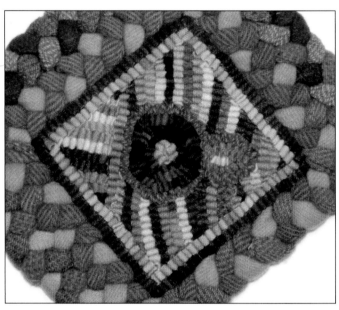

A hooking pattern can be both geometric and curved.

A hooking pattern can be a geometric shape.

A hooking pattern can be a combination of very simple designs such as hearts and stars.

BLOCKING

If the hooked piece lies flat, it may not need to be blocked. However, if it curls up or appears bumpy, blocking will improve the overall look by smoothing out the hooking. Place the piece on a hard protected surface, with the design side down. The surface should be large enough for the entire piece. A floor can be used, if it is protected. Wet and wring out a washcloth, and set an iron to High with Steam. Place the washcloth over the hooking and press for 5 seconds. Repeat as needed until the hooked piece is uniformly smooth. Completely dry flat before proceeding.

PADDING AND LINING

If the hooking is part of a combination piece, it needs to be padded and lined to even the height of the hooking and braiding. Making the heights of the hooking and braiding equal assures even wearing and a more finished appearance.

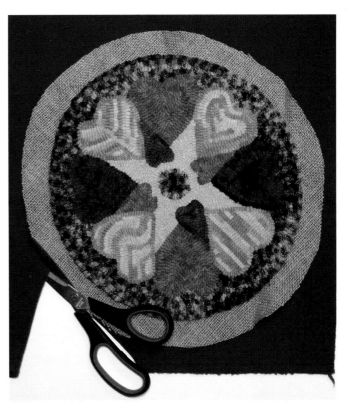

2. Cut a piece of thin wool suiting fabric the same size and shape as the rug backing. This fabric will become the finished underside or lining of the hooked piece. Any color will work, but it looks neater to see black, or a color found in the hooking, as in this photo.

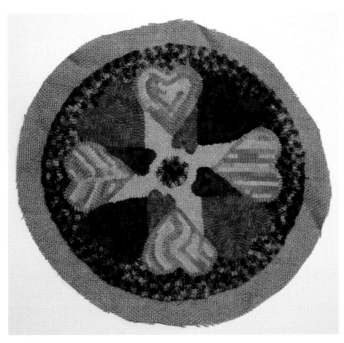

1. Cut around the hooked piece 1-1 1/4" beyond the last hooked row. The outside edge of the rug backing does not need to be reinforced by sewing; leave the cut edges of the rug backing unfinished.

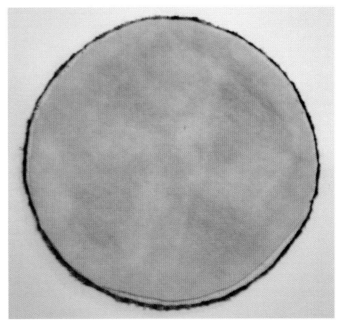

3. Cut a piece of cotton, wool or polyester quilt batting 1/8" smaller than the finished hooked piece. The thickness of the batting sheet depends on the thickness of the braids. Stack the hooking, padding, and lining to see if their height matches the braids. If the height does not match, add or subtract batting to make them approximately equal.
The rug backing has been finger pressed to the back of the hooked piece.

4. Layering: Layer the piece in the following fashion: wrong side of finished hooked piece, batting, and thin wool lining. Pin the three layers together using large safety pins or diaper pins at the following locations around the piece: 12 and 6 o'clock, then 3 and 9 o'clock. Make sure that the outside row of hooked loops is standing up straight and not folded down.

Place more pins if needed to keep the lining flat and evenly distributed around the hooked piece. Don't place the pins close to the outside edge of the hooking as room is needed to turn under the lining.

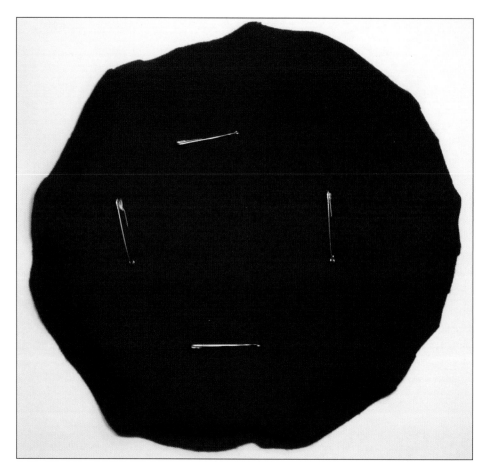

5. Folding and Sewing: Begin to turn under the lining so that the excess is folded around the batting. With matching thread, whip stitch the folded edge of the lining to the thin rim of the rug backing visible next to the edge of the hooked loops. The stitches can be about 1/2" apart. Do not worry too much about the appearance of the whip stitches, as they will be covered when a braided border is attached.

It is important not to stretch the wool lining fabric or to sew it too tightly. Try working on finishing the edge in 2" increments: finger press the rug backing, fold the lining and sew as above for a 2" area before moving to the next 2". The 3 layers should lie flat. If there is any cupping, take off the lining, loosen, and sew again. The padded and lined hooked center is now ready to have a border of straight braid attached, which is described in Chapter 8, Borders.

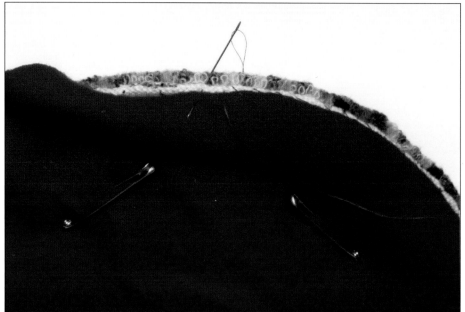

Special Shapes

Special shapes do require finishing in a slightly different way since there may be points, as in a hexagon or an inverted "V," as in a heart. The padding and lining are cut using the above techniques but the corners or points require more attention. When folding the rug backing and lining around outside

Sunny Days, Kris McDermet. 8" Diameter. 2009.
Photographed by Laurie Indenbaum
Adding a straight braided border to a hooked center is the best place to begin learning techniques to make a combination rug, combining hooking and braiding. One row of braid protects and hides the edges of the padded and lined hooked center, and frames the center so that it can stand alone or become the center for more hooked and braided borders.

corners, such as a square, the corners do not need to be mitered; they are simply folded along one edge, then folded again when turning under the next edge. If the corners appear too bulky, cut out some of the excess lining or rug backing fabric, and refold. Sew the layers together as in the instructions above, being careful to maintain sharp angles at the corners, as in the hexagon shown in the photo at right.

Inside curves or corners, such as the upper 'V' of a heart design, or inner curve of a scalloped pattern, are handled differently. Ease cuts will need to be made in the rug backing and lining to keep the layers flat. Make multiple small cuts around a curve, or one diagonal cut to the point of a corner, to fold the layers and keep them flat. The cuts can be made 1/8" to 1/4" from the outside row of hooking. It is better to cut too little with the first cut than too much. This is described in more detail with photos in the Chair Pad Project, Chapter 12.

The hooked hexagon center with its sharp corners may require more manipulation in the lining, folding, and sewing of the layers.

5 *Braiding Basics*

Overview

Although braiding is an ancient technique, the use of scrap fabrics to create braided rugs is thought to be a purely American invention. The earliest known mention of a braided rug is found in the records of Essex County, Massachusetts, from 1827, when a Miss M. Locke of Andover was awarded $2.00 at an agricultural show for: "a Rug of braided rags, very pretty...." [1]

Since that era, braiding has continued to be one of the favorite techniques for making hand-crafted rugs in America. Its popularity has persisted because of the simplicity of the technique and the rugs' practicality and durability. New England states were particularly prominent in maintaining the craft to protect against cold and drafty floors. New England states also

Techniques Discussed in this Chapter

- Braiding Supplies
- Preparing Fabric for Braiding
- Enclosed End Start
- Named Parts of a Braid
- Making a Practice Braid
- How to Splice Lacing Thread

benefited from the prevalence of woolen mills in this region, where scraps and remnants were given away or sold cheaply.

Braiding has progressed from its purely utilitarian beginnings to become an art form. Stunning braided pieces now are displayed on walls instead of floors.

Braiding Supplies

The essential supplies for braiding are simple: fabric, lacing needle, darning or tapestry needle, and lacing thread to connect the braids. Other supplies and equipment listed below are optional; they may make braiding easier, but are not essential. Most if not all of the items described below can be bought either new or used, or may be found in the house used for another purpose. More expensive, optional items, such as cloth cutters and sewing machines, can be found reasonably on websites such as eBay. As discussed in an earlier section, wool is the desired fabric, although other fabrics may be used.

Braiding Supplies.
Basic Rug Braiding Supplies. Beginning on the left and going clockwise: antique bird clamp; wool winder; cloth cutter; cotton splicing lacing thread; leather finger thimble; braidkin, clothespin; hemostat; needle-nose pliers; Vari-Folders®; flat table clamp.

LACING NEEDLE

Also called a braidkin, the lacing needle is flat with a curved, pointed tip that can easily be pulled between the braided loops. The lacing thread is loaded through two eyes at the lacing needle's square end. Some additionally "lock" the lacing thread by throwing the end under the loop of thread between the two holes in the braidkin; see the end of this chapter, where loading and splicing lacing thread are diagrammed.

LACING THREAD

There are several lacing threads used by braiders. The most popular are cotton splicing thread and waxed linen. The advantage of splicing thread is that it does not need to be knotted from one piece to another. The end of the old thread is threaded into the beginning of the new thread piece, locking it in place. See instructions at the end of this chapter. Cotton splicing thread is available in sizes 7, 8, and 9, with the smaller numbers having smaller diameters. They are available in several neutral colors.

Waxed linen is knotted with an overhand knot and its ends buried; see Hand Sewing Techniques in the Appendix. The wax can leave a visible residue on the loops. Waxed linen is also available in several colors.

DARNING OR TAPESTRY NEEDLE

A semi-blunt needle with a large eye is useful for piercing fabric, when starting a knotted length of lacing thread, and for joining one length of cotton splicing thread to another. #16 or #18 tapestry needles are commonly used.

SCISSORS

Should be sharp for cutting threads and fabric.

CLOTH CUTTER

A cloth cutter is not necessary, as most fabrics with high wool content tear easily and accurately on the fabric grain. A cutter can be useful when preparing a wool blend fabric that does not tear easily, or when using a wool fabric that has a loose weave that pulls or frays when torn. Cloth cutters are manual, with an adjustable strip size up to 2", which accommodate most braiding widths. Popular brands include Rigby and Fraser. A less expensive alternative to a fabric cutter is a quilter's rotary cutter and mat.

BRAIDING STAND OR CLAMP

Although not necessary, most braiders prefer to secure the braid in a clamp or stand to create tension when braiding. Clamps can be flat and spring-loaded, or hold the braid with a saw tooth holder and attach to a table. Stands are more portable since they are free-standing. If neither is available, braiders are creative

and use heavy books or other items to weight the braid and provide the desired tension.

Braiding Stand, showing Vari-Folders® and wool strips.

SAFETY PINS

An assortment of several sizes of safety pins is useful when marking areas of a project for butting, or for starting a braid. Diaper pins are especially handy because they are so sharp, and are a good size for anchoring folded strands to start braiding.

PINS

Straight pins with colored balls or colored flat heads are useful for marking the increases in braid loops around curves, so that future increases can be evenly spaced.

SEWING MACHINE

A sewing machine is useful for enclosing ends to start a braided project, and for sewing on additional strips diagonally. A sewing machine is not necessary, however, as a strong hand-sewn backstitch can be used in lieu of machine stitching. Several hand sewing stitches are described in the Hand Sewing Techniques in the Appendix.

THIN NEEDLE-NOSE PLIERS OR HEMOSTAT

These instruments are useful for turning the ends of the Enclosed End Start right side out, for pulling fabric under loops in butting or tapering, for reforming/reshaping braid loops after butting, and for twisting any tweaks back into shape.

BRAID-AIDS® AND VARI-FOLDERS®

Braid-Aids® are metal cones that help fold the wool strips for braiding. They are bought in packages of 3, one for each strip, and can be used for thinner fabric or narrow strips, e.g., 1.5". They may make braiding easier for people with hand weakness. They are optional; some braiders prefer to use them, while others do not.

Vari-Folders® are similar to Braid-Aids®, but accept wider strips, up to 2.25".

MARKERS

Marking pens can be used to mark where color changes should occur, or to mark the cutting line in the Enclosed End Butt. Although safety pins or dressmaker's tacks can be used for these tasks, it is much quicker to mark the sites with a marking pen. Black or red markers can be used on light-colored fabrics; Sharpie® metallic silver markers are best for marking dark fabrics.

RULER

A small 6" sewing gauge ruler is useful for measuring and cutting fabric widths to tear into strips. The movable gauge assists in correct measurement.

WOOL WINDER

Wool winders assist in winding wool strips quickly and efficiently. Five inch diameter rolls or smaller are easiest to work with when braiding.

RUBBER BANDS

Rubber bands are also used to roll up strips for strand management. Traditionally, the "right" side of the fabric faces outward on the roll. Shorter lengths of fabric do not need to be rolled as described.

Braiding Basic Techniques

STRIP PREPARATION

First, the fabric must be cut or torn into strips. A basic strip size for wool is 2", although there are reasons to cut fabric wider or narrower. Different strip widths can result in interesting "looks," as in tiny braid projects, see Chapter 9.

For a practice braid, make a 2" wide cut in each of 3 fabrics along a straight edge, and see if the strips tear cleanly. The fabric can be torn either lengthwise

or crosswise, but if the fabric has a stretch in one direction, avoid cutting or tearing with the stretch. Try to use 3 fabrics of similar weight, e.g., thickness of the fabric.

If the fabric(s) cannot be torn, use one of the following to cut 2" wide strips: a cloth cutter, a quilter's rotary cutter and mat, or scissors

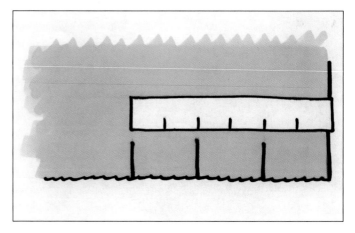

Shows a ruler laid across the end of the fabric. Cuts have been made every 2" to mark where to tear the wool into strips.

FOLDING THE STRIPS

There are 2 commonly used methods of folding the raw edges of the strip inward while braiding.
- Finger Folding
- Braid-Aids® or Vari-Folders®

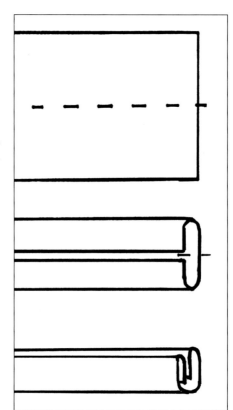

Finger Folding. The raw edges of each strip are folded into the center, and folded inward again while braiding, so that no raw edges are visible. Seamstresses may see the similarity to making double-fold bias tape. Although the hand movements necessary for making these folds while braiding can be frustrating to the novice braider, if one simply keeps at it for about 30 minutes, the natural rhythm of braiding sets in and it becomes quite simple. See below for other finger folding techniques that lead to plumper strands for braiding.

Some braiders prefer using Braid-Aids® or Vari-Folders® to the finger folding method. They fold the edges into the center tightly while braiding. They are placed onto the strip before it is sewn to another strip, and they slide down the strip as it is being braided, making folds as they slide. It is a matter of preference regarding how close to hold the braiding cones to the working braid; some braiders have them close, in their hands; some have them just below their hands, a few inches away.

Vari-Folders® have a moveable tab which adjusts the fabric tension for braiding.

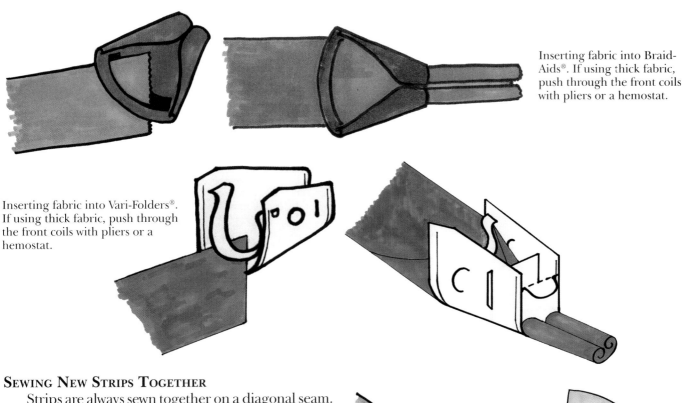

Inserting fabric into Braid-Aids®. If using thick fabric, push through the front coils with pliers or a hemostat.

Inserting fabric into Vari-Folders®. If using thick fabric, push through the front coils with pliers or a hemostat.

SEWING NEW STRIPS TOGETHER

Strips are always sewn together on a diagonal seam. With the strip held vertically, right side up, the seam should go from the 8:00 o'clock location to the 2:00 o'clock location in order to be hidden while braiding.

Place the old and new strips' right sides together at right angles. The strip on the right should be face down on top of the other strip, as above. Sew with a double or triple seam on the sewing machine, or hand sew with a backstitch. Trim the seam to 1/8".

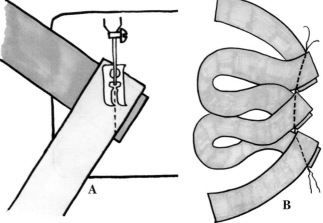

Sewing Multiple Strips by Machine.
Lay the end of the old strip right side up coming from the upper left of the machine. **(A)** Lay a new strip right side down across the old strip, perpendicular to the old strip, so that it drapes across the lower left of the sewing area. Sew the seam forward, reverse, then forward again. Do not lift the presser foot, nor remove the fabric. Find the end of the newly added strip and flip it once, right side up. Position this end so that it is now coming from the upper left. **(B)** Lay a new strip face down on top of the other strip. Sew as before, and continue.

STRIP MANAGEMENT

When braiding, long strips entangle. It is efficient to take the time to roll the strips up before braiding. Make the rolls no larger than about 5 inches in diameter, or the rolls will catch on each other too much while braiding.

Some braid with 1 or 2 strip rolls but keep the 3rd strand short, sewing on new strips as needed while braiding. The short strip is easy to pull through any tangles in the ends.

DIFFERENT FABRIC WEIGHTS

Wool is available in several different weights. It can be found thin enough to be suitable for blouses, or thick enough to be horse blankets. The best weights for braiding are in between these extremes. The best weights for braiding are "skirt weight," which is medium weight, or "coat weight," which is heavy weight. Tiny braids successfully use thinner wool because the strips are cut in much narrower strips.

It is important to keep the 3 loops of the braid equal in appearance, whether the 3 fabrics are of equal or different weights. If one strand's loops are noticeably larger or smaller than the other two strands, the braid will appear lopsided. If the project is a rug, the surface will be uneven and not wear as well. The goal is for a pleasing braid with equal height and plumpness of the folded strips.

There are several adjustments that can be made to keep the loops equal. First, thicker fabric can be cut more narrowly than the other fabrics, and thinner fabric can be cut wider. At times, a thin fabric can be completely doubled over and used as a double-thickness strand.

Over-folding is another technique that can be used when the strips are different weights. The result is a thicker loop of the lighter weight fabric. See diagrams to right which contrast normal folding with over-folding techniques.

(A) Standard 4-Fold Technique for Folding Strips. Fold both edges in to the center, then fold in half.

(B) Over-fold or 5-Fold Technique. The first fold from the left crosses over the center, then the right edge is folded to the center. The strip is then folded in half.

(C) 6-Fold Technique. Fold a strip in half. Fold the raw edges inward, then the folded edge over the raw edges.

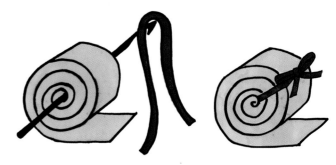

Rolling up a Strip and Hooking a Tie through the Center.
Roll up a strip, use a crochet hook to pull a thin length of waste fabric through the center of the roll, and tie it around the outside of the roll. As the thin length becomes loose around the roll, it can be re-tied.

Rolling a Strip around a Rubber Band.
Place the end of the strip in the center of a rubber band, and roll tightly, keeping the outer edge of the rubber band on the outside of the roll of fabric. If the rubber band is loose, knot it.

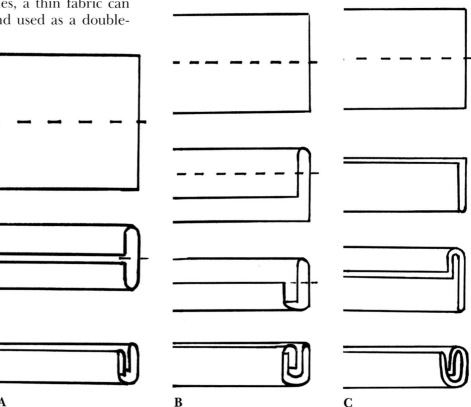

A   B   C

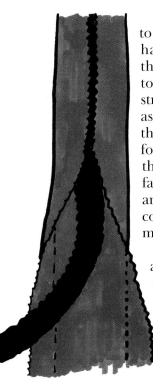

Strips can be "faced" or "stuffed" to increase bulk. A thin fabric can have waste scraps placed along the lengthwise center of its strips to "plump" it to match the other strands. The scraps can be as narrow as 1/4" to as wide as the full width of the strip. Try to use the same fabric for stuffing strips as for braiding; if the braid becomes worn, the same fabric will show through the worn area. If the waste wool is a lighter color and there is wear, it will be more noticeable.

There are no firm guidelines as to how wide or narrow to cut the strips of stuffing material. It

simply requires experimentation, with the goal of having approximately equal loops of braid throughout the piece.

Getting Started

ENCLOSED END START

The Enclosed End Start is one of several possible ways to start a continuous braid. The authors have selected this technique because of its simplicity, and because the skills learned here will be used, with modification, in the butting technique shown in a later chapter.

1. Start with 3 different strips of fabric for the practice braid. If planning to use braiding cones, place them on each strip now.

Stuffing a Strip to Make It Plumper.
Lay the scrap of fabric inside the folds before braiding.

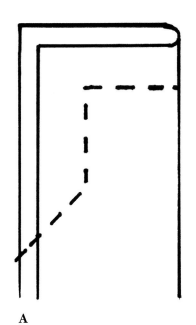

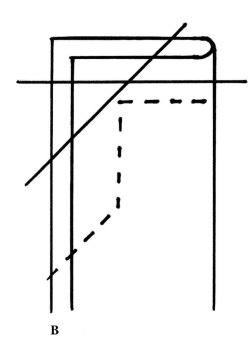

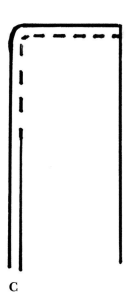

A   **B**   **C**

1. Enclosed End Start.
(A) Fold the end of each strip right sides together lengthwise. Start sewing at the fold, about 1/4" from the top raw edge. Sew a distance just a few threads wider than the width of a folded strip. Reverse the stitching, and come forward again to the same place in order to reinforce the seam. Make a sharp right angle turn by lifting the presser foot and turning the fabric with the needle down. Sew along the side of the raw edge about 1/2". The seam can either end here, or some choose to veer off to end the stitching. If hand stitching, use a narrow backstitch.
(B) Clip the raw edges at the end seam to 1/8". Clip closely at the corner with a diagonal cut. Do not trim the side seam.
(C) Turn the sewn strips right side out by using a hemostat or pliers to grasp the inside seam at the end and help turn the strip. Push the corners outward with the hemostat or pliers.

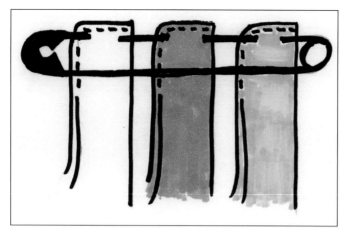

2. Placing Enclosed Ends on Start Pin.
Using a large safety pin, pierce each folded strand very close to the sewn end so that the open folds are facing left.

START BRAIDING

Braiding is simply the sequential crossing over of three strips of fabric after folding in the raw edges. Once folded, the strips are called folded strands. The crossing of the strands is done by "throwing" the right-most strand over the center strand, then the left-most strand over the center. While braiding, the folded edges are kept to the left at all times. When looking at the sides of the braid, the right side has smooth edges, and the left side has folded edges. In this book, all instructions are given for left-opening folds.

Make sure that the folded edges are staying to the left; the smooth edges to the right. Cross the folded strands "high" on the braid so that it is firm, not loose, and not too tight, either. If there are long loops and the braid flops over, it is too loose. If the braid is hard to bend, it is too tight.

After braiding a few inches, consider placing the end of the braid in a table or floor clamp to add stability and tension while braiding. When needing to pause in braiding, place a clothespin, or other clip, to secure the ends and prevent unraveling.

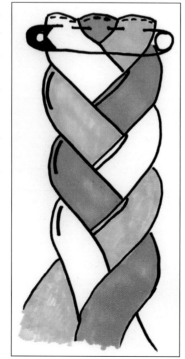

Making a Braid.
Bring the right-most strand over the middle strand and into the center. Bring the left-most strand over the middle strand and into the center. Repeat.

Practice braiding for at least 20 inches. Make sure that the loops are even. When comfortable with the basic technique of braiding, start with the easiest shape: an oval braided center, Chapter 6.

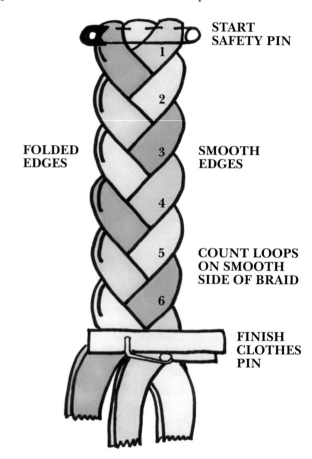

Named Parts of a Braid

LOADING A BRAIDKIN

The braidkin lacing needle is perfectly designed for slipping between braided loops.

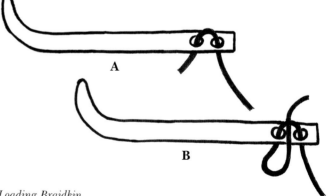

Loading Braidkin.
(A) Cut lacing thread and insert the thread up through the 1st hole and down through the 2nd. The thread can be almost doubled for lacing; shorten the tail by pulling the thread back through the holes.
(B) Some choose to "lock" the thread by throwing the end through the loop between the braidkin holes. While lacing, when the long tail starts to be caught in loops, loosen it by pulling back on the locked thread between the loops.

SPLICING LACING THREAD

Cotton splicing thread is hollow, so its ends can be tunneled inside each other and locked like a Chinese monkey puzzle. The advantage of splicing ends is that no knots are made, so no ends need to be buried.

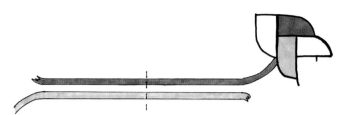

2. Cut a new length of lacing thread at least 36" long. Lay the ends, as above. The dashed line in the center indicates the point where each short end of thread is inserted into the long end.

1. When the end of a piece of lacing thread is reached, take the braidkin off. Free up at least 6" of thread, unlacing if needed.

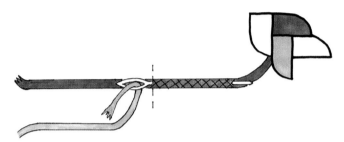

3. Thread a tapestry needle with the short end of the new thread, and tunnel it into the old thread for at least 2".

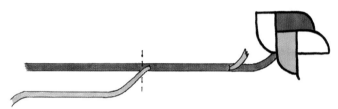

4. Often the tunneled end has a tail that is very long. Pull the tail of the new thread back until only 1/2" is showing, as above.

5. Thread a tapestry needle with the short end of the old thread, and tunnel it into the long end of the new thread for at least 2".

6. Trim both ends. Thread the other end of the new thread into a braidkin, and resume lacing.

1. Little, Nina Fletcher. *Floor Coverings in New England before 1850*. Old Sturbridge, Inc., Sturbridge, Massachusetts, 1967, p. 32.

6 Braided Centers

Overview

This chapter provides instruction for several braided shapes which can become centers for fancy braided borders or for hooked borders. Oval, round, square, rectangular, and heart-shaped braided centers are discussed with specific instructions for each shape. All of the shapes start with an Enclosed End Start, as described in Chapter 5. All of the centers are "continuous," meaning that they start in the center of the shape and spiral outward. The shapes are ended either with a taper for rounded shapes, or with a blunt ending for right-angled shapes, such as squares and rectangles. After the taper or blunt ending, most braiding artists add one butted row before attaching any further hooked or braided borders. The techniques presented in this chapter build on each other and on techniques presented in the Braiding Basics, Chapter 5.

Techniques Discussed in this Chapter

- Oval Center
- Round Center
- Square Center
- Rectangle Center
- Heart Center
- Tapering
- Blunt Ending

Oval Center

OVERVIEW

The oval is the classic shape of a braided rug and, along with the round shape, is the best shape for beginners to learn the basics of braiding. It is a shape that is easy to place in a room as a floor rug, and can be made in sizes as small as a doormat to as large as a room-sized rug. The oval is used for stair treads, for dresser scarves, and as the base for tote bags and some baskets.

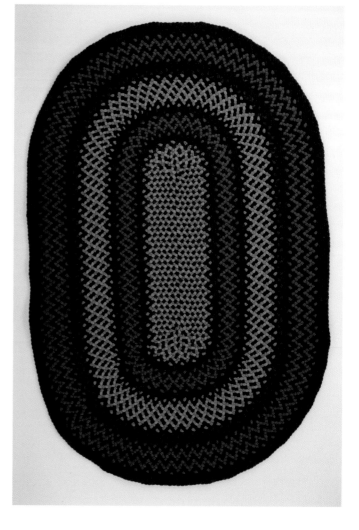

Moss and Mauve, Christine Manges.
4'2" x 6'4". 2008.
Continuous oval braided rug.

38

There are several different methods for starting a braid, lacing the center line, and braiding around the first two sharp corners. The techniques that the authors present here were chosen because they are adaptable to fancy borders, discussed in Chapter 8. The Resource section in the Appendix includes excellent references for instruction in alternative techniques.

DEFINING PARTS OF THE OVAL CENTER

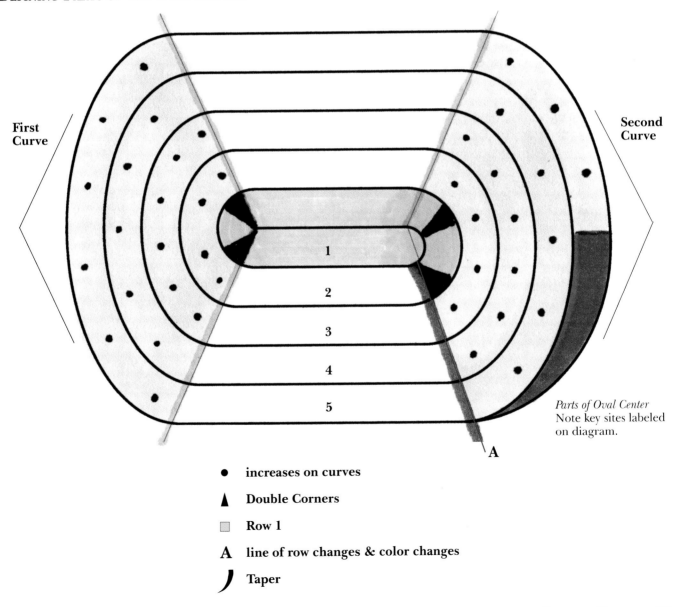

First Curve

Second Curve

1
2
3
4
5

A

Parts of Oval Center
Note key sites labeled on diagram.

● increases on curves

▲ Double Corners

▢ Row 1

A line of row changes & color changes

❩ Taper

SIZE PLANNING FOR AN OVAL RUG

To make a rug of a particular size, the length of the center row must be calculated. The formula is:

Length – width + 1"/foot = Length of Center.

For example, if a 2' x 3' rug is planned, then 3' minus 2' equals 1', plus 1" per foot. The length of the center row would be 1'1" or 13".

Another example is a planned 5' x 9', oval rug. 9' minus 5' equals 4', plus 1" per foot. The length of the center row would be 4'4".

The extra inch per foot of center row is necessary to allow for shrinkage of the braid during center row lacing. With each added row of braid, the width and length of the entire oval grow in proportion, until the project reaches the planned size.

BRAIDING THE FIRST ROW

1. Start: Prepare an Enclosed End Start as described in Chapter 5. Place 3 strands on the Start Safety Pin. Start braiding with the right strand: right, left, right, etc.

2. Braiding the First Side of Row 1: Make a straight braid of the length calculated above under Size Planning.

3. Making the First Turn by Braiding Two Double Corners: The braid needs to reverse direction and travel back along the length already braided to make the first row. If one were to take a straight braid and turn it back, the corner would turn upward and never lay flat. To make the hairpin turn in the braid and keep it lying flat, 2 double corners are necessary.

Remove the braid from its table or floor clamp, if one is being used, because it is not possible to make corners well while the braid is being held straight.

4. Make a double corner by braiding two loops on one side of the braid before bringing another loop, the crossover loop, from the other side. A double corner can be made to curve in either direction, but at this site for the oval shape, it must bend to the left by braiding Right, Right, Left (RRL). See diagram below.

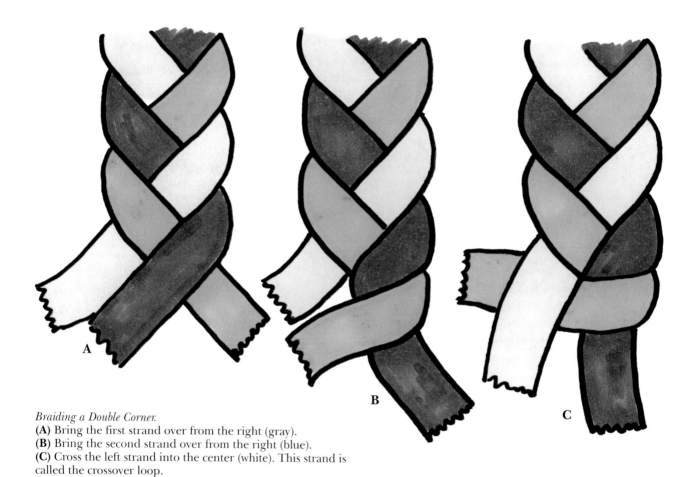

Braiding a Double Corner.
(A) Bring the first strand over from the right (gray).
(B) Bring the second strand over from the right (blue).
(C) Cross the left strand into the center (white). This strand is called the crossover loop.

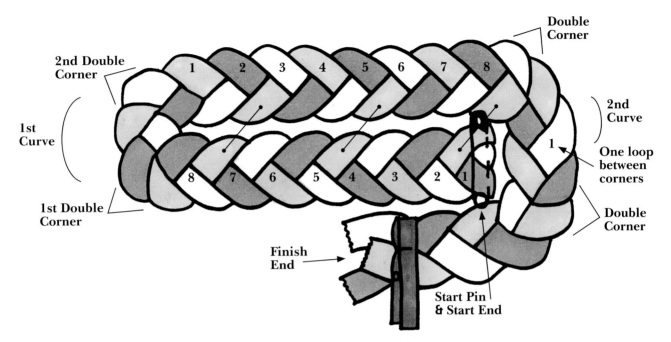

Loop Counts and Double Corners in the First Row of an Oval Center.
This diagram illustrates steps 1-7, specifically the 2 double corners at the first curve, 2 double corners at the second curve separated by a loop, and matching loop counts on either side of the center row. Note that the light blue loops match up across the center.

The "left," the crossover loop, is pulled firmly to make the corner sharp. Immediately follow this first double corner with a second one: Right, Right, Left (RRL). Resume straight braiding.

5. After a few inches more of straight braiding, put a clothes pin on the end of the braid and examine the 2 double corners. The braid should have a sharp turn back toward the Start. If the turn is very loose, unbraid back to the corners and re-braid the crossover loops more tightly.

6. Braiding the Second Side of the First Row: In order for the oval center to be symmetric, there must be an equal number of loops on both sides of the first row. Count the loops on the first side of the braid, starting with the smooth side loop in the Start Pin. Count down to the first double corner, but do not include either of the double corner loops. The result is the number of loops that should be braided on the other side of the braid after the first 2 double corners. See diagram, above.

Braid the determined loop count to make the second side of the first row.

7. Completing Row 1 by Braiding around the Start: Braid the second turn, which curves around the Start, by braiding the following: braid a double corner Right, Right, Left (RRL); then 1 smooth loop: right, left; then another double corner: (RRL).

Braid straight for a few inches and place a clothespin on the ends of the braid.

Note: a frequent mistake when counting loops before making a corner is to braid the number of smooth side loops, then immediately start making a corner, so that the last loop of the counted loops is the first loop of the corner. This makes the counted loops short by one loop. To avoid this mistake, always remember to separate the counted loops and the corner by one loop on the left. Note on diagram above that loop 8 is separated from the double corner loops by one loop on the left.

At this point, the braids are ready to be laced together. No more double corners are needed for the rest of the oval center; the braiding is straight from here to the end.

CENTER ROW LACING

Center row lacing is different from lacing anywhere else on the rug. At this location only, a braid running in one direction is laced to a braid running the other direction. At all other points on the rug, the braid is laced to other braids going in the same direction.

There are several methods for lacing the center row. Some simply sew the two braids together with sturdy thread, catching loops on the inside center by piercing the fabric loops with a needle. More commonly, a lock-stitch known as reverse e-lacing is used. It is called reverse e-lacing because the lacing thread travels in a script "e" sequence in reverse. For instructions on e-lacing, see references by Norma Sturges and Verna Cox in the Resources section of the Appendix.

The center row lacing method that is presented here is called "shoe-lacing" because the loops are laced from side to side down the center, with 2 "shoe laces" of lacing thread, similar to lacing shoes. Each thread goes back and forth to catch every other loop, alternating with the other lacing thread. This technique was chosen because it is also used, with a modification, in one of the fancy borders. The earliest

reference the authors have found to shoe-lacing is in Dorothy Parks Putnam's 1960 edition of *Beautiful Braiding*[1], although it is possible that shoe-lacing was described earlier elsewhere.

SHOE-LACING

1. Cut a long, 3' length of lacing thread. Thread one end with a braidkin lacing needle, and the other end with a tapestry needle. When lacing with a tapestry needle, lead each lacing stitch with the eye end, not the point, to slide more easily between the loops.

2. Lay the braid vertically so that the First Curve is at the 12 o'clock location, and the Second Curve is close to the 6 o'clock location. Note that the loops along the center are going in different directions: the loops on the center right are slanting upward to the left, and the loops on the center left are slanting downward to the right. The loops should pair up on the diagonals. One "matching set" will have identical fabric loops; the other two will not, as seen in the earlier diagram of braiding the first row.

3. Anchor the Lacing Thread for Shoe-lacing. See the diagram below, which shows how the shoe-lacing begins by lacing the top 3 loops counter-clockwise.

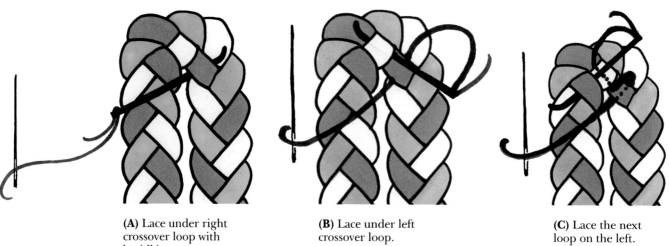

(A) Lace under right crossover loop with braidkin.

(B) Lace under left crossover loop.

(C) Lace the next loop on the left.

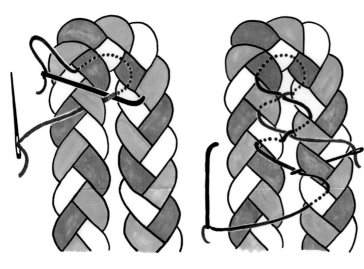

4. The two lacing threads are passed alternating left and right, lacing every other "eyelet" loop, as with shoe laces. The thread passing to the right must go UNDER a left-crossing strand, diagram on left; the thread passing to the left must go OVER a right-crossing strand, diagram on right, so that the lacing thread does not show between loops.

Shoe-lacing alternates between tapestry needle (pink thread) and braidkin (brown thread).

5. Repeat these passes until the only set of paired loops unlaced includes a loop in the Start Pin. Tie the lacing threads together tightly between the braids. Bury the shorter end under 3 loops and cut it close to the braid. All further lacing is done with one needle only.

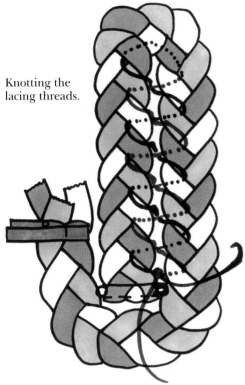

Knotting the lacing threads.

LACING AROUND THE START

1. Lacing around the Start:
Load the long end of the lacing thread into a tapestry needle. Lace the loop on the right that pairs with the loop in the Start Pin; lead the pass with the eye of the tapestry needle.

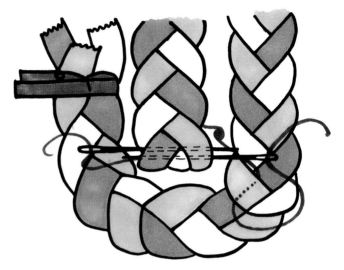

2. Sewing the Start:
Drive the needle point through all 3 strands as close to the Start Pin as possible, driving the thread from the open edges side to the smooth side of the braid. Remove the Start Pin. Turn the needle and drive it back again, starting and ending close to the original path.

3. Continuing to Lace around the Start:
Switch to a braidkin lacing needle. Lace the thread under the Start End's folded edge loop, then under the center loop of the curving braid, between the crossover loops.
Lace the smooth edge loop of the Start End, then the next loop of the new braid after the 2nd crossover loop. Pull tightly to create a "nesting" of the Start End into the 2nd Curve.

REGULAR LACING ON THE STRAIGHT SIDES

1. Turn the braids so that the Second Curve is to the right; the First Curve is to the left. This position is always used for lacing on a new braid, with the "rug" or base braid further away and the new loose braid close. The rug-side braid is called the "base braid;" the braid being laced on is called the "new braid."

Regular Lacing on the Straight Sides: When the braidkin is on the bottom (**A**), it drives the thread up under the next loop and into the space between braids. When the braidkin is at (**B**), it drives the thread down under the next loop and into the space between braids. Every loop is laced, alternating side to side, from base braid to new braid.

2. After lacing under each loop, pull the thread forward to make it fairly tight, then back to hide the thread between loops. Do not pull the thread so tightly that it distorts the braid, nor leave the thread so loose that it shows between loops.

The forward-then-backward pulls on the lacing thread are critical for two reasons. First, lacing thread should not be visible on either side of the rug. The proper tension, as described above, tucks the thread in the valleys between loops. Second, the forward-then-backward pulls tighten the lacing thread, so that there are no loose spaces between braids.

3. About every 5 to 8 loops, pull the thread very firmly to make sure there is no looseness in the lacing.

LACING AROUND CURVES

With knitting or crocheting, increases in the stitch count must be made to keep additional rows flat around curves. The same principle applies to braids: increases in the loop count must be made on the curved ends of the oval. If too few increases in loops are made, the piece will curve upward like a bowl. If too many increases are made, the piece will have ruffled edges.

To make an increase, skip a loop on the new braid and lace the next loop to the base braid instead. By skipping loops, 2 loops of new braid are effectively laced to 1 loop on the base braid, and the loop count is increased. See diagram below.

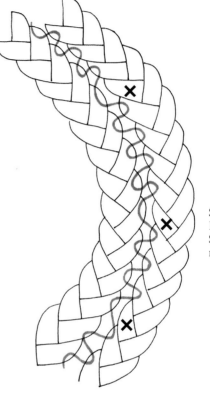

Skipping Loops to Make Increases: Skipped loops are marked with "X."

INCREASING TIPS

Remember when increasing:

• With an oval, the number of increases must be kept equal on both curves of the oval. If one side has more increases than the other, the piece will become egg-shaped rather than nicely oval.

•An increase is never made on the straight sides of the oval, only on the curved ends. Note that the straight sides become longer as the piece grows.

•Every loop of the base braid is always laced, only the new braid has skipped loops.

• A very rough estimate is that about 6 increases are needed on each curve per row, after the first couple rows. This estimate works most of the time, but every 4 to 6 rows, no increases will be needed at all to maintain a nicely curved, flat rug.

• If braiding a design, to keep the pattern of colored loops the same on both straight sides, make increases on the First Curve that are a multiple of 3. See Design section later in this chapter.

Did Not Increase and Should Have:
Note lacing thread is visible because no increase was made and should have been. Green loop of new braid was laced and should have been skipped.

Increased/Skipped Loop:
Note lacing thread is not visible because proper increase was made. Green loop of new braid was skipped and tweed loop was laced.

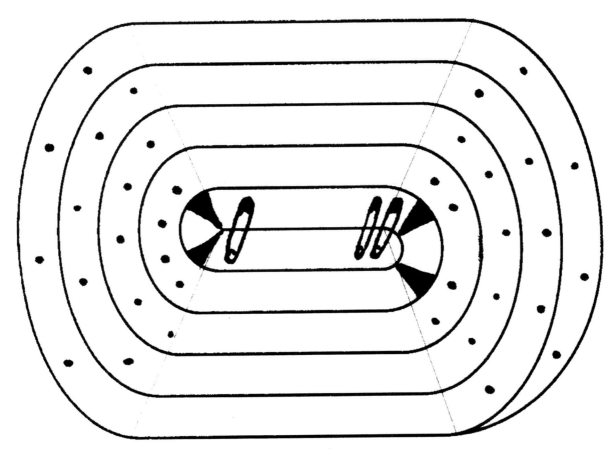

Marking and Matching Increases on Curves:
To mark an increase, place a headed pin in the base braid loop next to a skipped loop or increase. To make sure the increases match on both curves, put one safety pin at the center of the First Curve and two safety pins at the center of the Second Curve. Within each row, the First Curve is encountered first (1 safety pin) and the Second curve is encountered second (2 safety pins).
Make sure that the number of increases (count the headed pins, shown here with dots) on the Second curve matches the number of increases on the First Curve for each row.

COLOR CHANGES

Color/fabric changes are done at about the 2 o'clock location on the piece, or roughly adjacent to the Start. It is easiest to make one color change at a time; two color changes are easier than three. Making more than one color change at the same time and location in a continuous rug makes a dramatic and often unwanted visual effect.

Try to avoid color changes in early rows of the center. A general recommendation is that the first 1/5 to 1/3 of the oval center's width remains one block of color.

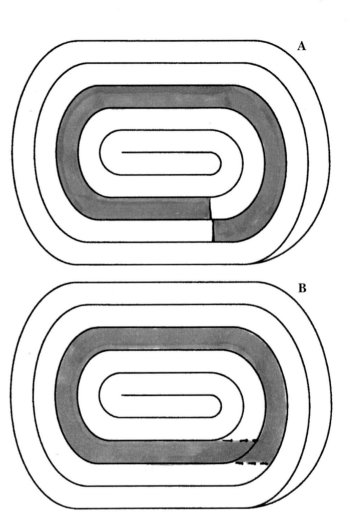

Color Change Site on Row 3:
(A) is made too far down on the curve; it is placed too far onto the straight side. This site makes the color change have an unattractive stair step effect.
(B) shows the color change in the proper site, hiding the color change just where the curve ends. It gives the illusion of being an oval ring.

COLOR CHANGE INSTRUCTIONS

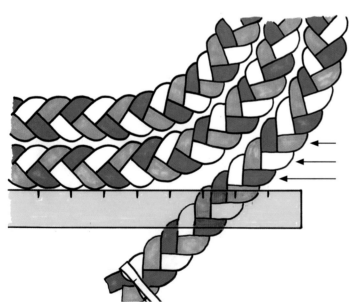

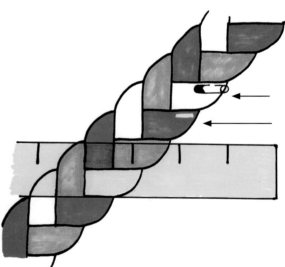

1. Choosing Loops for Color Change.
Lace the braid until a couple inches before the approximate color change site, making any needed increases. Place a yardstick or ruler along the straight side of the base braid below the color change site.
The color change should occur on the outside of the new braid and just before the edge of the yardstick. The arrows indicate the 3 loops that are good options for where a color change could occur.

2. Marking Loops for Color Change.
A small safety pin or marker can be used to mark the upper outer corner of the loop which will have a new color attached. Select a marker pen that shows on the loop color. Choose black or red for light fabrics; metallic silver for dark fabrics. Draw a short line in the upper outer portion of the selected loop, just as it emerges under the previous loop. The blue loop above is marked with metallic silver marker. If a pin is used, pin into only one layer of fabric.

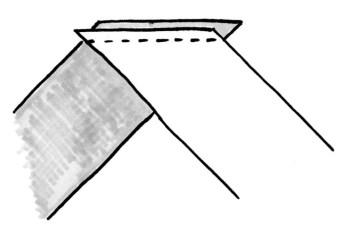

ENDING THE OVAL BRAIDED CENTER

Oval braided centers are finished off with a tapering braid before adding a hooked or braided border. When holding the Second Curve vertically, as in the diagram below, the taper is performed by narrowing the width of the braid over the 12 to 3 o'clock location. The tapering technique is explained at the end of this chapter.

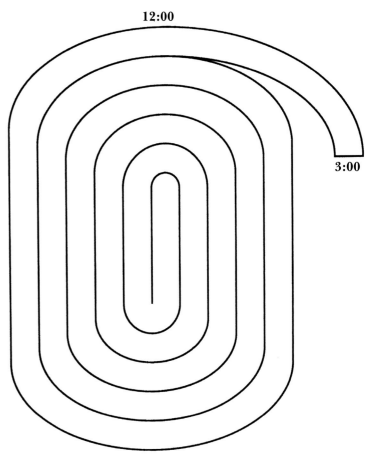

3. Cutting Strips for Color Change.
Unbraid a few inches. Open the strip right side up so that the marker line or safety pin is easily visible. Lay the new strip right side up under the old strip, as drawn. Cut both strips, right side up, from 2:00 to 8:00 o'clock location, exactly across the marker line.

Ending the Oval in Preparation for a Taper:
Lace the last row of braid up to the 12:00 position, then continue a braid of normal width until it fits easily around the remaining curve to about 3:00. Put a clothespin on the braid and leave it loose.
Instructions for tapering are found at the end of this chapter.

4. Sew on New Strip for Color Change.
Flip the new strip over so that the right sides are together, with raw edges matching. Machine stitch or backstitch by hand, 1/4" below the cut edges. Trim the seam to 1/8", and re-braid the strip.

Round Braided Center

OVERVIEW

Round braided rugs are classic. Along with ovals, they are the most frequently braided shapes. Many braiders start by making a round chair pad or decorative table mat for under a lamp or houseplant. Round rugs provide a useful center for anchoring a seating arrangement in a large room.

More innovative work with braided rounds connects them in long rows for table mats or hall runners, or spaces them equally around a large central circle for a flower shape. See Chapter 8, Bordering Challenging Shapes.

Braided rounds can be combined with hooking, such as a hooked border around a braided center to make a chair pad, wall hanging, or floor rug. Hooking can fill in the spaces between joined braided rounds in either curved diamonds or a curved triangle shape, depending on the arrangement. Braided rounds are also a good base for many of the fancy braided borders presented later.

> **Techniques Discussed in this Section**
>
> • Starting a braided round
> • Spacing increases
> • Color changes

> **Prior Techniques Needed for Round Center**
>
> • Enclosed End Start
> • Double Corners
> • Increasing

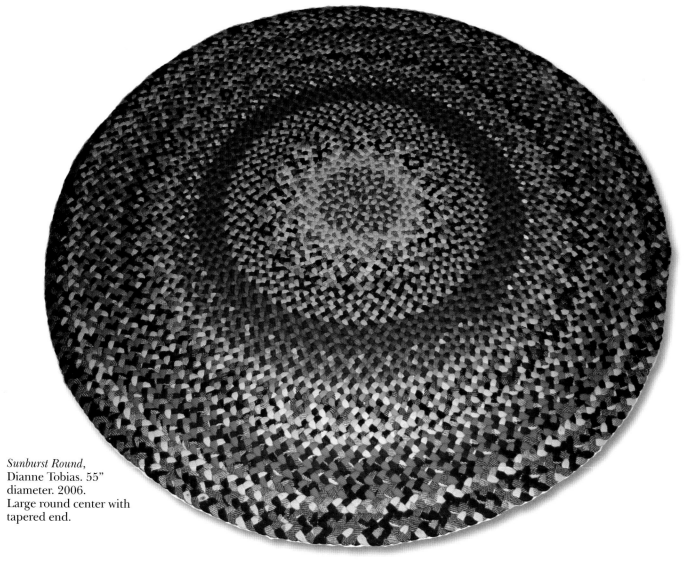

Sunburst Round,
Dianne Tobias. 55"
diameter. 2006.
Large round center with
tapered end.

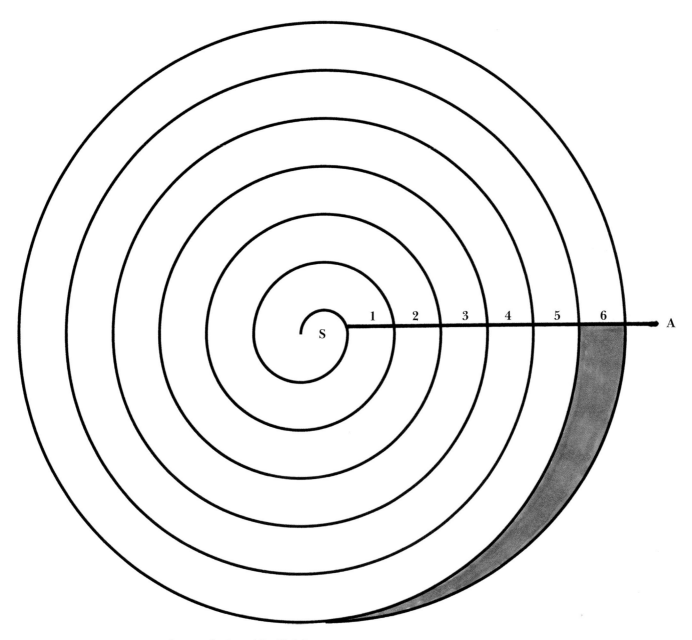

Named Parts of a Round Braided Center:
(S) Start
(A) A line is drawn adjacent to the Start and continued outward to count rows.
Taper: Noted in pink, the taper occurs over 1/4 of the circle. The location of the taper can occur anywhere on the round, but should complete a full row of any recent color changes and maintain the circular shape.

Size Planning

For a round braided center, size planning is easy. Braid until the center is large enough to fit the desired space, allowing for borders if they will be added.

Round Center Start

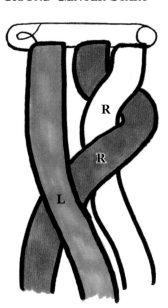

1. Start:
Prepare 3 strands as for the Enclosed End Start, see Chapter 5. Place the strands on the Start Safety Pin with folded edges facing to the left.

2. Starting to Braid the Center:
Make the first of 6 double corners by throwing the right strand to the center, then the right strand again, then the left strand to the center. This double corner is abbreviated (RRL).

3: First Double Corner Pulled Tight:
Pull the strands firmly to make the double corner.

6. Count the center loops to find the 5th loop. It is the same color as the first inside loop on the Start Pin. The 6th inside crossover loop is not needed at this time.

4. Row 1 of Round Braided Center:
Continue braiding a total of 6 (RRL) double corners. The braid coils tightly as above. Each of the "left" strands is called a crossover loop. The crossover loops are pulled firmly to turn the braid. Note that the loops in the center alternate between only 2 fabric colors.

5. After completing 6 double corners, braid a few inches of straight braid and secure with a clothespin.

7. Bury the Knot:
Thread a tapestry needle with about 2 feet of lacing thread. Put an overhand knot at the long end of the thread. Bury the knot inside the 5th loop by driving the needle between the folds, through the fabric on the smooth side of the 5th loop. Make sure the knot is hidden; trim any protruding ends.

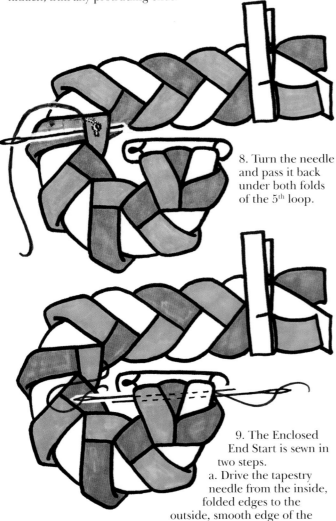

8. Turn the needle and pass it back under both folds of the 5th loop.

9. The Enclosed End Start is sewn in two steps.
a. Drive the tapestry needle from the inside, folded edges to the outside, smooth edge of the braid. Catch the full width of all three strands, and keep the path of the needle as close to the end seams as possible. Pull the thread tight.
b. Remove the Start Pin and drive the needle back to the folded edges side. Keep the second needle pass close, but different from the original pass. Pull the thread tight.

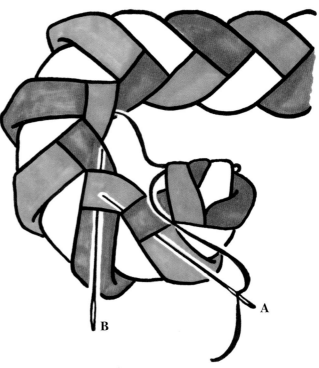

10. Lacing Inner Loops of Row 1:
Use the tapestry needle to lace under loop 2, see "A" in diagram. Lace the needle under loop 3, see "B" in diagram. Continue lacing the inside loops until loop 5, where the starting knot is hidden. If the point of the needle is catching fabric, then lead with the tapestry needle's eye.

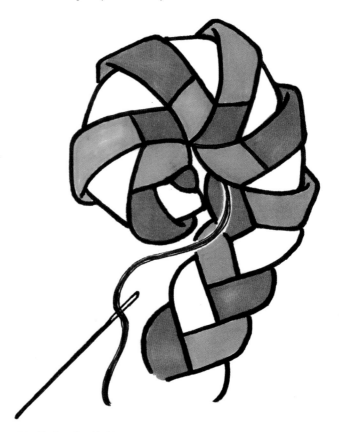

11. Closing the Circle:
Pull the lacing thread tight where it emerges under loop 5. Note that the 5 inside loops fall into a 5-petalled star design. There should be little if any opening between loops in the center.

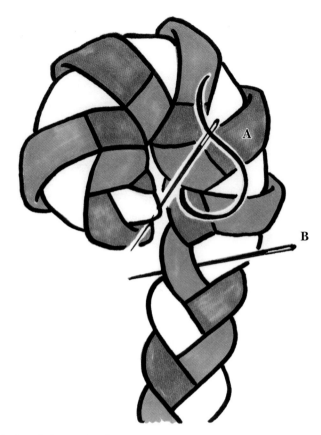

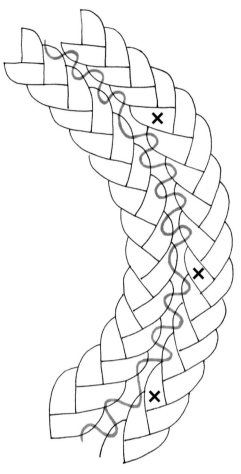

12. Completing Lacing for Row 1:
(A) Use the tapestry needle to pierce the lacing thread through the outer start loop (white loop in diagram).
(B) Skipping loop 6, lace through the next loop on the new braid as drawn.

Increasing Loops on a Curve.
This diagram shows a new braid laid alongside the base braid. In this diagram, increases are needed about every 3 to 4 loops to keep the braid flat. The skipped loops are marked with an "X." Keep the braided center round in shape. If an area seems to be losing its roundness, make a few more increases in this region to increase fullness.

If too few increases are made on the round center, the edges will start to curl upward like a bowl. If too many increases are made, the edges will begin to ruffle. The goal of making increases is to keep the round center both flat and shaped nicely in a circular shape.

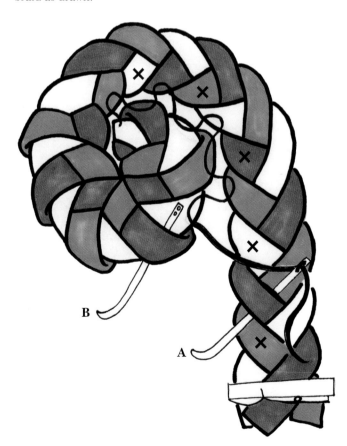

13. Lacing and Increasing on the Second Row:
Each single loop on the 1st row must have 2 loops from the 2nd row laced onto it. This doubling of loops is needed to keep the new braid flat as it coils tightly around the base braid, the round center. Note in the diagram to the left that each loop on the outside of Row 1 is laced, but only every other loop is laced on the new braid, or Row 2. Each skipped loop is marked "X" and indicates an increase.

Lacing from side to side is shown as the braidkin laces under the new braid (A) then under the base braid (B) Continue lacing in this fashion, skipping every other loop of the new braid, until the braid is back around to the area of the Start.

14. Lacing Further Rows:
Place a safety pin on the second row to mark the site of row changes, adjacent to the Start. As each row is braided, changes in the number of increases per row are made. Row 2 skips every other loop, Row 3 skips every third or fourth loop, and later rows require longer stretches between increases.

Did Not Increase and Should Have:
Note lacing thread is visible because no increase was made and should have been. Green loop of new braid was laced and should have been skipped.

Increased/Skipped Loop:
Note lacing thread is not visible because proper increase was made. Green loop of new braid was skipped and tweed loop was laced.

COLOR CHANGES

Unlike other shapes, there is no specific site recommended for color changes, because all points on the circle should appear the same. However, there are a few guidelines for incorporating new fabrics:

- Color changes are more noticeable when they occur in the center of the round. Further out toward the edge, they are less detectable. Try to avoid dramatic changes in color in the first 12" diameter of any round.
- When making color changes, avoid stacking the changes by making them at the same point in the row structure. Varying the color change location draws less attention to the change and is more visually appealing.
- The 2 best methods for arranging color changes are either in a spiraling pattern out from the center, or in random locations, see diagrams below.

ENDING THE BRAIDED ROUND

As with the oval braided center, the round center is tapered to end the braid. See the end of this chapter for instructions on tapering.

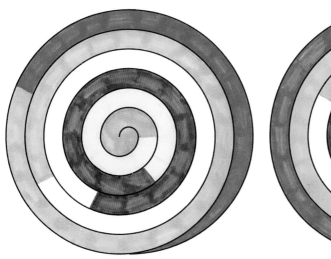

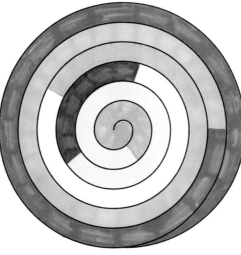

Spiral and Random Color Change Sites: On the left, color changes start at the 3 o'clock location, and spiral outward at 5 o'clock, 7 o'clock, 8 o'clock, and 10 o'clock locations. On the right, color changes occur randomly at the 5 o'clock location, 8 o'clock, 1 o'clock, 10 o'clock, and 3 o'clock locations.

Square Braided Center

OVERVIEW

A square is a practical shape offering plenty of design opportunities. Squares can be arranged as tiles, with every other square a hooked design. In a small size, a square makes a nice trivet or chair pad; larger, it can be used on square stair landings, or for other interesting square spaces. And squares, because of the ease of color changes at one braided corner, are adaptable to many patterned designs. One butted row is usually added after completing the blunt ending; after that, other fancy hooked or braided borders can be added.

Historically, squares were made with double corners at each corner. The resultant squares were less than satisfactory; the sides bulged outward and gave a sloppy appearance to the shape. Most contemporary

Christmas Square, Christine Manges. 10" x 10". 2009. Continuous braided square with one butted row.

braiders now have switched to using triple corners to keep braided squares well-shaped, with sharp right angles at the corners.

Triple corners come with a slight challenge when they are stacked row upon row, as in square or rectangular shapes. Instructions for stacking triple corners are discussed in this section.

Prior Techniques Needed for Square Center

• Enclosed End Start
• Regular Lacing

DEFINING PARTS OF THE CONTINUOUS SQUARE

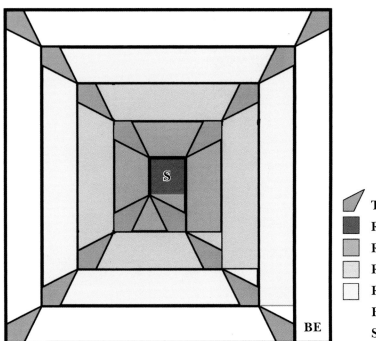

Triple Corners
Row 1
Row 2
Row 3
Row 4
BE Blunt Ending Site
S Start

Continuous Braided Square.
Note labeled parts of the square.

INSTRUCTION

1. Start:
Prepare 3 strands as in the directions for the Enclosed End Start, Chapter 5. Place the 3 strands on the Start Pin with folded edges to the left.

2. Braiding First Row:
Row 1 of the continuous square is very short: it consists of only 3 thrown loops of braid: Left, Right, Left. Note that while most Start instructions begin with a throw from the right, for this shape it works out better to start with the left strand.

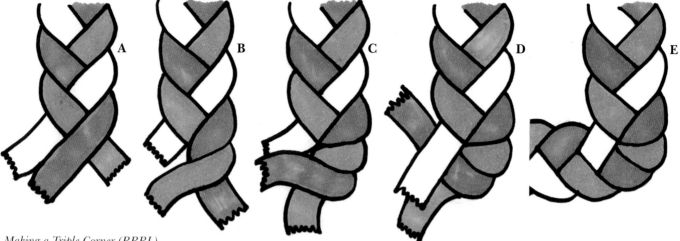

Making a Triple Corner (RRRL).
(A) Loop 1 (gray) is thrown on the right.
(B) Loop 2 (blue) is thrown on the right.
(C) Loop 3 (gray) is thrown on the right.
(D) The crossover loop is thrown on the left to complete the corner.
(E) The appearance of a completed triple corner.

3. Triple Corners: Row 2 starts with a triple corner, so it is first necessary to review how to make them. Triple corners have 3 loops at the corner, whereas a double corner has only 2 loops. Triple corners are made in much the same way as double corners, just with one extra loop. For a square, 3 loops are thrown on the right before a crossover loop is thrown from the left (RRRL). It is important to have the crossover loop firm and tight in order to make the corner angle sharp. For a continuous square, all of the corners are (RRRL) because the braid spirals clockwise.

In order to know where to place the corner, it is necessary to know where the last loop on the other side prior to the corner is placed. This loop is called the "B" loop, or the Before loop. In the diagram below, note the location of the B loop.

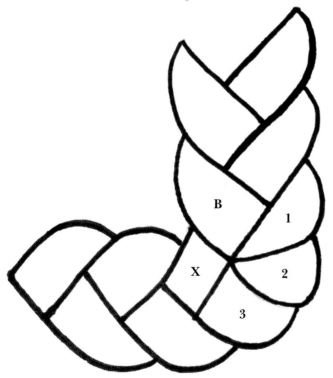

Triple Corner with Named Loops.
(B) "Before" loop; last loop thrown before the triple corner loops on the other side of the corner
Loops 1, 2, 3: Loops making the outer triple corner
(X) The crossover loop
Note that loops 1 & 3 of the triple are always made with the same strand, and that loop **(B)** is made with the same strand as loop 2.
When two loops have been thrown beyond the crossover loop, pull on the crossover loop strand firmly to make the corner sharp.

Interestingly, a triple corner does not change the strand order before and after the corner, whereas a double corner does change the strand order. This fact becomes important when butting certain shapes and borders, discussed later.

4. Braiding Rows 2 & 3:
Triple corners (RRRL) are noted in pink. The (**B**) loops, the loop before the triple is thrown, are drawn in blue. The yellow loops are crossover loops. Note loop counts on the smooth sides do not include the triple loops, or the crossover loops.
Row 1: Enclosed End Start. Row 1 is very small: Left, Right, Left.
Row 2: Starts in lower right corner A in diagram. Triple at A, Triple at (**B**), 1 loop (or: right, left) Triple at (**C**), 1 loop, Triple at D, 3 loops.
Row 3: Triple at A, 3 loops, Triple at (**B**), 4 loops, Triple at C, 4 loops, Triple at D, 5 loops. Further rows are indicated in a later diagram.

5. Lacing the First 2 Rows:
(A) Orient the braid so that the
Start is at the 12 o'clock location.
Load a tapestry needle with a
knotted length of lacing thread.
Drive the point of the tapestry
needle between the folds of the
crossover loop to the left of the
Start Pin, as drawn, which buries
the knot between the folds.
(B) Pass the needle back under all
layers of the same loop.

6. Sewing the Enclosed End Start:
Use the pointed end of the tapestry
needle to drive through all 3 strands
at the Start Safety Pin very close to
the end seams. Displace the needle
slightly and drive the needle back
through all 3 strands.

*7. Lacing the Loops on the Inside of
Row 1:*
These diagrams show how the space
is closed between the inside loops of
Rows 1 & 2.
Switch from a tapestry needle
to a braidkin and work counter-
clockwise:
(A) Pass the braidkin under the
loop adjacent to the Start.
(B) Pass under the 2nd thrown
crossover loop, as shown.

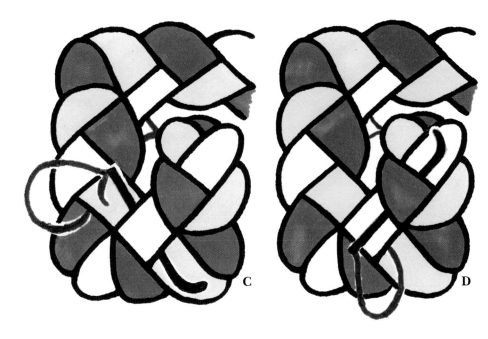

(C) Pass the braidkin under the 1st thrown crossover loop. The crossover loops are never laced from this point onward in the square.
(D) Pass under the inner loop below the Start.

8. Lacing around the Start:
(A) Pass the braidkin under the left start loop.
(B) Pass the braidkin under the loop above the Start.

9. Regular Lacing:
Turn the piece so that the Start is pointing to the right. Regular lacing starts along this first side. Begin by passing under the right Start loop, then skip the crossover loop, and pass under the next regular loop. Lacing proceeds right to left, catching every loop, alternating side to side until the next corner.
Increases, or skipped loops, are never made. All of the needed increases in the loop count per row are naturally made by having triples at each corner, which increases the loop count of each side by 3 for each row.

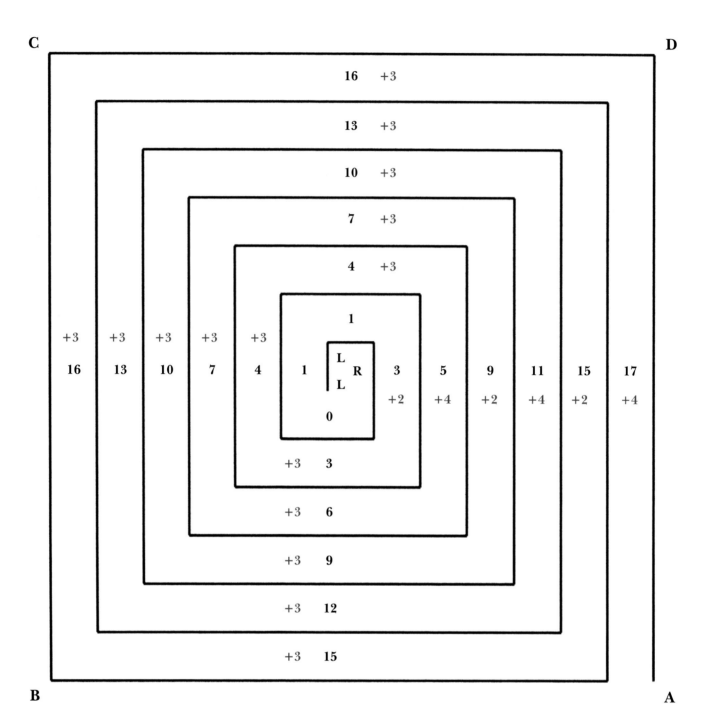

10. Loop Counts for Additional Rows:
This diagram shows the loop counts on the smooth side of the braid between triples corners.
Remember, the loops of the triple corners are NOT counted.
For larger squares, follow the following guidelines to determine additional rows' loop numbers:
Side AB: add 3 to prior row.
Side BC: add 3 to prior row.
Side CD: add 3 to prior row.
Side DA: add 4 to next row alternates with adding 2 to the next row.

TRIPLE CORNER THEORY

Triple Corners can be a challenge. When they are stacked row on row, they must be stacked in a particular way that alternates between rows. If they are not stacked properly, the shape of the braided square will be misshapen.

Triple corners consist of 3 loops. As they are braided, they "naturally" seem to have 2 loops fall on the first side, and 1 on the second side. If they are laced in this fashion, the greater number of loops on the first side of the corner will hump up, creating the shape in the diagram to the right.

In order to prevent this unequal distribution of loops, there are 2 techniques that can be used:

1. Loop counts: see discussion above. If the loop counts are followed exactly, a perfect square will result.

2. Marking loop B: Alternating the placement of the B loop by keeping track of its location with a safety pin at each corner. This last technique requires some explanation, but is simple to carry out. When stacking corners, the first thing to understand is that the B loop acts as a pivot for the corner cluster of loops. Wherever the B loop is laced, the outside corner loops turn around this site to make the right angle.

When stacking **double corners**, the B loop is always laced in the exact center of the prior row's double loops: between loops 1 & 2. The same holds true for **quadruple corners**; the B loop is always laced in the exact center of the prior row's corner loops: in between loops 2 & 3.

Misshapen Square Braided without Alternating Corners

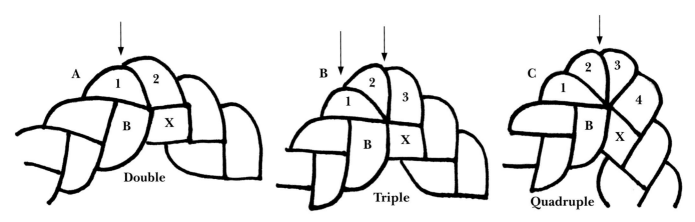

B Loop Locations for **(A)** Double, **(B)** Triple, and **(C)** Quadruple Corners

With odd numbers of loops in a corner (**triple and quintuple corners**) the challenge is that there is no exact center *space* between loops, because a *loop* is in the center. To lace the B loop of the new braid to the base braid's center, the B loop needs to skip back and forth between the spaces that are before or after the exact center loop. This alternation places B between loops 1 & 2 of the triple in one row, and between loops 2 & 3 in the next row.

To keep track without counting loops, place safety pins in between triple loops 1 & 2 for one row. When lacing up to each pin, once B has been braided at the site identified by the pin, move the pin to the outside of the new braid's triple corner, but place it at the alternate location, between loops 2 & 3.

In this way, simply changing the location of the safety pin at each corner from row to row, and braiding B at the safety pinned site, will result in a perfect square, without counting loops. This technique is particularly useful when braiding very large squares, for which counting loops is time-consuming.

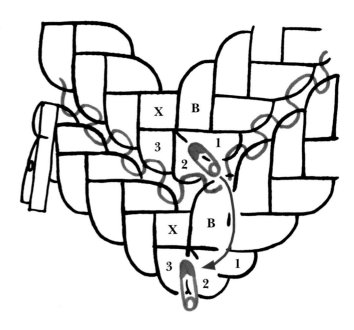

Changing Location of Safety Pin from One Row to the Next

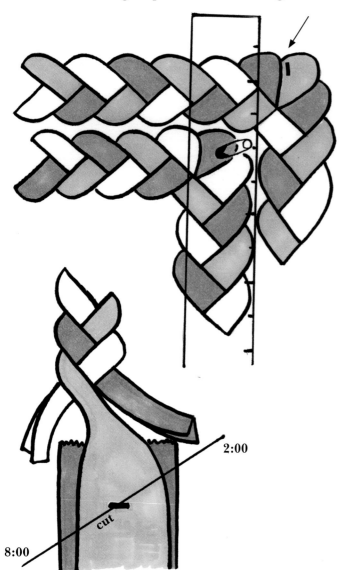

COLOR CHANGES

Color changes need to occur within the triple at corner A, where row changes occur. If possible, make color changes in loops 1, 2, or 3, and not in the crossover loop, X, unless absolutely necessary. The X loop sometimes appears to be located partly in the prior row and does not give as crisp a color change.

1. Identify Color Change Site:
Just as with color changes in an oval rug, braid beyond where the color change should occur. Lay a ruler along the outer edge of the next side, and pick a loop for the color change that is just beyond the ruler. See arrow.
2. Mark Color Change Site:
Place a marker line in the upper outer aspect of the chosen loop, using red or black markers for lighter fabrics, and a metallic silver marker for dark fabrics. Alternatively, mark the color change site with a small safety pin, catching only one layer of fabric
3. Unbraid a few inches. Open the strand that is safety pinned or marked, right side of fabric up. The safety pin/marker line may fall at an unusual angle because of the triple corner. Cut the fabric diagonally from the 8 o'clock to 2 o'clock location. The cutting line should cut through the center of the safety pin/marker line.
4. When cutting, place the new strip right side up underneath the old strip, so that the diagonal cuts match exactly. Flip the new strand over so that right sides are together, and sew with a 1/4" seam. Trim to 1/8", and rebraid. The seam line should be hidden 1/4" above where the safety pin/marker line was placed, underneath the previous loop.

ENDING THE CONTINUOUS SQUARE

The square shape is ended bluntly at Corner A. When braiding the 4th side of the row that ends at Corner A, straight braid 2 to 3 inches beyond the corner, and secure the ends. Do not braid a triple corner at this last corner.

Instructions for making a blunt ending are at the end of this chapter.

Rectangular Braided Center

OVERVIEW

A rectangular center is a practical shape. It can be braided as small as a table mat, or as large as a room. The shape can be used in long hallways, as a runner, or in stairways, as individual treads. Other unusual spots for rectangles include: a pew seat, a coffee table cover, or the back rest of a rocker. A braided rectangle can be combined with hooking, making a stairway runner that has the risers hooked and the treads braided for an interesting use of both art forms.

Techniques Discussed in this Section

- Counting Rows on a Rectangle
- Color Change Sites
- Braiding the First Row of a Rectangle

Continuous Braided Rectangle, Christine Manges. 18" x 24". 2009.

DEFINING PARTS OF THE RECTANGULAR CENTER

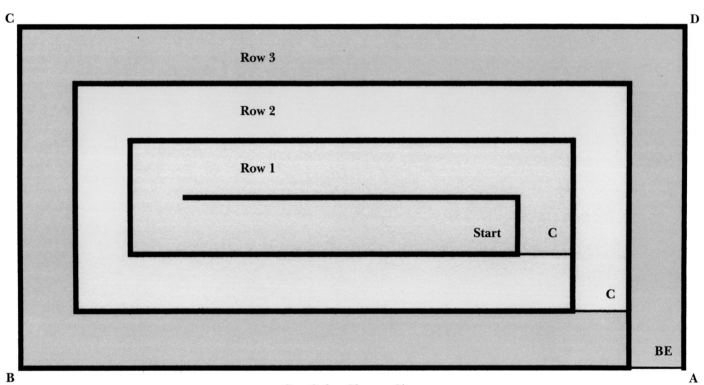

C = Color Change Site
BE = Blunt Ending Site

Parts of a Rectangular Center.
Start Corner A is the site of color changes, row changes, and blunt ending.

SIZE PLANNING

To make a rectangle for a particular space, measure the length and width of the space. Subtract the width from the length, adding 1 inch per foot. This measurement determines the length of the center row of the rectangle.

Formula: Length minus width, plus 1" per foot.
Example: 5' x 3' rug desired.

5' – 3' = 2'. Add 1" per foot: 2"
The center row should be 2' 2."

The same general guidelines for color that apply to an oval rug also apply to a rectangle. Try to keep the central color block fairly wide, at least a fifth to a third of the total width of the rug, before making dramatic color changes.

BRAIDING THE FIRST ROW

Triple   1   2   3   4   5   **Triple**

Triple

5   4   3   2   1

6   5   4   3   2   1   **Triple**

Braiding the First Row.
1. Start with an Enclosed End Start. Throw the first loop on the right. Braid until the length of the braid is the determined measurement.
2. Make two triple corners: (RRRL), (RRRL). Resume straight braiding for a few inches, then clamp the braid with a clothespin.
3. Count loops on the smooth side of the braid from the first throw on the Start Pin until the loop prior to the triple corner. Braid this number of loops on the other side of the center row, after the 2 triple corners.
4. Make another triple corner (RRRL), then right, left, then another triple corner (RRRL). Resume straight braiding for a few inches, then clamp the braid with a clothespin.

LACING THE CENTER ROW

The steps for lacing the center row are identical to those found in the oval braided center—the Shoe-Lacing technique.

Once laced, the center row of the rectangle should look like the following diagram, with the 2 ends of the lacing thread knotted.

The Center Row, after Shoe-Lacing

1. Load the longer end of the lacing thread with a tapestry needle.
Drive the eye of the tapestry needle under the B loop of the triple corner, as above.

2. Using the point of the tapestry needle, drive the needle through the 3 Enclosed End Start loops, very close to the end seams. Turn the needle and come back along a slightly different path through the 3 loops. Remove Start Pin. Remove tapestry needle and replace with braidkin.

3.
(A) Lace under the folded edge of the Start loop.
(B) Lace under the middle loop between the triple corners.

4. Turn the braid so that the Start is off to the right.
(A) Lace under the Start loop as drawn.
(B) Lace the next loop on the new braid, after the crossover loop.

LACING AROUND THE START

Start regular lacing, alternating from new braid to base braid, catching every loop. Continue until the next corner is reached.

STACKING TRIPLE CORNERS

Just as for a continuous braided square, the triple corners of a rectangle must be stacked properly or a distorted shape will result. The corners stack properly simply by following the loop counts in the diagram below. For an alternative approach to stacking corners, see the discussion of Triple Corner Theory in the prior section of this chapter on Square Centers.

A rectangle of any size may be made following these rules:

• The size of rectangles is changed by varying the length of the center line.
• For every rectangle, the loop counts on the short sides, BC and DA, should always be identical.
• All sides increase by a loop count of 3 on each row, except for side AB.
• After the first 2 rows, increases on side AB alternate between increasing by 2 loops and then increasing by 4 loops.

COLOR CHANGES

Color changes for a rectangle occur at Corner A, adjacent to the Start, but are otherwise identical to making a color change for a continuous braided square—see the previous section.

COMPLETING THE RECTANGLE

Continue braiding until the rectangle is the desired size for the center, subtracting the width and length for any desired border rows. End the center by continuing a straight braid beyond the corner adjacent to the Start, and then securing the braid.

A blunt ending is described in the Tapering/Blunt Ending section later in this chapter.

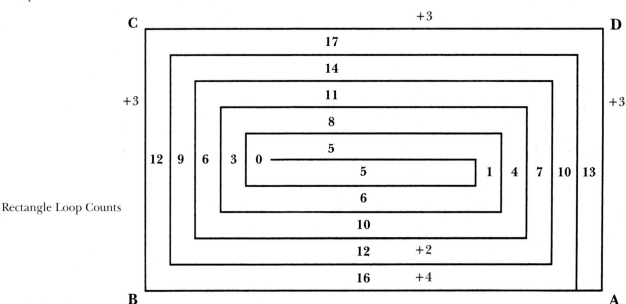

Rectangle Loop Counts

Heart Braided Center

OVERVIEW

Two types of hearts can be braided, but only one type is presented here. A heart can either be braided with triple corners stacked along the vertical center line, or with stacked double corners. While both shapes are pleasing, the double corner heart is easier; instructions for the double-corner heart are presented here.

A small braided heart can be a lovely center for a hooked border. Imagine a braided heart surrounded by a hooked border, which is then surrounded by a straight braid, followed by one of the openwork borders such as the triple picot for a final fancy border. Combining multiple techniques in this fashion would provide the artist with the pleasure of trying new things while creating a lovely little piece.

The heart shape is not for the beginner, however. The stacking of double corners, the need to maintain similar curves on both sides, and lacing an "inside corner," one that points *into* the shape, all make the heart a challenging shape.

Techniques Discussed in this Section

- Lacing a Double Corner in the Middle of the Center Line
- Stacking Double Corners

Prior Techniques Needed for Heart Center

- Double Corners
- Lacing the Center Line
- Regular Lacing
- Increasing

Multistrand Heart, Lois Stauffer.
36" x 29". 2005.

DEFINITIONS

A heart can be thought of as an oval rug that has been "cracked open" across the center, with braids filling in the crack. Thinking of the heart this way cues the braider to the known locations of the start, the row change site, the color change site, and the taper site.

Heart of Blue, Christine Manges. 29.5" x 33". 2008.
Heart center with multi-strand border.

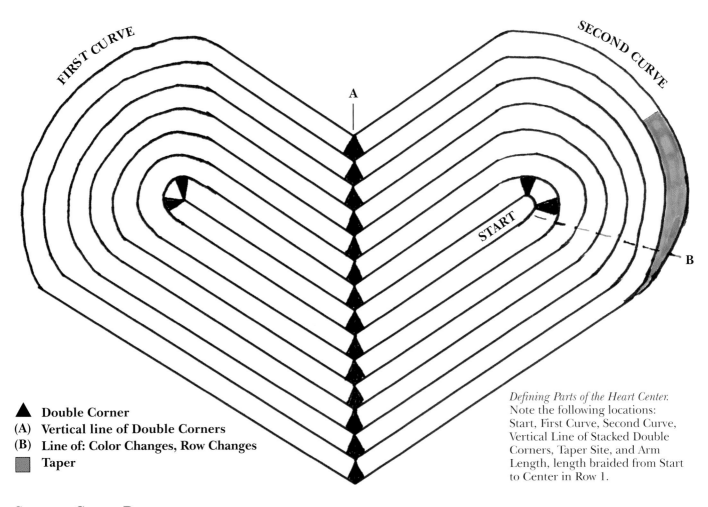

FIRST CURVE

SECOND CURVE

A

START

B

▲ Double Corner
(A) Vertical line of Double Corners
(B) Line of: Color Changes, Row Changes
▨ Taper

Defining Parts of the Heart Center.
Note the following locations:
Start, First Curve, Second Curve,
Vertical Line of Stacked Double
Corners, Taper Site, and Arm
Length, length braided from Start
to Center in Row 1.

SIZE AND COLOR PLANNING

A heart is a difficult shape to plan precisely. Hearts can have some differences in basic shape. Some prefer a fat heart shape; some prefer a leaner, longer one. In terms of braid width, tiny braids require more rows, and fat braids fewer.

A very rough estimate is that, for a given arm length (distance braided from Start to Center in Row 1), the height of the completed heart will be about 3 times that length, and the width will be about 4 times that wide.

Color for Hearts: Avoid dramatic dark/light changes in the central bands of the heart. The inner rows are quite thin; dramatic color changes between rows only emphasize this skinny, "V" shape. As the heart becomes bigger, the rows become rounder and more traditionally heart-shaped, and dramatic color changes are more pleasing in appearance. Try to keep sharp color changes limited to the outer third of the heart.

One of the delightful things about a heart shape is that even the most color-restrained of braiders feel free to use vivid pinks, reds, corals, and purple colors.

Pink & Brown Heart, Christine Manges. 15" x 19". 2009. Note how solid row sets off the decorative double picot border.

INSTRUCTIONS FOR A BRAIDED HEART CENTER

The instructions are written for a 21" x 28" heart. Other sizes can be made using these instructions, but substituting a different loop count for the initial arm length, indicated by "x."

A heart is started by braiding one arm of the heart from the outside right toward the center. A double corner is made at the center, and the braid continues out to the left end of the other arm. Two double corners reverse the course of the braid, which turns back and makes another double corner at the center. The braid continues to spiral around itself.

First Row of Braided Heart.
1. Prepare 3 strands as for the Enclosed End Start, Chapter 5. Place the 3 strands onto the Start Pin.
2. Braid 7 (or, "x") loops, making the first throw from the right, and counting loops on the smooth side of the braid. Include the first loop on the Start Pin in the loop count. Make a double corner (RRL).
3. Braid 7 (or "x") loops. Make 2 double corners (RRL), (RRL).
4. Braid 7 (or "x") loops. Do not count any loops from the double corners. Make a double corner (LLR). Note different direction. Count to make sure there are 7 loops between your last 2 double corners.
5. Braid 5 (or, "x – 2") more loops.
6. Braid around the Start: (RRL), right, left, (RRL).
7. Braid a few more inches and clamp the braid with a clothespin.

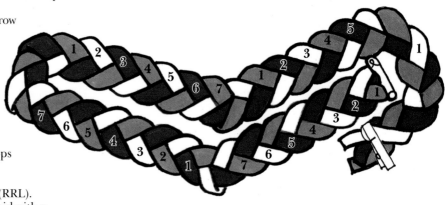

Shoe-Lacing Center Row:
Overview on left, close-up of double corner region on right.

8. Lacing the Center Row:
Shoe-lacing is used to lace the center row. This technique is discussed in the first section of this chapter, Oval Center. Follow these instructions until the double corners in the center are ready to be laced.

9. Lacing the Center Row's Stacked Double Corners:
Note that on the left-side braid, the left crossover loop and the loop just above it are effectively treated as one loop and are laced together. When the right-side braid's lacing thread is passing downward to the left, it must skip the crossover loop.

10. Continue shoe-lacing as per the Oval Center diagrams. Then lace around the Start End, following the diagrams for sewing and lacing around the Oval Start, which follow immediately after the shoe-lacing diagrams.

11. Stacking Double Corners at the Bottom Corner:
To maintain symmetry in the heart shape, it is important to properly stack the double corners that run up and down the center of the heart.

To align double corners correctly, remember this phrase: "B is laced between loops 1 & 2."

12. Braiding the Bottom Double Corner:
Braid and lace until the loops from the base braid's double are seen. Lay the new braid alongside the base braid to see which loop falls between loops 1 & 2 of the base braid's double. This loop is the **(B)** loop of the new braid's double; the next loops thrown on the right will be loops 1 & 2 of the new braid.

If you are having trouble identifying the loops of the double, place a safety pin in the valley between the base braid loops 1 & 2. Braid to this point, and remember that the safety pin marks where the **(B)** loop should be braided and laced. After braiding the new double corner, clamp the braid and move the safety pin to the new braid's valley between loops 1 & 2.

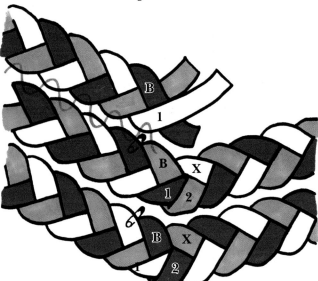

13. Stacking Double Corners on the Top Corner:
Stacking double corners above the center row is more challenging. The phrase "B is laced between loops 1 & 2" still is true, but the base braid does not have loops 1 & 2 showing; instead, it has a **(B)** loop showing.

14. Braiding the Top Double Corner:
Braid until a loop falls right before the base braid's **(B)** loop. This loop is the first loop of the new braid's double. Throw another loop on the left, which is the 2nd loop of the new braid's double. Complete the corner with a crossover loop on the right. Loops 1 & 2 of the new braid straddle the base braid's **(B)** loop. If a safety pin is used to remind the braider where to place the double corner, it should be placed in the valley before the base braid's **(B)** loop. The safety pin identifies where the 1st loop of the new braid's double is laced.

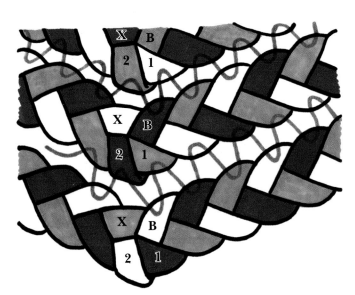

15. Lacing the Bottom Corner:
Lacing proceeds from right to left. Note that in the above diagram, loop **(B)** of the new braid is laced between the base braid's loops 1 & 2. The crossover loop on the new braid is not laced.

Lacing double corners is the time to check that the corner has been properly braided. Loops 1 & 2 must straddle loop **(B)** The corner is laced by skipping the crossover loop completely. Skipping this loop is essential for a crisp corner. If the loop is laced, two problems occur: the corner will straighten out, losing its angle; and there is the risk of a "hole" or opening being created where the crossover loop is pulled away by the lacing thread.

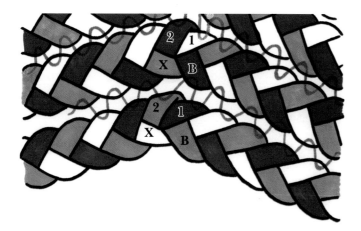

16. Lacing the Top Corner:
Note that the heart has been turned upside down so that lacing can proceed from right to left. Loop 1 of the new braid's double is laced to the space prior to the base braid's (**B**) loop, and loop 2 to the space just after (**B**). The crossover loop on the base braid is not laced.

Tapering

COLOR CHANGES

Follow the guidelines for making color changes, discussed in the Oval Braided Center section, earlier in this chapter.

THOUGHTS ABOUT THE HEART SHAPE

A heart is rounder at the lower portions of both outer curves than on its upper portions. The lower portions need an occasional increase in loops, even down onto the straight lower sides, to give some fullness. These increases have their greatest effect if made in the first few rounds of the heart. Later increases simply make the edge of the braid ruffle, and contribute less to the roundness of the heart.

It is imperative to keep both sides of the heart equal and symmetric. Use pins to mark increases on the first curve. When lacing the second curve, the Start curve, make the increases equal to, and similarly spaced, as those of the first curve.

Do not assess symmetry of the sides at any point other than when the row change site has just been laced. At any other site, there *should* be asymmetry, because an incomplete row is asymmetric.

It is possible to have too many rows. If the indentation at the top of the heart is flattening out, then remove some of the outer rows of braid until a more classic heart shape is regained. If planning to attach a fancy border, leave room for these rows in the planning.

TAPERING

The heart should be tapered on the curve adjacent to the Start. See instructions for tapering, next.

OVERVIEW

Tapering is a way of ending a continuous round, oval, or heart-shaped braided project by narrowing the braid along a curve. In the past, traditional braided projects were mostly oval or round rugs, finished almost exclusively with a tapered end or "rat-tail." Today, many braiders still finish beautiful rugs in this manner, with only a taper.

To taper, the width of the strands is narrowed gradually, re-braided, and then the ends are buried in the rug. The goal is to maintain the shape of the piece while gradually narrowing the last row. Although careful examination can reveal the taper, the taper should not be evident at a distance because the outside shape is maintained.

Although a taper can serve as the final ending to a project, adding at least one additional row of butted braid after the taper is recommended. A butted row is created when the braid's end is joined to the braid's beginning, such that each row is a complete circle or oval, similar to a ring. The extra butted row(s) after a taper provide a professional finish. Butted rows also protect the weaker tapered area, which is more likely to unravel or fray over years of wear. A discussion of butting is in Chapter 7.

A different method is needed for finishing braided centers that do not have curves, such as squares and rectangles. These right-angled shapes are finished with Blunt Endings, which are discussed in the section following Tapering.

Still other shapes are best finished with neither a taper nor a blunt ending; these shapes are discussed at the end of this chapter.

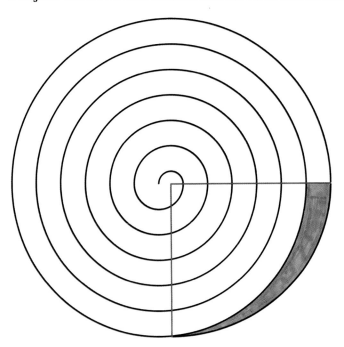

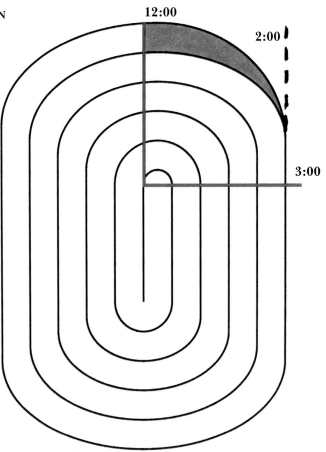

Taper Site of Round Braided Center.
The taper site is shaded in pink and occurs over 1/4 of the circle, as drawn. Try to identify the quarter circle for the taper which will best maintain the roundness of the shape. This site is usually near the row change line of a round, shown in the diagram extending from the center to the 3 o'clock location. The most important consideration for choosing a taper site is where the round shape is best preserved.

Taper Site of Oval Braided Center.
The taper site is shaded in pink and occurs between the 12 o'clock and 2 o'clock locations, adjacent to the Start. The oval is somewhat different from a round; it cannot use a full 1/4 circle (e.g., 12 – 3 o'clock) for the taper because the straight sides begin at the 2 o'clock location. The taper must finish before the dotted line indicating the start of the straight side, or there will be an unsightly bump outward in the oval shape between 2 and 3 o'clock.

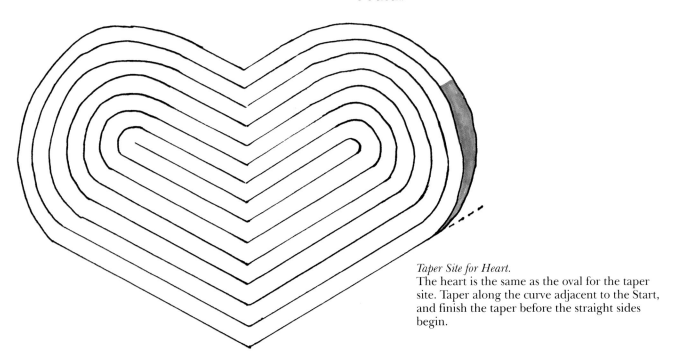

Taper Site for Heart.
The heart is the same as the oval for the taper site. Taper along the curve adjacent to the Start, and finish the taper before the straight sides begin.

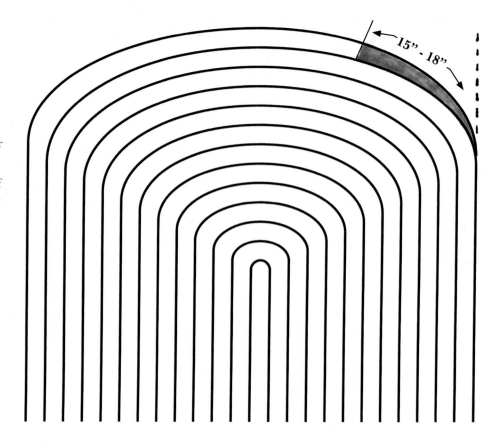

Taper Site for a Large Oval.
If the oval, or other curved shape, is large, e.g., over 3 feet wide, the taper can be done over a shorter distance. Choose the same site as determined by shape, but only the last 15"-18" of braid at this site needs to be tapered.

15" - 18"

COLOR CONSIDERATIONS FOR TAPERING

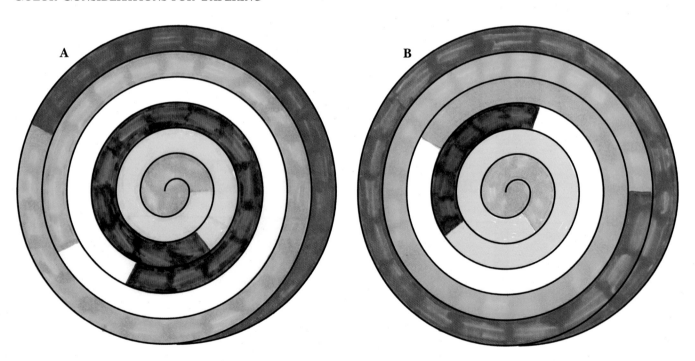

A

B

Color Considerations for Tapering.
(A) The outer row has an incomplete round of blue, which is unattractive.
(B) The outer blue row is completed, giving more of a framed look to the piece.
While the most important consideration in selecting a taper site is the project's shape, it is also important to keep this color guideline in mind when planning a taper. This guideline applies to all shapes.

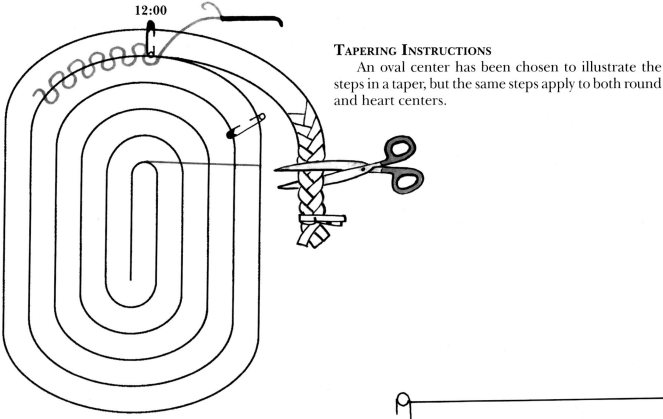

TAPERING INSTRUCTIONS

An oval center has been chosen to illustrate the steps in a taper, but the same steps apply to both round and heart centers.

Starting a Taper.
1. Make a braid long enough to reach the 3 o'clock location, and clamp the braid.
2. Lace the braid up to 12 o'clock.
3. Place 2 large safety pins: a Start Pin at the beginning of the taper, at 12 o'clock on the new braid; and a Finish Pin on the base braid marking where the taper must be finished, 2 o'clock.
4. Cut the braid 3" below the Finish Pin.

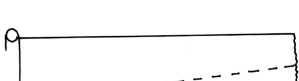

Trimming Strands.
6. Trim each strand to 1/2 of its original width. The cutting line is indicated by the dashed line in the diagram. It does not matter which side of the strand is trimmed.
7. Fold as for regular braiding, tucking raw edges in, as far as is possible. Place a clothespin to secure ends from unbraiding. (not pictured)
8. Lace up to the clothespin, allowing increases when lacing to accommodate the smaller size of the tapered braids' loops. (not pictured)

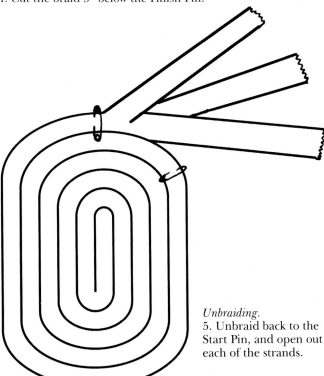

Unbraiding.
5. Unbraid back to the Start Pin, and open out each of the strands.

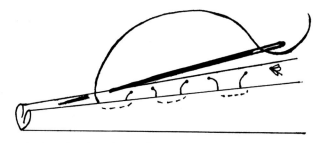

Blind Stitch Trimmed Strands.
9. Using a needle and matching thread, blind-stitch the remaining length of the strips into narrow tubes.
10. Braid and lace the narrow, sewn strands until about 2" - 3" before the Finish pin.

Bury First Strand.
11. Working from the front and using a hemostat or pliers, bury one strand by pulling it under a loop. The strand being buried is most easily hidden if it matches either the loop before, brown, or the loop after where it is buried, green. Anchor the end in place with a safety pin.

Alternative Method to Bury a Tapered End.
In this diagram, an alternative method for burying a tapered end is shown. Working from the front, the tapered end is pulled across an outside loop and under an inside loop. This method works best when the outside loop and the tapered end are matching colors. Anchor the end with a safety pin.

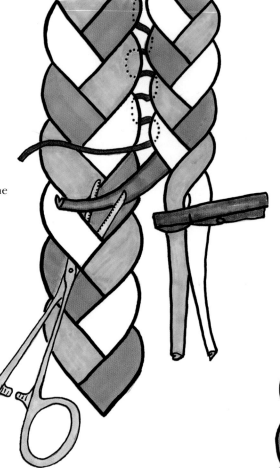

Twisting the Remaining 2 Ends.
12. Working from the front, twist the remaining 2 strands so that the right strand crosses forward and to the left. The direction of the twist is important; it needs to mimic the outer loops of the braid. There should be 4 twists of the 2 remaining strands.
13. The twisted ends naturally straddle the front and back of the base braid. Bury the front strand, the 4th twist, on the front of the base braid. Bury the back strand, the 3rd twist, on the back of the base braid (see arrow right). Use either method of burying strands, as shown in the 2 prior diagrams. Anchor the ends with safety pins.

Assess the taper and make any adjustments or redo if necessary to make the taper neat and invisible along the braid edge. Depending on the shape of the piece, fabric weight, and width, it may take several attempts to obtain a satisfactory taper.

- Does the edge of the taper end before the Finish Pin?
- Is the edge of the project smoothly contoured, or does the taper create an unsightly bump?
- Are the ends neatly stitched shut, or are raveled edges showing?

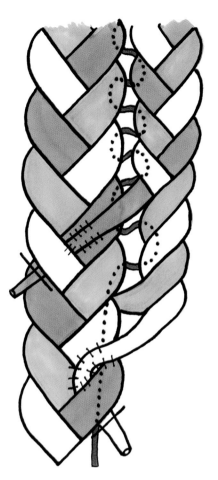

Lacing the Taper and Stitching Down the Ends.
14. Lace the tapered area to the base braid. Bury the lacing thread by lacing through 10 loops. Cut the lacing thread flush with the rug.
15. The tapered ends are stitched on 3 sides with matching thread before they are buried under a loop. An alternative method is to anchor the tapered ends by stitching multiple times through the taper and the full thickness of the braid, in the valley just before where the tapered end is buried under a loop. After the ends are stitched down by either method, cut the ends where they emerge out from under their burying loop.
16. If additional butted rows will be added, do not stitch down the tapered ends until *after* lacing on the butted border row. The stitches will interfere with the ability to place the braidkin through the tapered loops and lace the next row on successfully. Leave the safety pins that are securing the tapered ends in place until after the butted border is laced on, then come back and stitch the tapered ends down.

Blunt Endings for Square or Rectangular Shapes

A different method of ending is needed for square or rectangular projects, since these shapes end with a 90° outside corner. For these shapes, the continuous braid is ended bluntly rather than tapered, and then finished with a butted row to protect the blunt ending.

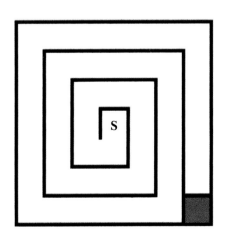

Blunt Ending Sites.
The blunt ending sites for the rectangle and square are shown highlighted in pink; both occur at the row change sites for these shapes.
For the rectangle, the blunt ending site is adjacent to the Start (S).
For the square, the blunt ending site is one corner down from the corner adjacent to the Start (S).

INSTRUCTIONS FOR BLUNT ENDING

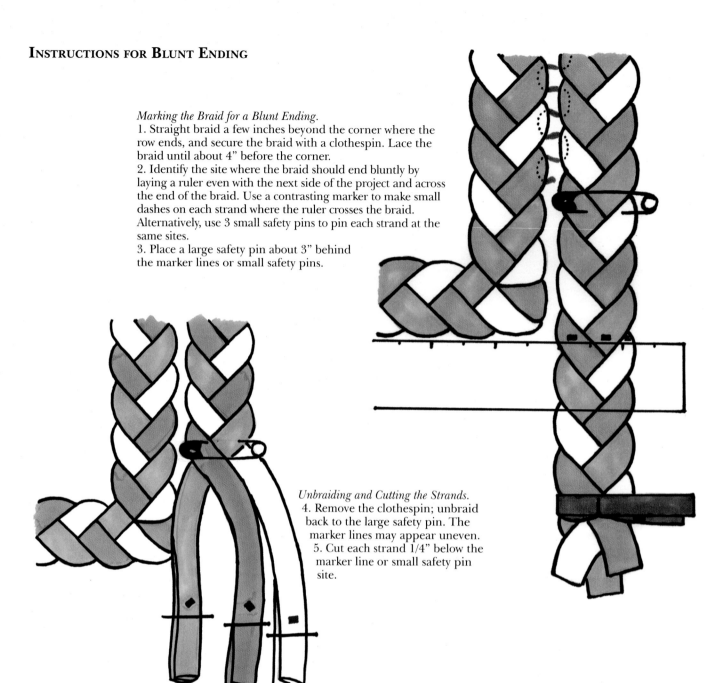

Marking the Braid for a Blunt Ending.
1. Straight braid a few inches beyond the corner where the row ends, and secure the braid with a clothespin. Lace the braid until about 4" before the corner.
2. Identify the site where the braid should end bluntly by laying a ruler even with the next side of the project and across the end of the braid. Use a contrasting marker to make small dashes on each strand where the ruler crosses the braid. Alternatively, use 3 small safety pins to pin each strand at the same sites.
3. Place a large safety pin about 3" behind the marker lines or small safety pins.

Unbraiding and Cutting the Strands.
4. Remove the clothespin; unbraid back to the large safety pin. The marker lines may appear uneven.
5. Cut each strand 1/4" below the marker line or small safety pin site.

Sewing the Blunt Ends.
6. **(A)** Fold a strand right sides together. Locate the marker line on the inside fold and make sure it is hidden by the seam. Sew across the bottom edge with a 1/4" seam allowance. Make the seam width a few threads wider than the width of a folded strand. If hand sewing, use a back-stitch; if machine sewing, reverse and re-stitch. Turn a right angle to the first seam and sew about 1/2" up the side. Veer the stitching off to the side.
7. **(B)** Trim the top and corner raw edges to 1/8" from the seams.
8. **(C)** Using a hemostat or pliers, grasp the end seam from inside the sewn tube and turn it right side out. Repeat steps 6-8 for all 3 strands.

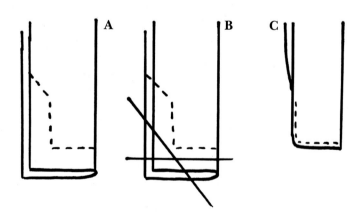

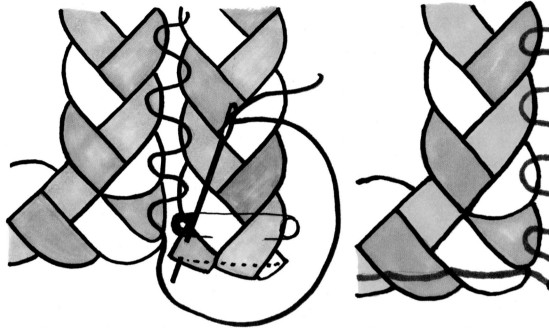

Rebraiding and Finishing.
9. Rebraid the ends; secure with a large safety pin.
10. Using matching thread, stitch the ends of the braid to each other.
11. Lace the blunt end to the prior row. It may be necessary to switch to a tapestry needle to secure the blunt end to the braid. See brown end in diagram which can only be laced by being sewn with a tapestry needle, because it is so short. Lace through 10 more loops and cut the lacing thread flush with the braids.

Completed Blunt Ending.
This diagram shows the appearance of the blunt ending when completed.

FINISHING OTHER SHAPES

For other shapes, with angles that are sharper than 90^0, e.g., flower, star, etc., there are options for ending. A blunt end in the valley between petals or star points may be the best way to conceal a braid's ending, or perhaps a taper on the curve of a petal would look best. Usually a row or two of butted braids will cover any uneven edges.

Diamond shapes are a special consideration. Diamonds can be long and slender, or wide enough to be close to a square in shape. While a blunt ending is easiest to rebraid and sew when it is made straight across, the blunt ending can be modified to end on an angle, for the corner of a diamond.

Certain shapes are better suited to all-butted rows, rather than continuous braids. For example, octagons and hexagons have 135 and 120 degree angles, respectively. If the final braid is tapered along the length of one side, the project's shape loses its symmetry and becomes irregular. If the final braid is ended bluntly at a corner, one side always appears longer than the others. The only method that preserves the hexagonal or octagonal shape is to butt all rows.

Instructions for octagonal and hexagonal all-butted centers are not given in this book, but are available in books listed under Resources, specifically those by Barbara Fisher.

1. Putnam, Dorothy Parks. *Beautiful Braiding.* Action, Massachusetts: Action Press, Inc., 1960, p. 53.

7 Butting

Overview

Butting is the process of joining the Start End of a braid to the Finish End of a braid, to create a ring with no beginning or end. In a braided rug or other piece, typically the center is made as a continuous braid, then the last 1 or 2 rows are butted to give a more finished look. Alternatively, every row can be butted in the braided portion of a project. For a hooked piece, a butted braided border can be added after the hooking has been padded and lined. Both straight braided rows and fancy border rows can be butted.

There are several published methods for butting; see Rug Braiding references in the Resources section in the Appendix.

Techniques in the past have included such wide-ranging approaches as turning under each end and hammering the bulging ends flat,[1] to starting and ending with overlapping tapers. Current techniques identify where overlapping strands match and sew each strand together at this site to make a complete ring.

The butting method chosen for this book is called the Enclosed End Butt. It was taught to the authors by Pam Rowan, taught by Betty Mutina, who learned it from Millie Pillsbury. The authors have made a modification that hides the seams more effectively than the original method. This method is also quite similar—although the strands are cut and joined in different sites—to the favorite method used by Helen Howard Feeley, who wrote an influential text on braiding in 1957.[2]

The Enclosed End Butt is easy to learn and adaptable to both straight braids and the fancy borders described in Chapter 8. Most of the other methods of butting do not work as easily for these fancy borders. The Enclosed End Butt does work for even the most complex braid.

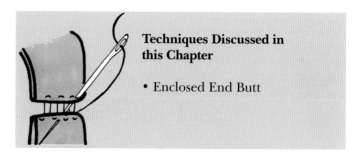

Techniques Discussed in this Chapter

• Enclosed End Butt

This method can be used when butting "on the rug," meaning that the row to be butted has been laced onto the project, except for 4 to 6" on either side of the butt area. Or this method can be used for butting "off the rug," in which the row is braided and butted as a ring before it is laced onto the rug or piece.

This butting method requires some hand sewing. While this is acceptable to some, it is daunting to others. See Hand Sewing Techniques in the Appendix for a description of the stitches.

Supplies Needed for this Technique

• Start Safety pin
• Finish Clothespin
• 3 small safety pins, 1 large safety pin
• Felt-tip markers, or more safety pins
• Scissors
• Needle nose pliers or hemostat

Enclosed End Butt

The Enclosed End Butt begins with the Enclosed End Butt Start. This Start is almost identical to the Enclosed End Start, discussed in Braiding Basics, Chapter 5. The difference is in the placement of the ends onto the Start Pin.

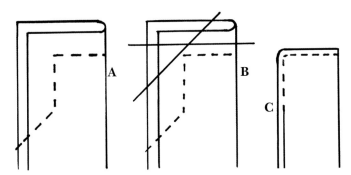

1. Enclosed End Butt Start.
(A) Fold the end of each strip right sides together lengthwise. Start sewing at the fold, about 1/4" from the top raw edge. Sew a distance just a few threads wider than the width of a folded strip. Reverse the stitching, and come forward again to the same place in order to reinforce the seam. Make a sharp right angle turn by lifting the presser foot and turning the fabric with the needle down. Sew along the side of the raw edge about 1/2". The seam can either end here, or some choose to veer off to end the stitching. If hand stitching, use a narrow backstitch.
(B) Clip the raw edges at the end seam to 1/8". Clip closely at the corner with a diagonal cut. Do not trim the side seam.
(C) Turn the sewn strips right side out by using a hemostat or pliers to grasp the inside seam at the end and help turn the strip. Push the corners outward with the hemostat or pliers.

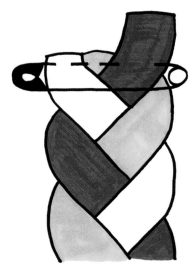

3. Beginning to Braid.
Begin braiding by throwing the right strand over the center. Braid a length long enough to overlap the Start at the butt site by a few inches. Place a clothespin to clamp the Finish End.

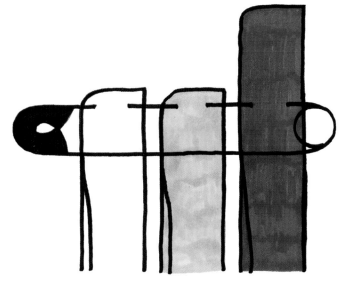

2. Arranging Strands on Start Pin.
Arrange the strands on the Start Pin in the following fashion: keeping folded edges to the left, place the right strand so that there is about 3/8" of a tail hanging off the Start Pin. The middle and left strands are pinned close to the end seams, as in the normal Enclosed End Start described in Chapter 5. For narrower strips and tiny braids, pin the right strand with about 1/4" hanging off the Start Pin.

4: Identify the Butt Site.
Lay the Start End on top of the Finish End, remembering that the smooth sides are on the right and the folded edges are on the left. Find where the loop colors match up exactly, shown here with marker lines and safety pin.

Start End

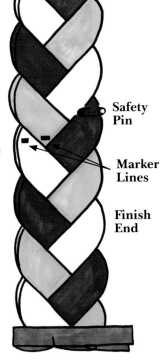

Safety Pin

Marker Lines

Finish End

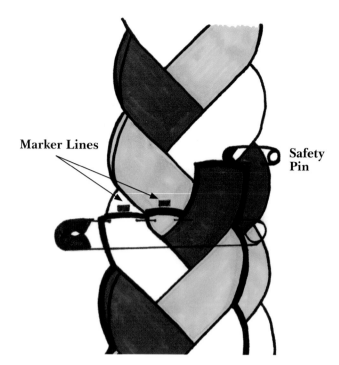

Marker Lines

Safety Pin

5. Marking the Finish Strands.
This diagram is a close-up view of the Start End laying on top of
the Finish End, so that the sites for marking the Finish strands
are clearly visible.
Mark the Finish strands just above each Start strand loop. Mark
them either with a small dash of contrasting felt-tip marker
(black or red for light fabrics, metallic silver for dark fabrics)
or with small safety pins, catching only one layer of fabric. Two
strands in the diagram above are marked with felt tip marker;
the 3rd strand is marked with a safety pin.

6. Place a securing
pin in the Finish
braid at least 2"
above the marked
sites.

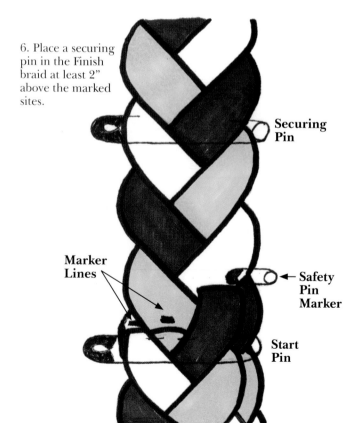

Securing Pin

Marker Lines

Safety Pin Marker

Start Pin

7. Unbraiding and Cutting the Strands.
Unbraid the Finish End back to
the securing pin. Cut the strands
straight across, 1/4" below the
marked sites.

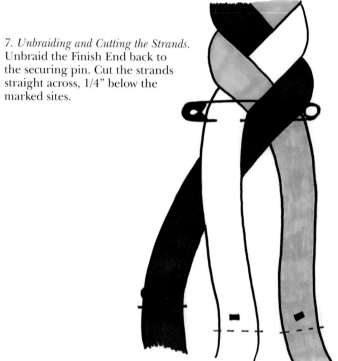

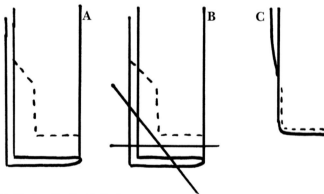

A   B   C

8. Enclose the Finish Ends.
Repeating the same steps used in the Enclosed End Butt Start,
enclose the ends of the 3 Finish End strands, as pictured. Before
sewing the seam, make sure that any marker lines or dashes will
not be visible once the end is turned right side out. Sew each
end seam 1/4" above the cut end, and trim the end seam and
corner as above. Use hemostat or pliers to grab the end seam
and help turn the end right side out, as with the Start.

9. Rebraid, and Secure Ends.
Rebraid the Finish ends. The shortest strand should finish braiding on the right, in preparation for matching up with the longer Start strand, shown in red. Pin at this site. The other 2 strands will usually be longer.

10. Throw the left strand over the center so that it matches to its mate, green in diagram. The middle strand will naturally match its mate on the left, white in diagram.

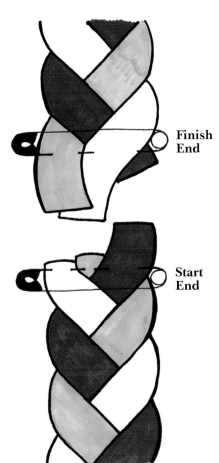

Finish End

Start End

12. Sew the Ends Together.
Taking each set of strands one at a time, pull on both strands to get some length to work with. Starting with the outer right strands (red in the prior diagram) and using matching thread, sew the front, sides, and back of the ends together. Try to keep the stitching invisible by entering the fabric where the last stitch ended, and redirecting the needle in a slightly different path. Do not continue the same needle and thread to tack the next strand; tie off the thread after sewing each strand, so that the strands can move separately from each other.

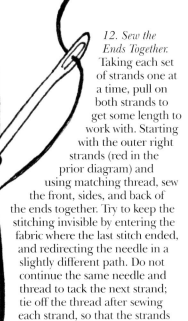

Some sew the backs together first, by putting the backs of matching strands together and whip-stitching the ends. To sew the front and sides of the strands, straighten the strand out so that the fronts touch each other, and sew. (no picture)

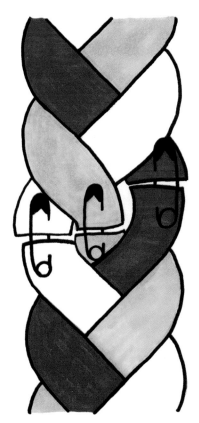

11. Pin the Matching Ends Together.
Using small safety pins, pin each matching set of strands together, as above. Remove the Start Pin and Finish pins, leaving only the small safety pins.

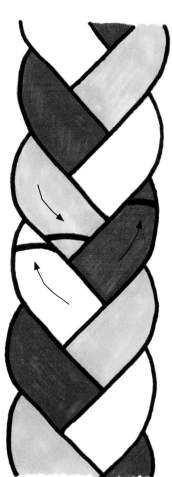

13. Move Loops to Hide Seams.
To hide the seams, move the seams upward or downward in the braid with a hemostat or pliers, so that the seam is buried under an adjacent loop.

1 & 2. Feeley, Helen Howard. *The Complete Book of Rug Braiding.* Coward-McCann, Inc., New York, 1957, p. 41.

8 Borders

Overview

As illustrated throughout this book, borders can make a braided or hooked center more interesting and unique. Borders can be either hooked or braided. They can be as simple as one straight braid laced around a hooked piece, or as complex as multiple borders, alternating between hooking and braiding.

Certain assumptions about borders apply to this chapter.

- First, all braided borders are butted.
- Second, before a border is attached, the center must have a single row of butted, straight braid laced and sewn onto it. This braid serves as the base onto which a border is attached.

Techniques Discussed in this Chapter

- Straight Braid Borders
- Straight Braid Borders for Previously Finished Hooked Centers
- Hooked Borders
- Braided Borders
- Designs/Patterns
- Fancy Borders

Pocket Knot, Kris McDermet. 14" x 18". 2010.
One straight braid border frames the braided center followed by three more hooked and braided borders.

• Third, all hooked borders are finished with at least one row of straight braid. Hooking can be finished without braids, but in this book, which encourages combination pieces, only finishing with braids is described.

• After the straight braid is attached, experimentation with the addition of "fancy" braided borders is encouraged.

This chapter is organized into the following sections:
• Straight braid borders for hooked or braided centers
• Straight braid borders for previously finished hooked centers
• Hooked borders attached to a braided center
• Braided borders

The braided borders are further divided into:
• Patterned design borders
• Fancy borders, solid and openwork

At the end of the chapter, there is a discussion of challenging borders, those that, because of the shape of their centers or the fact that the centers are attached, are challenging to border. Both braided and hooked solutions are discussed.

Prior Techniques Needed for this Chapter

• Braiding Basics
• Hooking Basics
• Enclosed End Butt

OVERVIEW

A simple border of a single, butted braid is needed to finish either hooked or braided centers, or a hooked border, before additional borders can be attached. In this section the technique for lacing on a straight braid border to braided and tapered round centers, braided and blunt-ended square or rectangular centers, and variously shaped hooked centers are described.

Glia, Cathy Mathiesen, Hooking; Kris McDermet, Braiding. 17" diameter. 2008.
Two simple straight braid borders surround the hooked center.

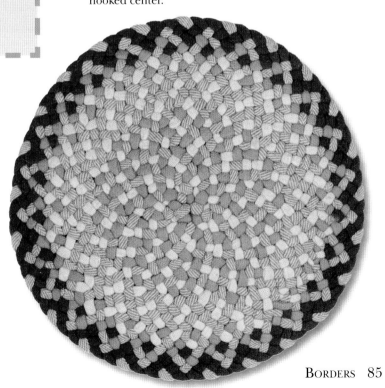

Starburst Pink Chair Pad, Kris McDermet. 17" diameter. 1988. Large braided center with 3 colors surrounded by 2 straight braid borders.

STRAIGHT BRAID BORDER: ROUND AND OVAL BRAIDED CENTERS

Attaching a straight braid around a round center is fairly simple. Increases or skips are made evenly around the circle, including over the taper. The butt site is not placed over the taper site. Once the straight braid has been laced over the tapered area, remember to go back and sew down any tapered ends that were left unstitched.

The same guidelines apply to an oval center.

When butting a straight braid, the butt can either be done "on the rug" or "off the rug." In general, on the rug—meaning that the braid is laced around the center before it is butted—is recommended, because it eliminates the possibility of having a twist in the braid, or of miscounting the number of needed loops. Butting off the rug is defined as butting the straight braid into a ring and then lacing the ring onto the rug or piece.

Instructions for lacing on the braid before butting:

1. To begin lacing, leave a tail of 4" of the start of the braid and 6" of lacing thread unlaced. Do not start the lacing over a taper.

2. Lace around the piece, spacing increases equally, until the Finish End overlaps the Start End by a few inches. Stop lacing a few inches away from the overlap. Make sure the loops match at the butt site. Unlace and relace if necessary to get the butt to match up without having to stretch the braid.

3. Perform the Enclosed End Butt, then complete the lacing. Where the lacing ends meet, tie them in a square knot, and bury the ends under 3 loops before cutting flush with the braid.

Lacing on an already butted braid: Some braiders are more comfortable butting off the rug. This method is more portable; less fabric and fewer tools are needed if done away from home, and the center of the piece does not even need to be brought along. It is possible to purchase patterns in which the loop count of every butted row has already been calculated. See Resources, specifically for Barbara Fisher.

1. Make sure that there are no twists in the braid.

2. Count the number of loops around the base braid; where there is a taper, count the half of the piece that does not have a taper and double the number of loops. To this number, add the number of expected increases. A very rough estimate is that each row of braid for a round or oval increases by about 6" in length, so increase by however many loops are in 6" of braid with the current fabrics. The final number of loops should be divisible by 3 in order to butt properly, e.g., match the strands with like strands.

3. Overlap the braid and perform the Enclosed End Butt.

4. After butting, start lacing the braid anywhere desired, spacing increases appropriately. Tie off the lacing thread ends when the lacing has been completed, as above.

ADDING ADDITIONAL ROWS OF STRAIGHT BRAID TO ROUND AND OVAL CENTERS

The same instructions above apply if additional rows of straight braids are added to an initial border row. Either braid and lace around the shape, adding increases as necessary, and butt where the braids overlap; or, butt off the rug, calculating the increases by adding the number of loops found along 6" of braid. Do not stack the butted areas of the rows on top of each other: distribute the butt sites around the shape for successive rows.

STRAIGHT BRAID BORDER: SQUARE AND RECTANGULAR CENTERS

Attaching a border of a single butted braid to either a square or rectangle is simple, because there are no increases. The 4 triple corners naturally increase each row by a loop count of 12. It is important to assure that the triple corners fall at the right location, and that the sides have the correct loop count.

Location for Butt: It is easiest to place the butt location, and start braiding the border row, about 6" further down the long side from where the blunt ending is located. The square is similar: start the braid and locate the butt about 6" down from the blunt ending. In this way, it is easy to assure that the loop count laced over the blunt ending is correct, because this area is one of the last sites to be laced before the butt occurs. It is easy to make sure that the lacing over the blunt ending preserves the correct loop count for that side, and if a mistake is made, it is not far to unlace.

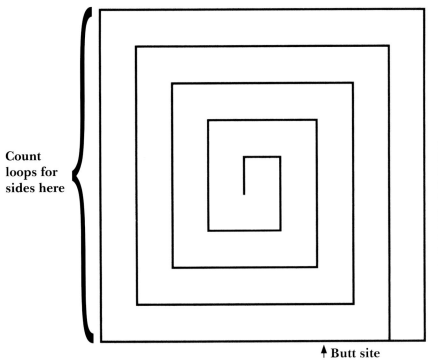

Count loops for sides here

↑ **Butt site**

Square.
For a square, the loop count should be equal on all sides. Count the number of smooth-side loops on the base braid *between* triples on a side that does not contain the blunt ending. Add 3 to this loop number. On the border braid, all sides should have this new number of loops between triples.

Count long-side loops here

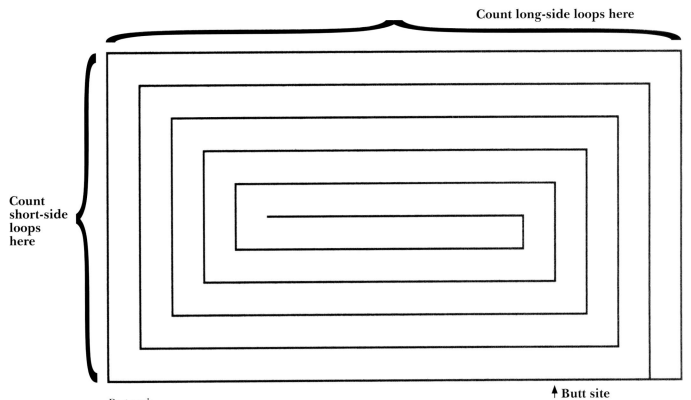

Count short-side loops here

↑ **Butt site**

Rectangle.
For a rectangle, opposite sides must have an equal loop count. Count the number of loops between triples on a short side that does not contain a blunt ending. Add 3 to this number; that is the number of loops between triples on both of the short sides. Do the same to calculate the number of loops for the long sides.

ADDITIONAL ROWS OF STRAIGHT BRAID BORDER: SQUARE AND RECTANGULAR SHAPE

If additional rows of straight braid are added, the loop count per side between the triple corners increases by 3 with each added row. For example, if a square has a loop count of 15 between triple corners on each side of the base braid, in the next row the count will be 18. For a rectangle, both the short side count and long side count increase by 3. After the first row covering the blunt ending, it is no longer necessary to butt 6" down from the ending; in fact, butting in the same site should be avoided. Space the butt sites of successive rows around the shape.

STRAIGHT BRAID BORDER: HEART SHAPE

A heart includes both a taper and corners. Adding a row of straight braid essentially follows the guidelines for rounds and ovals: make both sides of the heart match in loop count, keep the loop count over the taper equal to other areas on the braid, and add increases as needed. The loop count found along 6" of straight braid is an estimate for the number of needed increases. Take care to place the corners properly, following the instructions used to make the heart-shaped braided center, found in Chapter 6.

ADDITIONAL ROWS OF STRAIGHT BRAID: HEART SHAPE

Additional rows of straight braid may be added around a heart shape. Make increases in loop count to keep the braid flat around the curves, and continue to follow the guidelines for stacking double corners. Space the butt sites around the shape for successive rows.

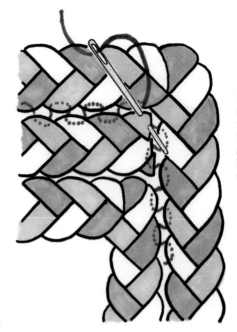

Lacing over a blunt ending usually requires switching to a tapestry needle, and piercing the blunt ends to lace to the new braid.

Straight Braid Border around Hooked Centers

Placing a border of a single straight braid around a hooked center is necessary to cover the whip stitching of the lining to the rug backing at the outer edge of the center. If the hooked center is a round shape, the braid should be about 3/4" larger all the way around than the finished center. Any needed increases should be spaced around the center equally in order to ease in the natural fullness of the circle.

Bird with Berries Chair Pad, Kris McDermet. 13" diameter. 2006. *Photographed by Laurie Indenbaum*

When placing a straight braid around a cornered piece, such as a square or rectangle, it is not necessary to have the 3/4" of extra space as described above. Braiding a square hooked center is done differently than a round hooked center. Instead, the braid should loosely but closely abut the edges of the hooked center. Loop counts should match on all sides for a square, and on opposite sides for a rectangle. Triple corners should be placed carefully at all corners.

An octagonal or hexagonal hooked center requires that all sides have the same loop count in between double corners. Butt the braid between corners on the straight portion of the braid. When lacing the braid to the center, make sure to sew each corner of the hooking as in the diagram below. The only difference is that a double corner is found in the braid at each corner, not a triple.

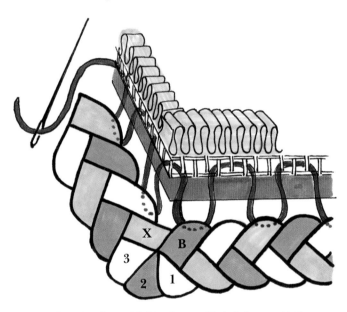

Sewing and Lacing the Braided Border to a Hooked Center with Corners. This shows the exaggerated distance between the padded and lined hooking and the straight braid border. The lacing thread should be tight between the braid and the rug backing; this diagram has them spaced apart to show the correct lacing and sewing sequence at the corner.

Attaching the braid involves alternating lacing through every other loop of the braid, and sewing 1/2" through the thin rim of rug backing visible on the side of the finished hooked center. Note that when lacing the corner, the B loop of the triple is laced, then the corner of the hooking, then the loop *after* the crossover loop.

ATTACHING A STRAIGHT BRAID BORDER TO A PADDED AND LINED HOOKED ROUND CENTER

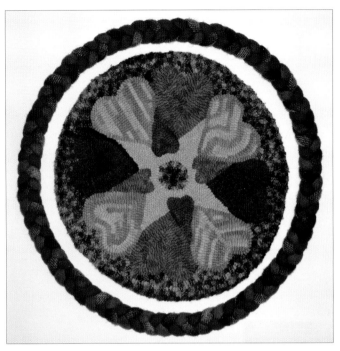

1. Make an Enclosed End Butt Start, and straight braid enough length so that when the circle of braid is placed around the center, there is 3/4" of air space between the braid and the hooked center. The braid can be butted either on or off the finished center. The photo shows a butted braided border before attaching it to the center.

2. Pin the butted braid in place at the 12, 3, 6, and 9 o'clock locations, using large safety pins.

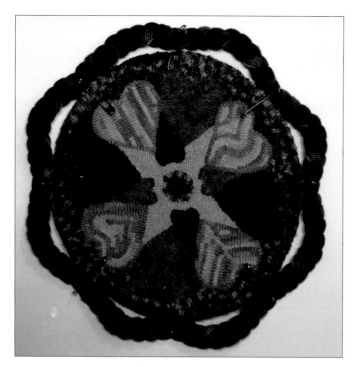

3. Place 4 more safety pins between the first pins, spaced evenly around the center. The braid is ready to be sewn and laced to the finished hooked center.

4. The finished hooked center with one row of straight braid attached.

ADDING ADDITIONAL ROWS OF STRAIGHT BRAID AROUND HOOKED SHAPES

Round Shape

When lacing on a new braid to a base braid sewn and laced to a hooked center, every loop is laced on the base braid which is different from sewing and lacing to a hooked center. Increases are made by skipping loops on the new braid as with all braided oval pieces. See the regular lacing instructions found in Oval Center, Chapter 6.

Square Shape

For a square shape, keep the loop counts of all sides equal; the loop count between triple corners on each side increases by 3 per row. Follow the guidelines for alternating triple corners in the section Square Braided Centers, Chapter 6. In one row, the new braid's loop B laces to the base braid triple's space between loops 1 & 2; in the next row, between loops 2 & 3. The same instructions apply to rectangles.

Heart Shape

For heart-shaped hooked centers, the corners are doubles, and additional rows of straight braid with double corners are stacked along the vertical center according to the guidelines discussed for Heart-shaped Braided Center, Chapter 6. Increase as necessary within each row to keep the braid flat around the curves.

Octagonal and Hexagonal Shape

For octagonal and hexagonal hooked centers, additional rows have an increase in loop count between double corners of 2 per row. For example, if the base straight braid has 20 loops on each side between double corners, the next row has 22.

For all shapes, space the butt sites of additional rows of straight braid around the shape.

ATTACHING A STRAIGHT BRAID BORDER TO A PREVIOUSLY FINISHED HOOKED CENTER

Hooked pieces that have been finished by a technique other than attaching braids can become the center for a braided border, especially if they have a rolled edge that has been whip stitched with wool or another fabric. This offers hooking artists the opportunity to experiment with braided borders without creating a new hooked project. After one border of straight braid is attached, any of the additional hooked or braided borders presented here can be added. These pieces are best suited as wall hangings or table mats, or if for the floor, in a low traffic area.

This rolled edge is one of many techniques that hooking artists use to finish a hooked piece for the floor or wall without attached braids. This square will be used as an example for how to attach braids after a hooked piece has been finished by another method.

This 8" square was made by Lucy Clark for a "green" square exchange at the 2009 TIGHR Conference, see Networking section in Appendix. The outside edge of the square was rolled and then whip stitched in matching green needlepoint yarn.

1. Cut out padding for the hooked center to within 1/8" of the outside of the rolled edge.

2. Cut out thin wool lining 1-1.25" larger than the finished hooked piece and pin, with large safety pins, to hold the layers together in preparation for sewing.
There are 3 layers: the finished hooked center, the padding on the inside of the hooking, and the lining.

3. Fold the lining around the padding. Using matching thread, whip stitch the folded lining to the wool yarn that was used to finish the hooking. Three layers are now showing when looking at the side view: the final row of hooked loops, the wool yarn whipped border, and the folded lining fabric. The hand sewn stitches also show, but this side view of layers will be covered by the first row of braid.

4. Choose 3 colors of wool, and prepare strips for braiding. Make the Enclosed End Butt Start and braid 2/3 of the length of one of the straight sides of the hooked center. If the finished hooked piece is round or oval, braid 1.25 times around the outside border of the hooked piece. (not pictured)

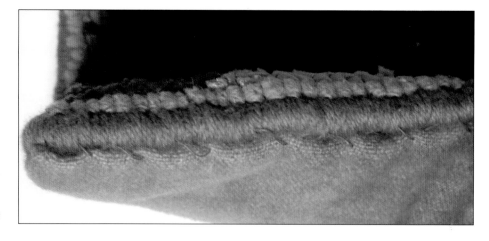

5. The braid is ready to be attached. The folded edge of the braid is facing the 3 layers of the hooked center. Load a darning needle with lacing thread. Leaving a 5" tail of lacing thread unknotted and a 4" tail of braid, begin lacing through a loop 4" down from one of the 4 corners. Place a 1/2" stitch through the wool that has been whipped around the rolled edge of the rug backing.

6. Use the eye end of the darning needle to lace through a loop, then switch to the pointed end of the darning needle and sew through 1/2" of the rolled edge. Lace every other loop, alternating with sewing through the yarn on the rolled edge.
Since this piece has straight sides, it is not necessary to make increases in the braid to add fullness, as would be necessary with a round center. Be careful not to stretch the braid when lacing and sewing it to the straight sides.

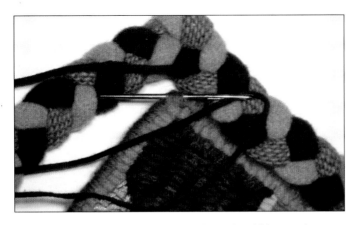

7. Lace and sew to the first corner. There should be one loop right before the point of the corner of the whip stitched rolled wool edge. Sew directly through the point at this corner.

8. Braid a triple corner (RRRL). Do not lace through the crossover loop, marked here with a red dot. This crossover loop should lie directly at the point of the corner. Lace through the next loop on the braid as pictured. Sew and lace along the 2nd side of the hooked square center to the next corner, then around the square back to the Start.
Count the loops on the sides of the braid. Make sure that loop counts are the same on matching sides of a rectangle, or the same on all 4 sides of a square.

9. When the sewing and lacing around the center are finished, complete the Enclosed End Butt. Sew and lace the butt site to the hooking, and tie a square knot in the lacing thread so that it is hidden in the valleys created between the loops of the braid. Run the excess lacing thread under 4-5 loops and cut off the excess.

OVERVIEW

Hooking can be used as both a center and a border in combination rugs and other pieces. In fact, the entire piece can be created so that braiding and hooking go back and forth as a series of borders. As an example, see the chair pad *Springtime Wreath*, which features a braided center, then a hooked border in the shape of a wreath, one straight braid butted row, and a final picot braided fancy border. Similarly, the table mat, *Turquoise Table Wreath* has a tiny braid center, a hooked wreath border, several rows of butted tiny braids, and a final border of picot braid.

The braided center can be a square, rectangle, oval, hexagonal, triangle, heart or a scalloped shape. The hooked border is designed, hooked, and attached so that it appears to be part of the entire piece. Using complementary or the same fabrics in the hooking and braiding can integrate the two even further.

Instructions given in this section are applicable to bordering any shaped center. Specific instructions for a chair pad project with a hooked wreath and braided border are in Chapter 12.

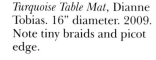

Techniques Discussed in this Section

• Finishing Inner and Outer Edges of Hooking
• Finishing Hooked Pieces of Different Shapes

Turquoise Table Mat, Dianne Tobias. 16" diameter. 2009. Note tiny braids and picot edge.

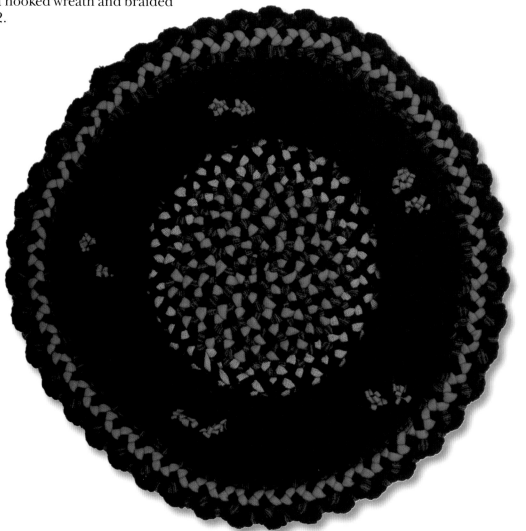

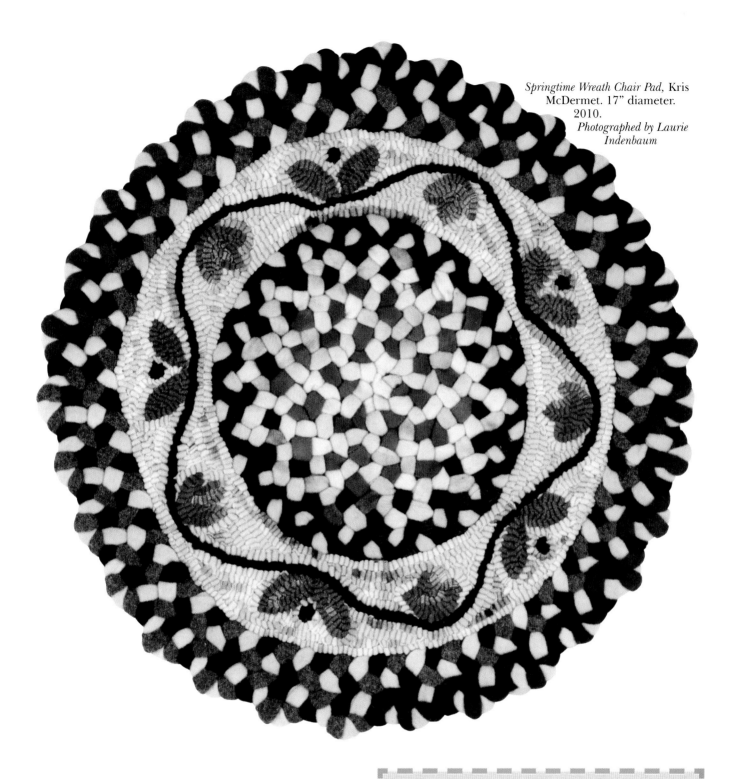

Springtime Wreath Chair Pad, Kris McDermet. 17" diameter. 2010.
Photographed by Laurie Indenbaum

Prior Techniques Needed for this Section

• Hooking Basics
• Finishing a Hooked Center
• Enclosed End Butt

SIZE & FABRIC PLANNING

After making the braided center, decide how large and what shape to make the hooked border. The shapes can mimic each other, as with concentric circles; or can contrast in shape, as with a round braided center and scalloped hooked border. Mats or rugs of this style with multiple borders can be planned ahead and carefully measured based on the size of the braided center, or the next step can be determined as each border is made.

The same wool can be used for the hooking and braiding, or hand-dyed hooked wool can be combined with complementary "as is" braided wool. Choices include vibrant and contrasting fabrics to make the hooked border become the focal point of the rug, or similar colors for both portions of the project, blending the center and hooked border evenly into each other.

Bittersweet, Kris McDermet. 30" diameter. 2009.
Painting by Lynn Hoeft
Photographed by Laurie Indenbaum

Pocket Knot, Kris McDermet. 17" x 23". 2010. Multiple braided and hooked borders.

INSTRUCTION

Before beginning the hooked border, choose and braid one of the shapes described in Braided Centers, Chapter 6. Finish the braided center with a butted row of straight braid.

Here the center is already a combination itself: small braided rectangle, hooked border, and one row of straight braid.

The instructions in this section apply to any hooked border, but they refer specifically to the larger hooked border which will be placed around the combination center, shown in the photo below.

If the hooked border is a simple circle or concentric square, determine the width of the hooked border, and use a ruler to measure outward from the traced line. Mark the width of the border at regular intervals, and then make the outer pattern line by connecting the marks. For example, if the hooked border will be three inches wide, lay the ruler around the traced line at regular intervals, and place a dot at 3" out from the line. Connect the dots and to outer edge of the pattern.

If the hooked border is not a concentric shape, for example, a scalloped edge, use a household object such as a plate or bowl to create regularly spaced scallops; measure the spacing carefully both between scallops, and outward from the center line to the peaks and valleys. Wavy line borders can either be drawn free hand, or traced onto a template that is repeated regularly around the edge of the pattern.

1. Make the hooked border pattern by tracing the outside edge of the finished braided center onto a piece of newsprint paper, making this traced line 1/8" larger than the braided center. This extra 1/8" allows some room for attaching the hooked border to the braided center, because the hooking often expands slightly.

2. Transfer the hooking pattern onto the rug backing using inexpensive netting, e.g., the kind used in bridal gowns. Place the netting with the traced design on top of the rug backing, tape it securely to avoid shifting, and retrace the design. The marking pen ink goes through the holes in the netting and transfers the design to the rug backing. Take off the netting and re-mark the design on the rug backing if the lines are too light.

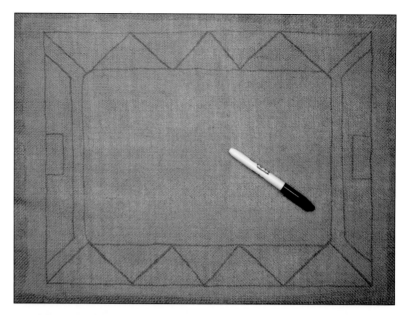

3. Hook the border design as follows: On the inside border line, hook 3-4 rows of the background fabric. These inner edge rows allow a row or two to be taken out if the finished hooked piece becomes too large to accommodate the braided center, due to expansion of the hooking.
Next, hook the outline of each design, then hook the inside of the designs. Outline the designs in the background fabric, and finally, hook the background. Block the hooked piece, if needed.

4. Make sure the braided center fits in the outer hooked border. The hooked piece is now ready to be padded and lined.

5. Cut the excess rug backing 1-1.25" from the outside border of the hooking.

6. Cut the padding for the outer and inner border of the hooking about 1/8" in from these two borders.

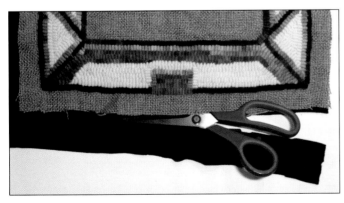

7. Cut thin wool lining for the outside hooked border the same size as the cut for the rug backing.

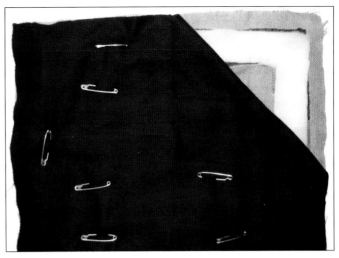

8. Pin the three layers together. "Ease" cuts are not necessary for turning the rug backing or lining on the outside of a round or square-cornered hooked border. If the rug backing and lining do not lay flat, either the lining has been sewn too tightly to the rug backing, or ease cuts may be needed.

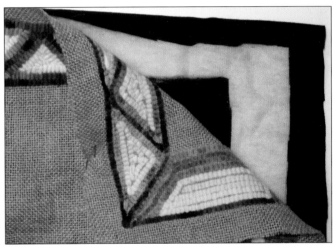

9. Turn the thin lining over the padding. Turn the rug backing to the wrong side and using a whip stitch, hand sew the lining to the thin rim of the outside of the hooked border's rug backing. These stitches stabilize the piece before cutting out the inner edges of the 3 layers.
Here, the inner border of the padding has been cut but not the inner border of the lining.

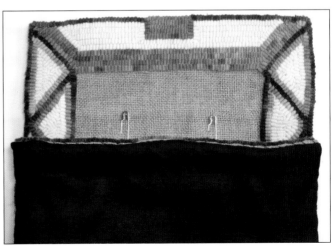

10. This shows the finished 3 layers: lining, thin rim of rug backing, and outside final row of hooking. The inner border has not been cut out.

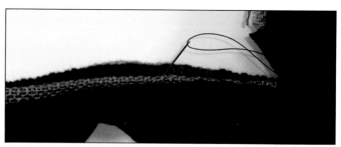

11. A hooked border differs from a hooked center in that there is an inside edge to prepare.

Cut out the braided center shape from the rug hooking backing and thin wool lining. Leave an extra 1-1.25" of extra rug backing and lining for turning under. With rounded shapes it is common to need ease cuts to keep the turned-under backing and lining laying flat. The inner edge of the padding has already been cut. The ease cuts can be made 1/8" to 1/4" away from the outside row of hooking. Start with 1/4" and re-cut if needed so that the piece lies flat.

14. Using a whip stitch and matching thread, hand sew the inner seam by sewing between the wool lining and the thin rim of turned rug backing. Sew around the shape and end with a knot. When looking at the edge of the finished padded and backed hooked piece, there are three layers: the hooked rug loops standing straight, the thin rim of rug backing, and the wool lining.

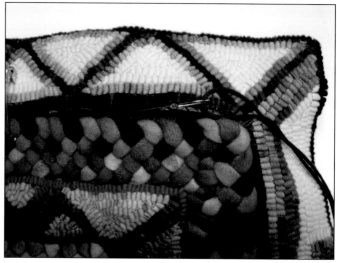

12. Cut through the wool lining and the rug backing 1/8" to 1/4" from the corners, in preparation for folding.

15. Attach the hooked border to the braided center by threading a tapestry needle with lacing thread. Leaving a 5" tail of lacing thread, make a 1/2" stitch through the thin rim of the rug backing visible on the inner hooked border an inch or two beyond one of the four corners.

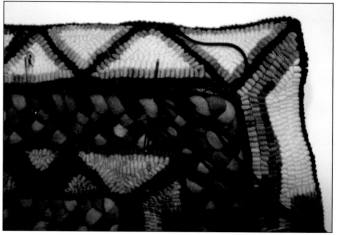

13. Fold the lining around the layer of padding.

16. Lace a loop on the outer edge of the braided center. Lace into every other braided loop. When the hooked border is fully sewn and laced around the four corners and straight sides of the braided center, tie the start end of the lacing thread to the finish end with a square knot. Hide the ends by lacing them under 4 to 5 loops of braid, and cutting off the excess.

The finished mat with multiple braided and hooked borders. The outer border can be followed by more straight braids and/or fancy borders, as described later in this chapter.

Braided Designs / Patterns

OVERVIEW

Braiding patterned designs into a butted border adds an appealing element to the braiding. With planning, it is possible to create patterns such as dots, diamonds, and slashes within the braids. These designs add sparkle, and mark the project as one made by a skillful braider. Braided patterns are also interesting when placed on the sides of baskets and bags.

Designs Presented in this Section

- Dots
- Right Slashes
- Left Slashes
- Alternating Slashes
- Flowers I & II
- Arrowhead
- Triangles
- Rick Rack
- Lacy Rick Rack
- Diamonds
- Back-to-Back Triangles
- Braids, or Double Diamonds

Multicolor Bag with Designs,
Donna Mickewich.
15.5" x 10". 2010.

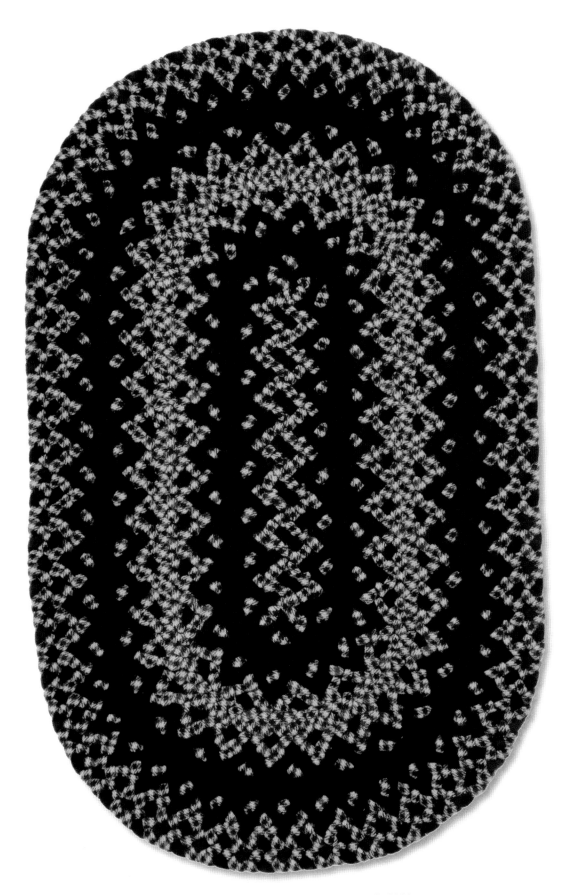

Ric Rac Magic, Myra Jane Ober. 28" x 44". 2010.
Note creation of designs with just 2 fabrics.

Designs require 2 elements to make them stand out:

• Contrast: The color creating the patterned design should have sufficient contrast against the background to stand out. For instance, black against white, or white against black, provide the most contrast, whereas medium gray against medium brown provide insufficient contrast to make the design visible. The contrast color is usually a solid fabric. The background color can have more texture, e.g., a tweed or plaid.

• Surrounding Calm: To make a design stand out, "calm" rows should be placed on either side of the design. If a beautiful diamond design is placed immediately adjacent to a busy 3-color braid, the edges of the diamonds will be poorly defined. However, if a design is surrounded by rows of braid made from 3 strands of the background color, the pattern can be dramatic.

Moss and Mauve, Christine Manges. 4'2" x 6'4". 2008.

Christmas Rug, Bobbi Mahler. 30" diameter. 2008. Note use of color and solid rows to highlight the design.

Designs for Different Shapes

It is easier to place designs into certain rug shapes than in others. Straight braids laced together are probably the easiest project in which to place a patterned design, because there are no curves or double corners to disrupt the pattern. Similarly, butted borders for bags and baskets lend themselves nicely to designs, because each row has the same number of loops; there are no increases and the loops stack up on top of each other perfectly. A rectangle or square adapts well to patterned borders; although these shapes have corners, the corners all are triples, which restore the chosen design after each corner.

Ovals and Circles: These are the most difficult shapes for maintaining a pattern because the curved shape requires increasing. When increases in loop count are made on the curves, the pattern is immediately thrown off.

As ovals and circles become larger, it is easier to add butted patterned borders. The curves become shallower, and fewer increases are required as these shapes grow. It becomes easier to add on several rows at a time without increasing at all, which is perfect for adding a design.

The rug must be at least 12" diameter, for a circle, or 12" measured across the curve, for an oval, before adding a design without increases can be considered. The larger the rug, the easier it is to incorporate a design.

With increasing border rows, the only way to keep a pattern on an oval or circle is to have each row of pattern be the same loop count. All the increases needed for the whole design must be made when lacing on the first row of the design.

For example, the rick-rack design requires 3 rows to complete its pattern. When the first row of this pattern is laced on, it must include all of the increases necessary to keep all 3 rows of pattern flat. Increases cannot again be made until the final row of solid background color is added on, or the design will be thrown off.

Basket or Bag: Baskets or bags are ideal shapes for designs, as each row is usually the same loop count as the previous row. Count the number of loops on the base row. As long as it is a number divisible by 3, start making butted design rows that incorporate that loop count around. If the loop count is not divisible by 3, add one or two increases when adding on the first row to make it divisible by 3.

Square/Rectangle: When adding designs in border rows to a square or rectangle, the triple corners take care of all needed increases. Each row naturally increases by 4 corners x 3 loops = 12 loops each row. As triple corners do not disrupt a pattern, the patterns continue perfectly after the corners.

Hearts: with double corners throwing off the design, and curves to consider also, hearts are very difficult to place designs around consistently. Only one pattern is easy to work with in hearts: Flowers II, see below.

Hexagon/Octagon: Maintaining patterned borders around hexagons and octagons is difficult. The double corners necessary for these shapes disrupt the design at each corner. Patterns are best saved for the occasional rows, about every 6 to 8 rows, when the double corners start to become too pointy, and 2 to 3 rows are laced on as a straight braid, e.g., no corners.

Maintaining Designs Around Curves

There are 2 ways to calculate the number of increases necessary to maintain a design around an oval or round shape. These increases are made in the first row of the design.

Rough Answer: As the first row of a design is being laced on, put in too many increases, even to the point of making the row start ruffling. Only increase on the curves, not on the straight sides. As each additional row of the design is added on, make no increases at all. By the final row of the design, usually all of the ruffling has been flattened out. Press the design area with a wet pressing cloth and steam flat.

More Precise Answer: As discussed when adding on a row of straight braid, each row around a round or oval shape increases by about 6 inches. This estimate is somewhat large for tiny braids, and somewhat small for very large braids; the estimate is best for braids about 1" in width.

Measure the number of loops on 6" of braid with the current strips. Multiply this number of loops by the number of rows needed to make the pattern. Increase by this number when lacing on the first row of the design. Do not increase again until after the last row of the design has been laced on.

> Ex: Number of loops in 6" of current braid = 11
>> Number of rows for diamond design = 4
>> 4 x 11 = 44 increases spaced over first row of pattern

For a small rug, in which the curve is tighter, fitting 44 increases around the curves is impossible. As this example illustrates, it is much easier to fit designs around large, shallow curves.

DESIGNS

Making a border of patterned designs requires the planning and arrangement of contrast and background colors while lacing.

DOTS

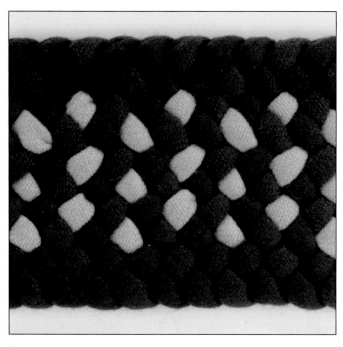

Dots Design

Dots. The dots design is easy and elegant.
• Rows required: At least 2; more rows are preferred
• Row 1: 1 contrast strand, 2 background strands
• Row 2 and any additional rows: same as Row 1
• Lacing: Lace the new braid's contrast loop between the base braid's 2 background loops, and repeat for each additional row

RIGHT SLASHES

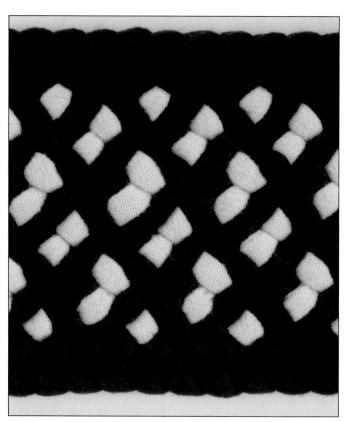

Right Slashes Design

Right Slashes. Several rows of slashes all pointing upward to the right make a pretty and effective design.
• Rows required: at least 2, more are preferred
• Row 1: 1 contrast color, 2 background colors
• Row 2 and any additional rows: same as Row 1
• Lacing: Lace the new braid's contrast loop just after lacing the base braid's contrast loop, e.g., the new braid's contrast loop should be below and to the left of the base braid's contrast loop

LEFT SLASHES

ALTERNATING SLASHES

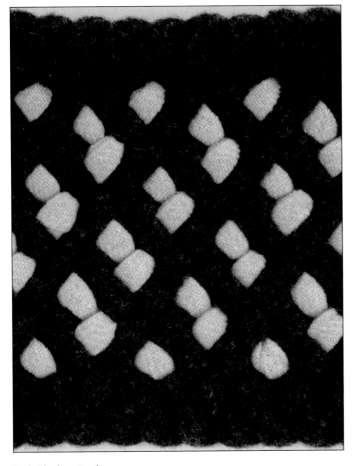

Left Slashes Design

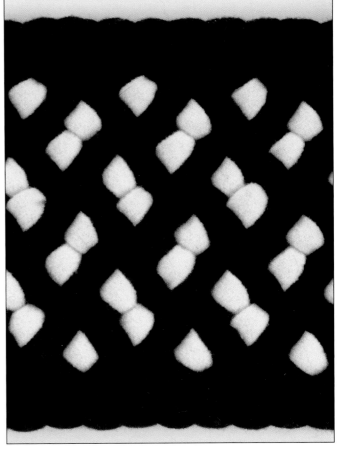

Alternating Slashes Design

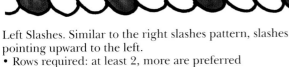

Left Slashes. Similar to the right slashes pattern, slashes pointing upward to the left.
• Rows required: at least 2, more are preferred
• Row 1: 1 contrast color, 2 background colors
• Row 2 and any additional rows: same as Row 1
• Lacing: Lace the new braid's contrast loop before lacing the base braid's contrast loop, i.e., arrange the new braid so that the contrast loop falls below and to the right of the base braid's contrast loop

Alternating Slashes. This pattern is created by alternating the slashes upward to the left and upward to the right. As with all slash patterns, they are most effective with at least 4 or 5 rows to establish the pattern.
• Rows required: at least 3
• Row 1: 1 contrast color, 2 background colors
• Row 2 and additional rows: same as Row 1
• Lacing: Alternate between the directions for left slashes, then the directions for right slashes, for each row

FLOWERS I

Flowers I Design

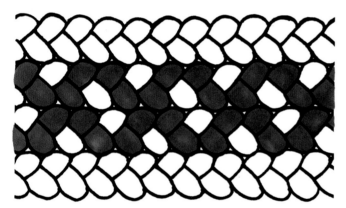

Flowers I. This design can be dramatic but must be set off by background rows to be seen. For this reason, the background rows, rows 1 and 4, are listed as part of the design.
- Rows required: 4
- Row 1: All 3 strands in background color
- Row 2: 2 contrast color strands, 1 background color strand
- Row 3: 2 contrast color strands, 1 background color strand
- Row 4: All 3 strands in background color
- Lacing: Slashes become the flower's center. When lacing row 3 onto row 2, it doesn't matter whether the slashes slant to the left or right

FLOWERS II

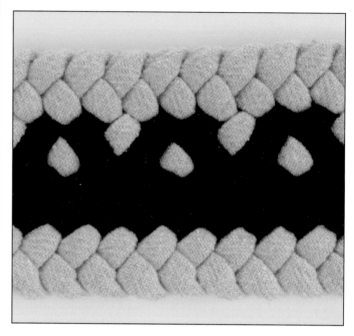

Flowers II Design

Flowers II. This simple design requires only 3 rows. The first and last rows are solid, with one patterned row. The simplicity of this design makes it one of the few that work around double corners, in an octagon, hexagon, or heart. The pattern is briefly altered at each corner, but then resumes quickly.
- Rows required: 3, but only one with patterned strands
- Row 1: All 3 strands in background color
- Row 2: 2 contrast color strands, 1 background color strand
- Row 3: All 3 strands in contrast color
- Lacing: No specific instructions

ARROWHEAD & TRIANGLES

These 2 designs are shown together, because they are the same design, but look quite different by changing the bottom row to either background or contrast color.

The arrowhead was one of the first designs ever described in braiding books and pamphlets. It creates a mirror image in its background color. The bottom row is the background color.

The triangle design is the same as the arrowhead but its bottom row is made from the contrast color, which completes the shape of the triangle.

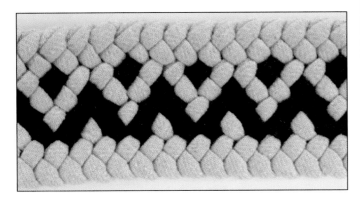

Arrowhead Design

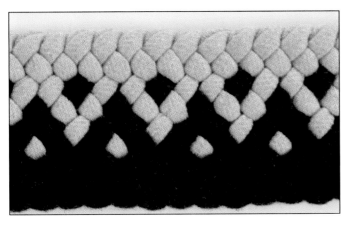

Triangle Design

A

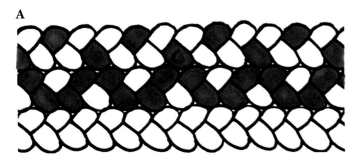

(A) Arrowhead & (B) Triangle.
• Rows required: 3
• Row 1: 1 contrast color, 2 background colors
• Row 2: 2 contrast colors, 1 background color
• Row 3: Arrowhead: 3 strands of background color
　　　　　Triangle: 3 strands of contrast color
• Lacing: Lace the 2 contrast loops of Row 2 to straddle the contrast loop of Row 1

RICK RACK

Rick Rack Design

Rick Rack. The rick rack pattern is beautiful and requires only 3 rows to develop the design. It can be "stacked" with the rick rack design appearing in both the contrast and background colors, and can be continued for as many rows as desired.
• Rows Required: 3
• Row 1: 1 contrast color, 2 background colors
• Row 2: 2 contrast colors, 1 background
• Row 3: 1 contrast color, 2 background colors
• Lacing:
　　Lace Row 2 by having the 2 contrast loops straddle Row 1's contrast loop
　　Lace Row 3 by having the contrast loop fall between Row 2's contrast loops

B

LACY RICK RACK

DIAMONDS

Lacy Rick Rack Design

Diamond Design

Lacy Rick Rack. This pattern creates a wider design than standard rick-rack, with loops of background color shining through to give it a "lacy," more open appearance. It is most effective when used as a single design and not "stacked" as in the manner often used with standard rick-rack.
- Rows Required: 4
- Row 1: 1 contrast color, 2 background colors
- Row 2: 2 contrast colors, 1 background color
- Row 3: 2 contrast colors, 1 background color
- Row 4: 1 contrast color, 2 background colors
- Lacing:
    Row 2: contrast loops of Row 2 straddle contrast loop of Row 1
    Row 3: background loop of Row 3 straddles contrast loops of Row 2
    Row 4: background loops of Row 4 straddle background loop of Row 3

Diamonds. Diamonds can create an impressive border pattern in a braided project and can clearly identify the braider as a skillful artist. The diamond's "center" is made of a slash of background loops; the slash can slant to the right or left.
- Rows Required: 4
- Row 1: 1 contrast color, 2 background
- Row 2: 2 contrast colors, 1 background
- Row 3: 2 contrast colors, 1 background
- Row 4: 1 contrast color, 2 background
- Lacing:
    Row 2: 2 contrast loops straddle Row 1's contrast loop
    Row 3: The background loop can be laced either before or after Row 2's background loop
    Row 4: The contrast loop fits between the 2 contrast loops of Row 3

BACK-TO-BACK TRIANGLES

DOUBLE DIAMONDS

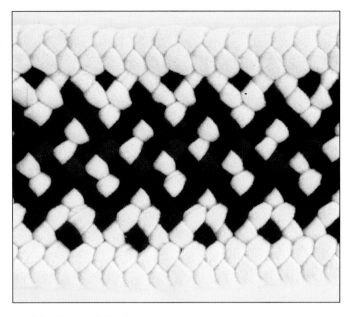

Back-to-Back Triangles Design

Double Diamond Design

Back-to-Back Triangles. This design is easy to continue around curves because, although it requires 5 rows, the middle (3rd) row is a solid, so increases can be made in this row which is the center of this design.
- Rows Required: 5
- Row 1: 1 contrast color, 2 background colors
- Row 2: 2 contrast colors, 1 background color
- Row 3: All 3 strands in contrast color
- Row 4: 2 contrast colors, 1 background color
- Row 5: 1 contrast color, 2 background colors
- Lacing:
    Row 2: 2 contrast loops straddle Row 1's contrast loop
    Row 3: Lace on; increase if needed around curves
    Row 4: Lace on; increase if needed. On any straight portions of the project, try to have the background loops of Row 4 approximately center on the background loops of Row 2. Note they will not match up exactly.
    Row 5: The contrast loop fits between Row 4's 2 contrast loops

Double Diamonds. Turned sideways, this pattern gives the appearance of braids, by stacking 2 diamonds which slant in opposite directions.
- Rows Required: 5
- Row 1: 1 contrast color, 2 background colors
- Row 2: 2 contrast colors, 1 background
- Row 3: 2 contrast colors, 1 background
- Row 4: 2 contrast colors, 1 background
- Row 5: 1 contrast color, 2 background colors
- Lacing (as per diagram):
    Row 2: Make the 2 contrast loops straddle Row 1's contrast loop
    Row 3: Lace the background loop BEFORE the background loop of Row 2
    Row 4: Lace the background loop AFTER the background loop of Row 3
    Row 5: Make the contrast color fit in between the 2 contrast loops of Row 4

Many other designs are possible, alone or by combining several designs, e.g., stack diamonds which alternate between contrast and background colors; stack rick rack in between rows of diamonds, etc. Use the following page to experiment!

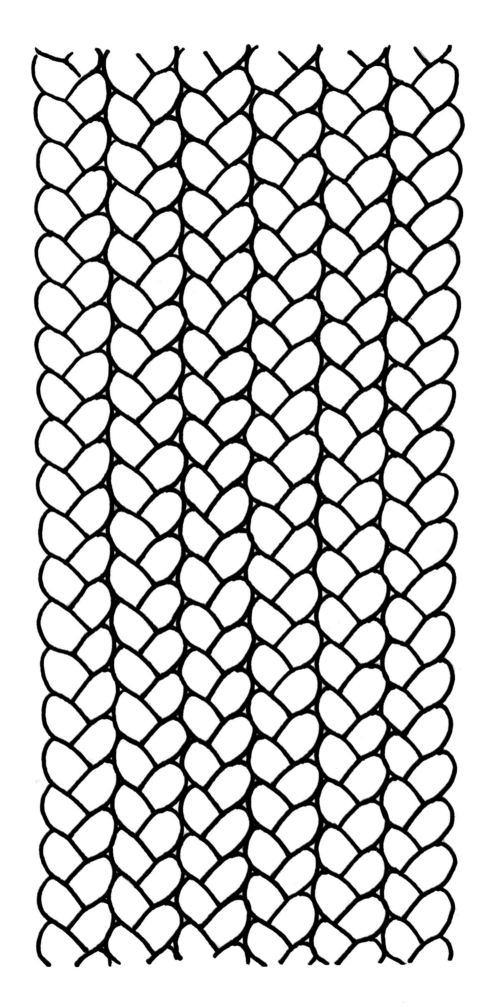

Fancy Borders

OVERVIEW

Fancy borders expand the possibilities of borders beyond straight braiding. They add eye-catching and attractive frames to a hooked or braided piece. Fancy borders may be as simple as a picot edge, or as fancy as several stacked borders.

The borders can either be "solid," meaning that there are no holes or "lacy," in which there is some openwork. Borders with larger openwork spaces are not ideal for rugs on the floor, but work well as borders for "off the floor" projects such as chair pads, table runners and mats, baskets, bags, and trivets.

Fancy borders often incorporate double and triple corners to make an edging have twists and turns. These corners are not difficult to learn; they are the same corners used in the first turn of an oval rug, or found in the corners of a square or rectangular rug.

Fabric and color variations can be used to produce interesting effects in fancy borders. For example, using a contrasting strand for the crossover loop in either the triple picot or the back-and-forth picot can create a very different look in the border than using 3 same-color strands.

Techniques Discussed in this Section

- Lunette Braids
- Shaker Picot
- Double Corner Braids
- Double Picot
- Triple Corner Braids
- Triple Picot
- Back and Forth Triple Picot
- Zig-zag
- Zig on Picot
- Knotted Arches
- Snowflake
- Stacked Triple Picots
- Scalloped
- Castle Top

There are many possible fancy borders. Only a few are detailed here. Once the basic techniques for braiding and butting these borders are learned, it will be possible for the reader to create more.

Christine Manges and Dianne Tobias. Chair pads/table mats with a variety of borders.

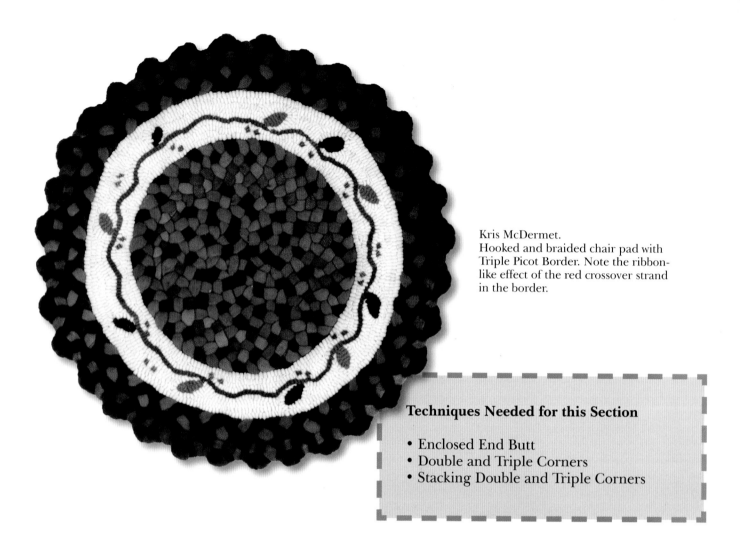

Kris McDermet.
Hooked and braided chair pad with
Triple Picot Border. Note the ribbon-
like effect of the red crossover strand
in the border.

GENERAL GUIDELINES FOR FANCY BORDERS

1. All fancy borders are started using the Enclosed End Butt Start.

2. Fancy borders are butted using the Enclosed End Butt.

3. If there is a double or triple corner in the border, pull the crossover loop firmly while braiding. A firm crossover loop makes the corner sharp, and the path of the braid more interesting.

4. Never lace the crossover loop… unless instructed to do so!

5. Fancy border elements that stand out from the straight braid base are called "motifs." Examples of motifs would be the points of zigzags or picots, or the arches of knotted arches. The number of base braid loops required to be able to lace on each motif are called a "repeat."

Motifs should be spaced evenly around a shape. Planning for fancy borders requires counting the loops available in the base braid and determining if the specific border will fit. If placed around a round center, there should be an equal number of loops on the base braid between motifs. If placed around a square, there should be equal numbers of motifs on

each side. This becomes important when the border is laced to the base.

6. Cornered shapes often look best when the fancy border emphasizes a corner. For example, if a double picot border is placed around a square, then a longer-than-usual space of straight braid could be placed on either side of the corner. In this example, perhaps a triple corner could be used at the corner, instead of a double.

7. Lacing tips:

• Space motifs evenly: Count the base braid loops, the number of loops around the straight braid laced onto the project. Divide by the "repeat" size, the number of loops required for lacing on each motif within the border. If the number does not divide evenly, spread the extra loops around evenly.

Example: A round hooked center has 58 loops around its straight braid border. The repeat size for the chosen border requires 6 loops of base braid. 10 motifs can be spaced evenly (6 x 10 = 60), and 2 increases must be made when lacing on the border.

The twists and turns of a border braid usually make any increases while lacing the border onto a curve unnecessary—unless required to space motifs evenly.

8. Color choices: A fancy border is something special: set it off from the rest of the piece by placing a solid-colored base braid beneath it.

9. Fabric choices: Any fabrics can be used in borders, and decorative fabrics with a sheen or metallic threads can provide a special look. Wool, however, is still the best fabric to use for borders. The many twists and turns in some of the borders—zigzag, for example—requires steaming and pressing to get them to lie flat. This degree of heat is not suitable for some of the novelty fabrics.

Fabric weight: Most fancy borders look better when made with thinner weight wool and thinner braids because of the twists and turns required. Although the borders can be made with whatever weight of fabric has been used in the rest of the piece, a daintier, lacier look is easier to achieve with thinner weight and narrower width of strands. If the center was braided with 2" wide strips of medium weight wool, consider narrowing the strips to 1.75" for the borders.

10. Butting comments: Although the Enclosed End Butt is used for each of the borders presented, the butt site may look a bit different. Specific instructions for a butt site within the pattern are given in the description for each fancy border, below. For several borders, there are stretches of straight braid within the pattern. In this case, the butt would be along the straight braiding. For other borders, in which there are many double or triple corners, e.g., back and forth triple, the butt site is more difficult to locate. Pay attention to the instructions for how to start the braid; this will dictate the butt site.

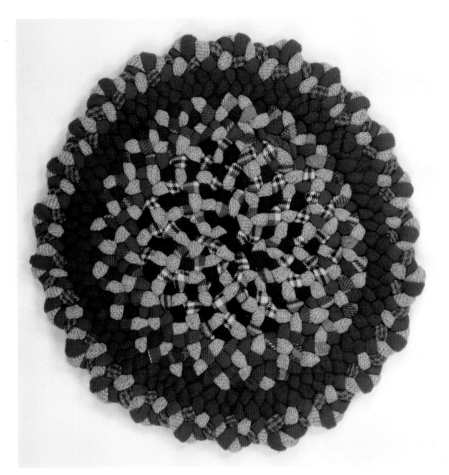

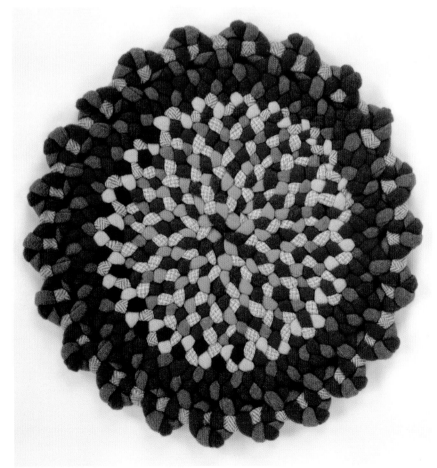

Top right:
Red Round with Triple Picot Edge, Christine Manges. 12" diameter. 2008.
Solid-colored braids set off the fancy border.

Right:
Chair Pad with Back and Forth Triples, Christine Manges. 14" diameter. 2008.
Note the fancy border is set off from the round center by solid-colored braids.

11. Shape comments: Round, square, hexagonal, octagonal, and basket shapes accept fancy borders fairly easily, but hearts and ovals have an interesting difference. These shapes have both straight and curved areas. On the straight sides, the motifs line up parallel to each other. Around curves, the motifs splay outward, and have more distance between their ends than their bases, as shown in the diagram.

This point is irrelevant for one-row borders, because they are "short" enough in their height that it makes no difference. On some of the taller borders, however, such as scalloped, the border will look different on a curved and straight portion. In later rows, it may be necessary to make changes in the loop count to accommodate the splay in the design on the curved portion, but not the straight. It is up to the reader whether this differing look of the same border within one piece is a problem, or just something interesting.

FANCY BORDER INSTRUCTION

This section describes each fancy border with specific instructions for how and where to start braiding, how to make the braid, motif size, color options, lacing, options for management of corners, and butting sites.

The first 2 borders presented are simple: they are made with straight, butted rows. What makes them interesting is how they are laced on and arranged.

LUNETTE BORDER

A Lunette border is composed of 3 to 4 rows of butted straight braid. The braids are anchored in specific sites around the base braid so that "petals" are created, with moon-shaped "lunettes" of open space between each row. This border is best suited for a round center, although it could be adapted to a square, rectangle, hexagon, or octagon with a special corner treatment. This border is unsuitable for a floor piece.

This oval piece is surrounded by a scalloped border. Despite being laced to the same number of loops on the base braid, the border has a slightly different appearance on the straight and curved portions, as the motifs splay outward on the curve.

Scarlet Poppy, Christine Manges.
15" diameter. 2009.
Border of 4 Lunette braids
around a round braided center.

Making the Border: Start the braids with an Enclosed End Butt Start. The lunette braids are simple, straight braided rounds. The instruction needed for this border consists of figuring how to stack the braids and create the open spaces between them.

Petal Spacing: Count the number of loops on the base braid. Decide how many "petals" will be spaced around the center: choose 6 to 8 for small centers; larger numbers of petals for larger pieces. Divide the base braid loop count by the number of desired petals.

Example: there are 58 loops on the base braid. Eight "petals" are desired. 7 x 8 = 56; the petals will be spaced every 7 loops… except twice, because of the extra 2 loops on the base braid, they will be spaced every 8 loops. Place safety pins or other marker pins every 7 (or 8) loops equally around the base braid. The two 8-loop petals should be placed on opposite sides of the base braid for balance.

Lunette Size: Decide how much space should show between the rows of braid. These rows appear best when there is a shallow crescent of unlaced "space" in between each row, not a huge crescent, which may distort the braid too much and make it difficult to lie flat. As in the example below, the inner braids often need only 2 or 3 loops more per row than the base braid loop count to make nice lunettes. With larger braids, larger loop count differences are required. Try to have the loop count for petals a multiple of 3, which is easier to butt.

In the *Scarlet Poppy* example, the base braid has 64 loops, and 8 petals are placed around the center. The petals are spaced every 8 loops on the base braid. The rows of border are attached every 10, 12, 15, and 18 loops successively. For another project, the petals may need to be spaced apart by larger numbers of loops, depending on the size of the project and the braid.

Color Options: Each row of border should be fairly uniform in its color choices between strands. For example, different shades of red are chosen in the 3rd strand of the border in the photo, and this strand shows off the crescent spaces nicely.

Lacing: Lacing is started in the new braid in the center of a petal, leaving a 6" tail of unknotted lacing thread. The thread is carried through the *inner* loops on the petal, which gathers the loops slightly to help them lay flat along the petal's inner curve. At the safety-pins on the base braid row, the lacing thread anchors the new braid as shown in the diagram to the right.

When lacing Row 1 to the base braid, the lacing thread encircles the safety-pinned loop twice so that it is firmly anchored, and also so the lacing thread arching through the petals will not slip and "gather" the petal curves. When lacing Row 2 onto Row 1, anchor the lacing thread in a double circuit through the loop directly above the safety pin in the base braid.

Butting: Butt where the correct loop count for each row will be obtained. For example, Row 4's petals are anchored every 18 loops, and there are 8 petals, so there would be a butt at the 144th loop (start counting with the longer Start loop called "zero.") Place the butts of each row in a different location around the center.

Scarlet Poppy Detail

Lacing the Lunette Border. Rows 1 & 2 are laced to the prior rows. Note the safety-pinned loop in the base braid. Loops that are used for anchoring additional rows are shown in gold.

Corner Options: Row 1 of the lunette border is shown in red in the diagram, with anchoring sites at each corner, and at 2 places on each side. Note that with increasing rows, the petals adjacent to a corner need increases of 1 or 2 more loops than the inner petals to make the same curve. This difference occurs because one of the anchoring sites for the corner petals extends outward at a diagonal at the corner, rather than perpendicular to the sides. This difference also applies to hexagonal or octagonal shapes, which should be anchored at each corner and then equally spaced along the sides.

Finishing: After adding on the final row, adjust any awkward loops with pliers or a hemostat, and try to hide seams that are showing. Steam iron with a pressing cloth, and dry flat.

SHAKER PICOT BORDER

The Shakers were known for their "borders on borders" style of finishing rugs, so it is fitting to have one of their borders in this book. The Shaker Picot border is mentioned in *Shaker Textile Arts*, by Beverly Gordon: "One rug has a picot on the edge: the outer strand of the last braid is pulled out loosely at intervals to form a scallop."[1]

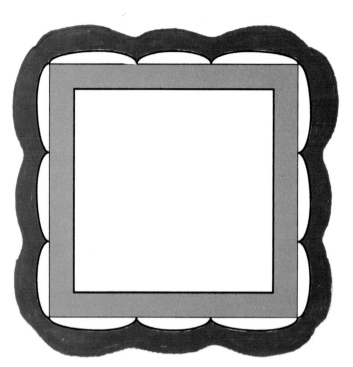

Corner options for Lunette Border

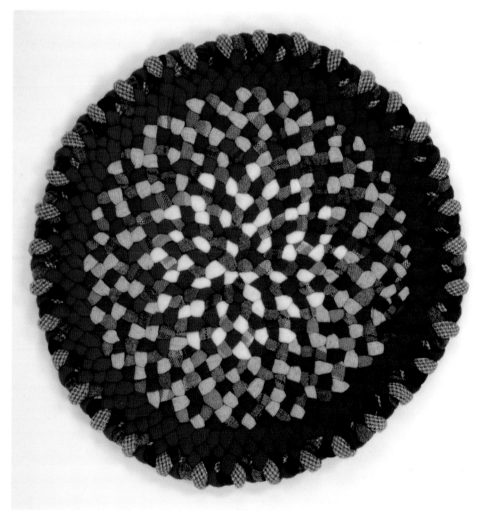

Shaker Picot Round, Christine Manges. 14" diameter. 2010. Note how the solid row sets off the border.

Although it is described, there is no image of this border, and the authors have not found a picture elsewhere. The following border is our best idea of what was meant by this description:

Making the Border: Make an Enclosed End Butt Start; begin anywhere on the border braid.

Make a straight braid that is 1.5 times the number of loops around the base braid. For example, if the base braid is 60 loops, make a straight braid of 60 x 1.5 = 90 loops. Butt the braid off the rug at the correct loop count.

Motif size: 2 loops on base braid.

Color Options: The pulled loop of the picot should contrast with the other two loops. A base braid of a solid color, in the photo below it is red, is recommended to set the border off from the rest of the piece.

Lacing: Two loops of the border braid are laced regularly to two loops of the base braid; the picot strand is never laced.

After the row has been laced on, hemostats or pliers are used to pull firmly on the outer picot strands. Pull until the inner loops of this strand almost disappear.

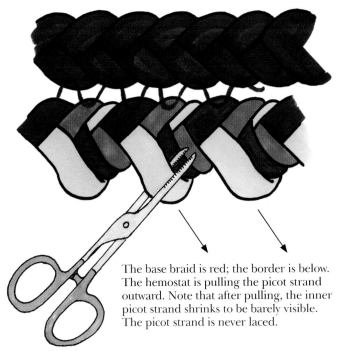

The base braid is red; the border is below. The hemostat is pulling the picot strand outward. Note that after pulling, the inner picot strand shrinks to be barely visible. The picot strand is never laced.

Corner Options: If choosing to place this border around a cornered piece, first figure out the number of loops to braid for each side: count the number of base braid loops on a side between triples, and add 3. If the base braid is around a hexagon or octagon, made with double corners, count the number of loops between corners on a side and add 2. Multiply this number by 1.5 to find the number of loops to braid between double corners on the border braid. Even if the border surrounds a square, the corners in the border braid must be made with double corners to have this border work out correctly. Make the picot strand fall as loops B and 2 of the double corner.

Finishing: When finishing a piece with a Shaker picot border, avoid steam pressing the outer row. If the outer row of this border is pressed, the picot flattens, and loses its unique appearance. The piece can be pressed everywhere else with a pressing cloth.

Detail of Shaker Picot Border. Note the 3-D effect, as the pulled loops stand up above the adjacent braid.

To place a Shaker picot around a corner, a double corner must be used and the picot strand must fall as loop B and loop 2 of the double corner.

DOUBLE PICOT BORDER

This border is one of the easiest. It employs only double corners, spaced between a couple of straight loops.

Pink & Brown Heart, Christine Manges. 15" x 19". 2009. Note how the solid row sets off the decorative double picot border.

Making the Border: Make an Enclosed End Butt Start. Place the strands on the pin, noting that if a contrasting strand is desired for the crossover loop, it should be placed on the right side of the Start Pin, e.g., the 3/8" longer strand.

Start braiding with the right strand: R, L. Make a double corner on the smooth edge side of the braid: (RRL).

Throw another 2 loops: R, L, and repeat the instructions. The braid should always have 2 straight loops between its double corner picots.

OR: *R, L, (RRL), R, L,* repeat.

Motif size: 3 loops on base braid.
Color options:
• All three strands of the same fabric, note heart photo, above.
• The crossover loop is a different color from the 2 loop strands. The crossover strand travels back and forth like "dots."
• All 3 strands can also be different, but no specific pattern is created.

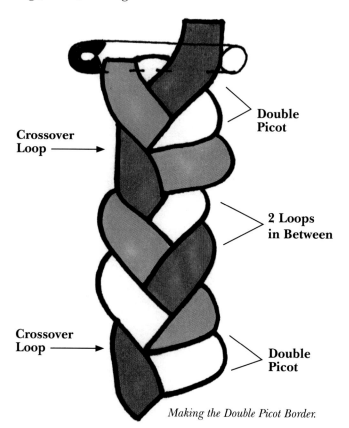

Crossover Loop →

Double Picot

2 Loops in Between

Crossover Loop →

Double Picot

Making the Double Picot Border.

Detail of double picot border.

Lacing: Leave a 4" tail of border unlaced at the Start, as well as a 6" tail of lacing thread. Start lacing in the B loop before the double corner picot. Lace the next base braid loop. The next loop on the border would be the crossover loop, but this loop should not be laced. Instead, lace the next base braid loop, so that two base braid loops in a row are laced. Proceed with lacing, skipping every crossover loop and lacing two base braid loops instead. Continue until back close to the Start, where a 4" tail of unlaced braid is left.

When lacing on this braid, increases are not generally necessary. If, however, the braids do not match up at the butt site, then it may be necessary to unlace up to 1/4 of the row to space 1 or 2 increases so that they will not be visible. The 1 or 2 increases should make the butt site match perfectly.

Butting: The Enclosed End Butt is the easiest method to join fancy borders. Overlap the Start End over the Finish End. Find where the loop colors match up, starting with the 3/8" longer Start loop on the right. Once this strand has been located, verify that the other 2 strands match up. If the other 2 strands do not match, move up or down 3 loops to find the match. Pin together, and make adjustments in the lacing, if needed, to get this butt site to match up easily.

Once the butt site has been identified, place a securing safety pin about 3" above the marker lines on the Finish End, and unbraid back to the pin. Enclose the ends as for the Enclosed End Start, checking to make sure the marker lines will be covered by seams.

Turn the strands right side out, rebraid *according to the border pattern*, and pin. Match strands with small safety pins, sew with matching thread, and bury the seams by moving the loops with a hemostat or pliers.

Corners: Management of corners is a matter of preference, however, corners often look best if they are emphasized. Instead of a double corner as usual for this border, a triple corner is thrown to emphasize the corner (see the diagram right). Another way to emphasize the corner is to place a longer section of straight loops on either side of the corner. However the corner is made, keep the number of straight loops between corners the same on either side of the corner.

Finishing: Adjust any misshapen loops; hide the seams if possible; and steam iron with a pressing cloth, laying flat to dry.

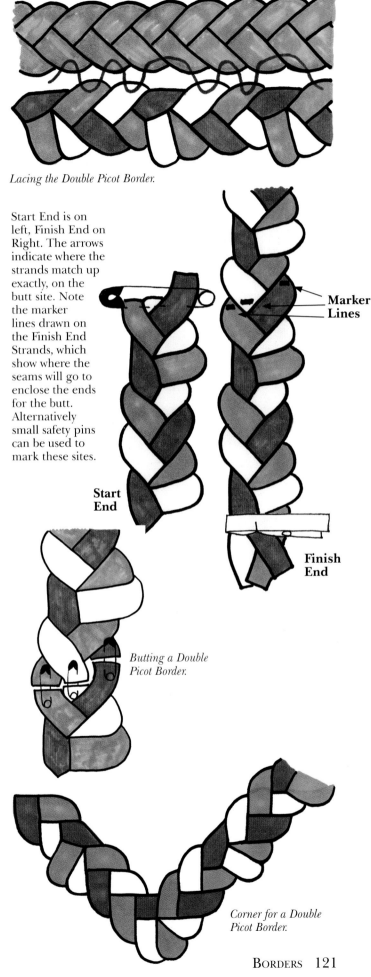

Lacing the Double Picot Border.

Start End is on left, Finish End on Right. The arrows indicate where the strands match up exactly, on the butt site. Note the marker lines drawn on the Finish End Strands, which show where the seams will go to enclose the ends for the butt. Alternatively small safety pins can be used to mark these sites.

Marker Lines

Start End

Finish End

Butting a Double Picot Border.

Corner for a Double Picot Border.

TRIPLE PICOT BORDER

This border is essentially the same as the Double Picot Border, but it is made with a triple corner instead of a double. It is one of the easier borders, and gives a nice decorative finish to projects. This border is quite safe for a floor rug.

The first published picture or description that the authors have been able to locate regarding this border is in the first edition of *The Braided Rug Book* by Norma Sturges.[2] A rug made by Lou Ann Mohrmann with a navy blue triple picot border is shown. The technique was later described by Nancy Young[3] and Donna McKeever[4] in newsletters devoted to rug braiding.

Making the Border: Make an Enclosed End Butt Start. Place the strands on the pin, noting that if a contrasting strand is desired for the crossover loop, it should be placed on the right side of the Start Pin, the 3/8" longer strand.

Make the first throw from the right, then left. On the smooth edge of the braid, make an outside triple corner. Throw 2 more loops (right, left) then pull firmly on the crossover loop to make a crisp, sharp corner. Braid so that the smooth edge has 2 straight loops between triple corners. Repeat the section between asterisks, as shown below.

* R,L, (RRRL), R,L,* repeat.

Making the Triple Picot Braid.

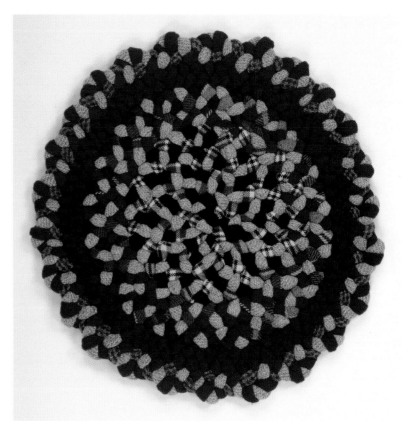

Red Round with Triple Picot Edge, Christine Manges. 12" diameter. 2008.

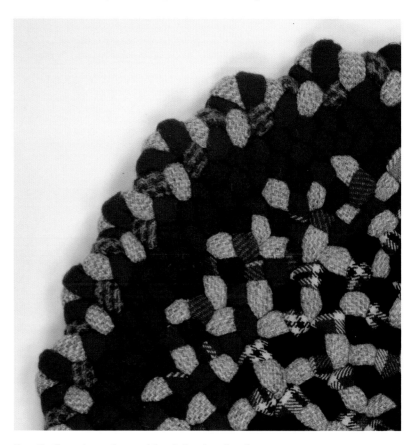

Detail of previous photo with triple picot border.

Motif size: 3 loops on base braid.

Color options: Note that when the loop count of the straight braid between the triple corners is 2, 5, 8, etc., the triple loops will always be identical (brown-white-brown in the diagram). If the loop count between triples is different from these numbers, then the triples will appear different from each other.

Color Option 1:
All three strands of the same fabric. This simple option can be made even more effective if the base braid has one strand that is the same color as the border braid. Lace the 2 border loops of straight braid on the folded edges side to straddle the same color on the base braid. The curve of the picot border follows the same color down into the prior row, emphasizing the undulation of the border.

Color Option 2:
The loops/strands of the triple are the same, with a contrasting crossover loop strand. A "dots" pattern appears, especially if the base braid also has this pattern.
Color Option 3: All strands are different, as seen in diagram below.

Lacing the Triple Picot Border, diagram oriented as for lacing.

Lacing: Leave a 4" tail of border unlaced at the Start, as well as a 6" tail of lacing thread. Proceed with regular lacing, but skip every crossover loop and lace through 2 base braid loops instead. Continue until back close to the Start, where a 4" tail of unlaced braid should be left.

When lacing on this braid, increases are not generally necessary. Only increase if needed to move the butt site by 1 or 2 loops into a matching location for butting.

Butting: The Enclosed End Butt is used. Follow the usual steps to overlap the Start End over the Finish End, and identify where the loops exactly match. Place marker lines (or safety pins) to identify butt sites on each stand.

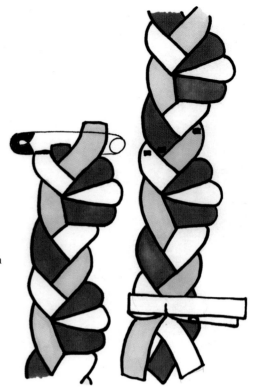

Identify Butt Site.
Start End is on left, Finish End on Right. The :e where the strands match up exactly has been entified. Note the marker lines drawn on the nish End Strands, which indicate where the ams will go to enclose the ends.

Place a securing safety pin about 3" above the marker lines on the Finish End, and unbraid back to the pin. Enclose the ends as for the Enclosed End Start, checking to make sure the marker lines will be covered by seams. Turn the strands right side out, rebraid according to the border pattern, and pin. Match strands with small safety pins, sew with matching thread, and bury the seams by moving the loops with a hemostat or pliers.

Resume lacing the butted braid. When the lacing thread ends meet, tie the ends together in a square knot. Bury the ends under 3 loops and clip close to the braid.

Corners: There are several ways to address corners.

A. Make increases or decreases as needed to make the corner of the base braid match up with one of the triple corners of the border braid, lacing border loop B to either the space between loops 1 & 2, or 2 & 3, on the base braid. In the diagram, B is laced to the space between loops 1 & 2 of the base braid's triple corner.

(A) Corner laced by placing triple picot exactly at the corner.

B. It is possible not to make any adjustments at all. The photo at right shows lacing around the corner as if it were a straight braid, without making any changes.

C. Replace the triple at the corner with a quintuple (5 loop) corner for emphasis. This suggestion is best for braids with all 3 strands the same color, because the extra loop may disrupt the strand order.

D. Another option for solid-colored braids is to place extra loops of straight braid before and after the corner. The elongated flat spaces on either side of a corner serve to highlight the corner.

Finishing: Adjust any awkward loops and hide seams. Steam iron with a pressing cloth, and dry flat.

(B) Note the triple corner is laced without changing the lacing at each corner. This method makes the corners each a bit different, but it does not detract from the piece.

BACK AND FORTH TRIPLE PICOT BORDER

This border differs from the Triple Picot Border in that triple corners are placed on both sides of the braid. This border has several interesting options for how it can be used: as an edging, to unite different areas within the same rug. See Judy Hartzell's piece *Fringe Flower*, in the Gallery, Chapter 14, in which this border is used to unite the leaves to the flower. Since this braid is symmetric side-to-side, it also works well to use it within the body of a piece, as "insertion lace."

The first use of this border that the authors have been able to identify is by Anne Eastwood in *The Braided Rug Book*.[5] In a personal communication,[6] Anne credits her design to 2 days of lessons in 1960 with Helen Howard Feeley, in which she was taught how to make "square corners." Later, Anne used this technique to create a distinctive edging by manipulating the square corners.

This border has tiny lace openings between the base braid and the border braid. The openings are quite small, and would be unlikely to catch a heel in a rug; however, use judgment about placing openwork borders on a floor.

Make the Border: Make an Enclosed End Butt Start. Place the strands on the pin. If a contrasting strand is desired for the crossover loop, it should be placed on the right side of the Start Pin (the 3/8" longer strand).

Chair Pad with Back and Forth Triples, Christine Manges. 14" diameter, 2008.

Make the first throw from the right, then left. On the smooth edge of the braid, make an outside triple corner. Throw 2 more loops: right, left, then pull firmly on the crossover loop to make a crisp, sharp corner. The last "left" thrown was actually Loop 1 of the next inside triple corner: Left, Left, Left, Right. Throw 2 more loops: left, right, then pull firmly on the crossover loop. The last "right" thrown was the start of the next triple on the outside, smooth edge of the braid. Repeat.

OR: *(RRRL), R, (LLLR), L,* repeat.

Motif size: 3 loops on the base braid.

Color options:
• All three strands of the same fabric;
• The loops of the triples (two strands) are the same, with a contrasting crossover loop strand; or
• All strands are different.

Interestingly, because the crossover loop is the same for both the inside and outside triples, it can be seen running as a straight "ribbon" between the triples. This ribbon effect can be emphasized by making the crossover strand a contrasting color.

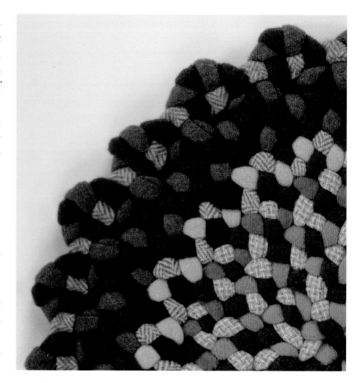

Detail of Back and Forth Triple Border.

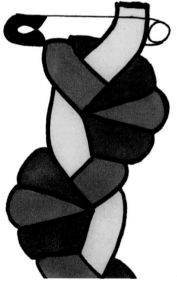

Starting the Back and Forth Triple Border.

Lacing: Start by regular lacing the first two loops of an inside triple to the base braid. After lacing the middle loop of the triple, lace through two loops on the base braid before catching the first loop of the next triple. Repeat around the rug.

Lacing Back and Forth Triple Picot Border. Note how the color choice for the crossover loop strand can emphasize the border, yellow in the diagram.

Lacing Alternative:
Lace only the middle loop of the inside triple, then lace through 3 loops of the base braid. While this method is less stable, it appears "lacier."
Note that this diagram shows the border used as "insertion lace," and laced between 2 straight braids. Lacing is carried out identically to the method above when adding on another straight braid after the border.

Butting: Place the Start End over the Finish End, and identify the butt site.

Place a securing safety pin about 3" above the marker lines on the Finish End, and unbraid back to the pin. Enclose the ends as for the Enclosed End Start, checking to make sure the marker lines will be covered by seams. Turn the strands right side out, rebraid according to the border pattern, and pin. Match strands with small safety pins, sew with matching thread, and bury the seams by moving the loops with a hemostat or pliers.

Resume lacing the butted braid. When the lacing thread ends meet, tie them together in a square knot. Bury the ends under 3 loops and clip close to the braid.

Butting Site:
Start End is on the Left, Finish End on the Right. The butting site is indicated by the short marker lines on the Finish End, which exactly correspond to the positions of each strand on the Start Pin.

Butting the Back and Forth Triple Picot Border.

Corners: This border has several options for lacing it around corners.

A. As per the diagram, lace the corners so that the last inside triple on a side is laced into the 2 spaces *before* the middle loop of the base braid's triple corner. After turning the corner, lace the next inside triple to the 2 spaces *after* the middle loop of the base braid's triple corner.

B. Perform the lacing as in option A, but emphasize the corner more by throwing a quintuple (5 loop) corner in the outside corner. Triple or quintuple corners are the only ones that will maintain the strand order.

C. Ignore the corner and simply lace around it as if the loops were on a straight braid. The corners may appear a bit irregular, but usually are still attractive.

Finishing: Adjust any misshapen loops and hide seams. Steam iron with a pressing cloth, and dry flat.

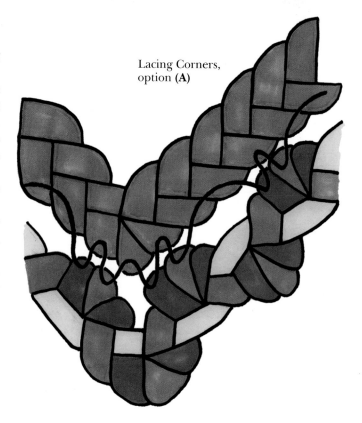

Lacing Corners, option (**A**)

KNOTTED ARCHES BORDER

This 2-layered border is more challenging because it includes knots in one of the strands. Knots are not typically incorporated into braids, but are quite attractive when surrounded by a second, arched layer of border. The arch may require some careful steam pressing after it has been laced on in order to get the desired curve around the knot.

Color Planning: Although technically there are only 2 rows to this border, it is best to think about it as 3, by including the base braid. The border looks best if the base braid and arch braid are a different color from the rest of the piece, but the same as each other. In the knotted row between the base and arch braids, the knot should be a fabric that contrasts sharply with the other 2 strands.

Making the Knot Row

1. Make an Enclosed End Butt Start. The strand that becomes the knot strand is placed on the right side of the Start Pin, 3/8" longer than the other 2 strands.

2. Start braiding with the right strand: R, L, R, L, R, L. Place a clothespin across the braid. There should be 3 smooth-side loops braided.

3. Stitching the Strand. The knot strand should be ready to be thrown on the right. Instead, take needle and matching thread, and blind stitch about 6" of the folds closed on the knot strand. This stitching is necessary to keep the knot appearing neat when it is tied.

Knotted Arches Chair Pad, Christine Manges. 16" diameter. 2008.

4. Throwing the knot. Make a loop and throw the end of the strand through the loop. Slide the knot down so that it is close to the braid. Do not tighten it so much that the knot becomes small; it should be a prominent element.

5. Continue braiding, placing a knot in the braid every 6th loop. The knot is always made with the same strand, and it needs to have the folds stitched shut 6" each time the knot is thrown. Try to keep the knots roughly the same size and appearance.

It is easier to throw the knot if this strand is kept short, with lengths added as needed, and not in a large roll.

Motif size: 6 loops on base braid.

Lacing: Lace knot row onto the base braid with regular lacing. Distribute any needed increases evenly.

Butting Knot Row: Review the Enclosed End Butt in Chapter 7. Since the butt occurs in the straight braid between knots, butt as for a straight braid.

Making the Arch Row: Make an Enclosed End Butt Start. Choose strands that match the straight braid around the center, or the base braid.

Start braiding with the right strand. Braid 3 smooth-side loops, then braid an inside triple followed immediately by another inside triple. Braid 7 loops on the smooth side of the braid between sets of triples. Repeat.

OR: R, L, R, L, R, *(LLLR) (LLLR), 7 smooth loops*. Repeat between **.

Motif size: 6 loops on knot row; one of the loops is a knot.

Lacing the arch row onto the knot row: The last 2 loops of the first triple, and the first 2 loops of the second triple, are laced onto Row 1 in the 4 spaces centered between knots, as drawn. When reaching the loops adjacent to the knot, lace down into the folded edge loops of Row 1 to lace under the knot, then return up to the smooth side loops of Row 1, as drawn. If the knot itself is laced, it is hard to hide the lacing thread.

It is normal for the crossover loops of the triples to become somewhat elongated once laced.

Butting the arch row: The Enclosed End Butt is used to butt the braid in the 7 loops of straight braid in between the triples. Count the loops of the arch that is being butted carefully to make sure there are 7 loops between sets of triples.

(A) Throwing an Overhand Knot.
(B) Sliding the Knot into Position, and Tightening.

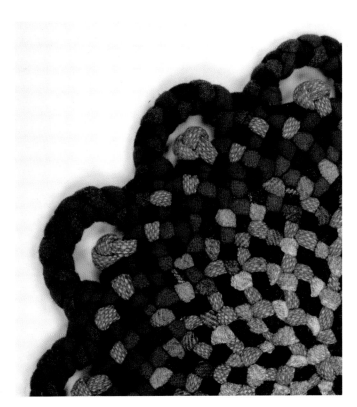

Detail of Knotted Arches Border

Lacing on the Arch Row.

Corners in Knotted Arches Border

1. In the knot row, an outside triple corner (RRRL) is placed at the corner between the knots. The 1st and 3rd loops of the triple are made with the knot strand. Braid, on the smooth side: the knot before the corner, 2 smooth side loops, an outside triple at the corner: (RRRL), then 2 more smooth side loops, then a knot.

2. In the arch row, an outside triple is also added, along with a few extra loops. At the completion of the arch around the last knot on a side, braid the first inside triple as usual (LLLR), then braid the following: R, L, R, outside triple: (RRRL), then R. The next inside triple begins the next arch: (LLLR), then 7 smooth side loops of straight braid, etc. Repeat the above steps for the next corner.

Finishing: This border may need some steam pressing. Without ironing, the arch is often too straight as it stretches between sets of triples. Spray the arch with water, shape the arch into a curve, cover with a pressing cloth, and press the arch on wool setting until it seems to have "set" into a curve. Repeat for each arch. Do not press the knot, which should have some height to it. Dry flat.

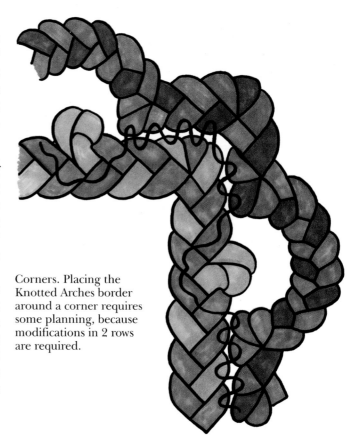

Corners. Placing the Knotted Arches border around a corner requires some planning, because modifications in 2 rows are required.

SNOWFLAKE BORDER

The snowflake border is an openwork border, with large lacy spaces. The border curves as it is braided, so it is more effective on a rounded base than on a straight one.

Do not be intimidated by the many twists and turns of the braid; the pattern is created by an arrangement of double and triple corners. Careful attention is required during braiding the first couple of motifs.

Making the Border: Make an Enclosed End Butt Start.

Snowflake Chair Pad, Christine Manges. 14" diameter. 2008.

Start braiding with the right strand: Right, Left, then make an outside double corner followed by a Right, then an inside triple corner. Braid a Left, then an outside triple, which is the center triple between pointy motifs.

Braid a Right, then an inside triple, a Left, then an outside double, then a Right and Left. Braid an outside Triple (the triple at the outside point of the motif), then a Right and Left. Repeat.

Or: R,L, *(RRL), R, (LLLR), L, (RRRL = triple between motifs), R, (LLLR), L, (RRL), R, L, (RRRL= triple at outside point), R, L.*

Motif size: 6 loops on base braid.

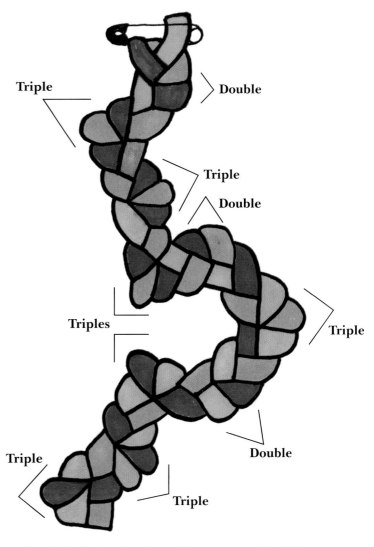

Snowflake Border. Start Loop is important in identifying butt site.

Detail of Snowflake Border.

Lacing: The "straight" portion between pointed motifs is laced to the base braid. The portion to be laced includes the last 2 loops of the inside triple, the B loop and crossover loop of the outside triple in the center, and the first 2 loops of the next triple.

Why is the crossover loop being laced, when it is usually avoided? It is usually avoided because lacing it can create a hole between the triple loops and its B and crossover loops. However, the border loops here are too tightly packed to develop a hole, and when the crossover loop is left unlaced, the border appears to be laced asymmetrically; there are 3 normal loops before the crossover, but only 2 after it.

Lacing Snowflake Border to Base Braid

Color options: Choose roughly similar-colored strands for the border, allowing the twists and turns of the braid to shine without the confusion of multiple strand colors. Set the border apart from the rest of the piece by making the base braid a different color from both the center and the border.

Butting: In this border, something interesting happens: it may be necessary to miss-butt, depending on the number of motif points in the piece. Miss-butting occurs when it is impossible to make the strand order match up correctly at the butt site. The shape of the braid is maintained, with the same number of loops found between corners, but the strands that match up to be sewn together may well be different colors from each other.

Is a miss-butt noticeable? Surprisingly, it usually is not.

Miss-butting: Place the Start End on top of the Finish End, and find the Finish loop that matches up with the long strand on the Start Pin. Ignore whether the colors match up or not; pay attention to the loop count and the location of adjacent corners. Pin the long strand and its mate together on the smooth side of the braid, and mark the Finish strand at the top where it will need to be butted.

Use the diagram below to match up strands for butting, realizing that the colors may not match.

Finish the Enclosed End Butt. Sew the ends with invisible stitching, and move the braid with hemostat or pliers so that seams are hidden.

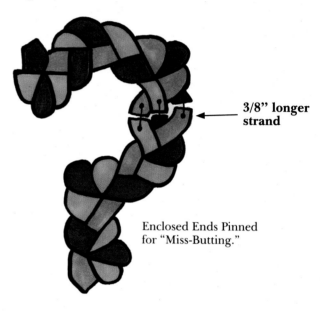

3/8" longer strand

Enclosed Ends Pinned for "Miss-Butting."

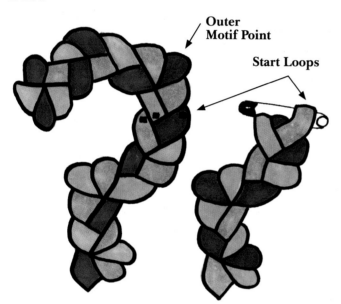

Outer Motif Point

Start Loops

Identifying the Butt Site.

ZIGZAG BORDER

The zigzag border is an easy border to make; it consists of either double or triple corners that make the braid sharply turn back and forth, with straight braiding between corners. There are large open areas that give the braid a lacy appearance. The braid can either be used as a border along the outside edge, or can be used inside the piece to link either hooked or braided portions. Note its use as both a border and insertion lace in the photo.

Examples are given with both triple and double corners used to make the border's sharp turns; either corner makes a decorative border. An advantage of the triple border is that all corners are made with identical loop colors, which is a quick way to verify that the count between corners is correct. The double-cornered zigzag has the same loop colors for the doubles along one side, but different loop colors on the other side.

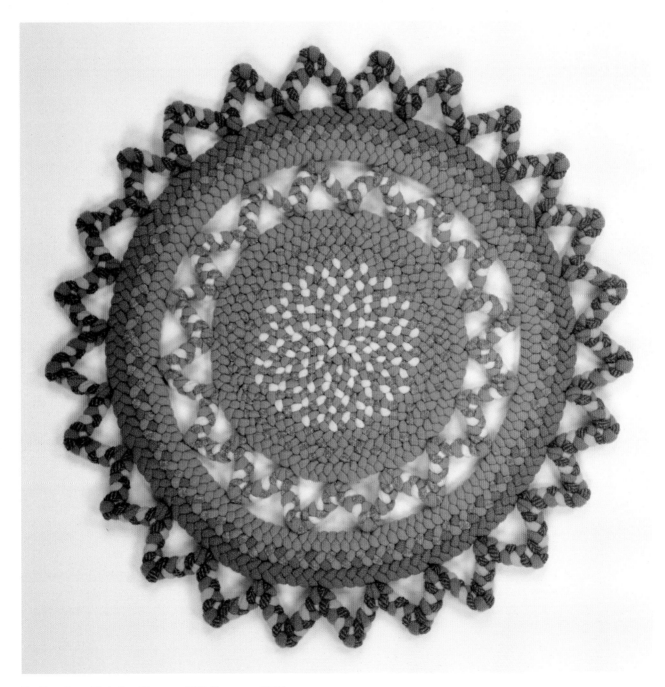

Radiant Sun, Christine Manges. 20" diameter. 2009.
Note use of zigzag border both inside and at the edge of the piece.

Making the Triple Cornered Zigzag Border: Make an Enclosed End Butt Start. Start braiding with the strand on the right. Braid right, left, right, then make an inside triple corner. Braid 3 smooth loops, then an outside triple corner. Braid 4 smooth loops, then an inside triple corner. Repeat.

OR: R, L, R, *(LLLR), L, R, L, R, L, R, L, (RRRL), R, L, R, L, R, L, R,* repeat.

Why are there 3 smooth loops between corners on one section of straight braid, and 4 smooth loops on the other? The reason is that the total number of loops—counting on both smooth side and folded edges side—is 7. On one length of braid, there are 3 smooth loops and 4 folded edges loops; on the other, 4 smooth loops and 3 folded edges loops. For simplicity, only the smooth side loops are referred to when counting.

Motif size: About 5 loops on base braid.

Color Options: All of the triple corners are identical in appearance. When keeping track of counts between corners, it helps to have different colors of strands, to make sure that all triple corners appear equal and can verify the count. Interestingly, the crossover loop, white in the diagram, never enters the triple corners, and appears to move in stair-step fashion between the turns of the braid. If this stair-step look is desired, place a bright or light strand at the left position on the Start Pin.

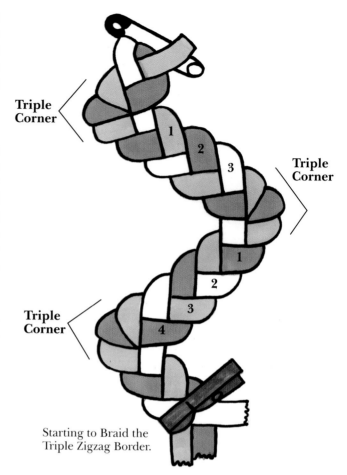

Triple Corner

Triple Corner

Triple Corner

Starting to Braid the
Triple Zigzag Border.

Lacing: Lacing proceeds from right to left. Lace the middle loop of the inside triple to the space after every 5th loop of base braid. Carry the lacing thread within the 5 loops in the base braid between triples.

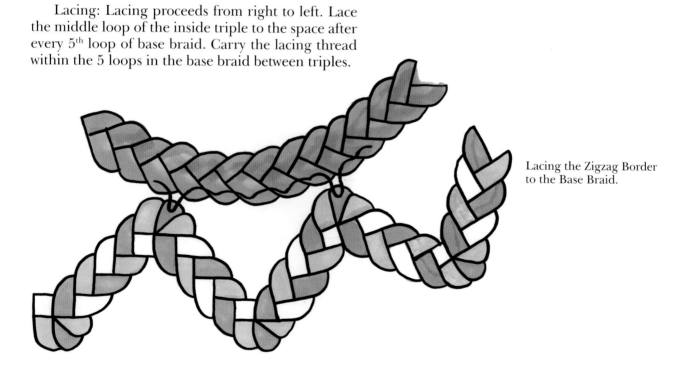

Lacing the Zigzag Border
to the Base Braid.

134 BORDERS

If the zigzag is placed between straight braids on a curved piece, as above, then typically the number of loops between the outside triple loops that are laced will increase. When lacing the border to the base braid, there are 5 loops between triples; when the outer straight braid is laced on, there are 7 loops. Depending on the curve—shallow or sharp—there may be fewer or greater numbers of loops needed.

Butting: Butt in the straight portions of the braid between corners. Make sure that the loop count between corners is correct at the butt site.

Lacing the Triple Cornered Zigzag Border between Straight Braids.

Making the Double Cornered Zigzag: Make an Enclosed End Start.

Start braiding with the right strand. Braid right, left, right, then an inside double corner, then straight braid for 2 loops on the smooth side, then an outside double corner, then straight braid for 3 smooth loops, then repeat.

OR: R, L, R, *(LLR), L, R, L, R, L, (RRL), R, L, R, L, R,* and repeat between **.

Motif size: 4 loops on base braid.

Color Options: no specific strand is emphasized in this border. Keep the strand colors similar to highlight the path of the braid, rather than certain strands.

Lacing: lace the second loop of each inside double after every 4th loop on the base braid. Carry the lacing thread within the 4 loops of the base braid, before catching the next double corner's second loop.

Butting: Butt in the straight portions of braid between corners. Make sure that the loop count between corners is correct at the butt site.

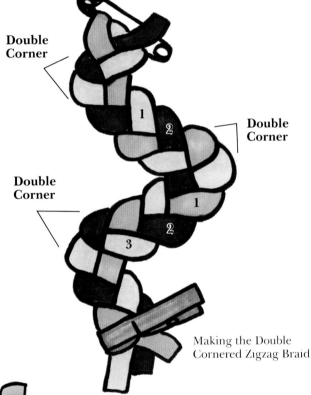

Double Corner

Double Corner

Double Corner

Making the Double Cornered Zigzag Braid

Lacing the Double Cornered Zigzag to Base Braid.

Making a Corner Triangle for a Triple Cornered Zigzag: Braid as usual for this border, having the middle loop of the inside triple fall at the space between loops 1 & 2 on the base braid. Braid 3 smooth loops, an outside triple corner, 2 smooth loops, an outside triple corner, and 4 smooth loops, inside triple corner. Have the middle loop of the last triple fall at the space between loops 2 & 3 on the base braid. Resume braiding as usual for this border.

The same technique—making a triangle at a corner—can be used with double cornered zigzag braids; braid to the inside corner, having the 2nd loop of the double fall at the space between loops 1 & 2 on the base braid's triple corner. Braid 2 smooth loops, outside double corner, 2 smooth loops, outside double corner, 3 smooth loops, inside double corner. Note: the strand order will be changed by making a triangle on the double-cornered zigzag border only. The strand order should revert to normal after 4 corners, but if it does not, follow the guidelines under "Miss-butting" in the Snowflake Border.

Finishing: Adjust any misshapen loops and hide seams. The zigzag points are prone to twisting to one side or the other instead of lying flat; mist the loose outer points with a spray bottle of water and arrange flat. Steam iron with a pressing cloth and dry flat.

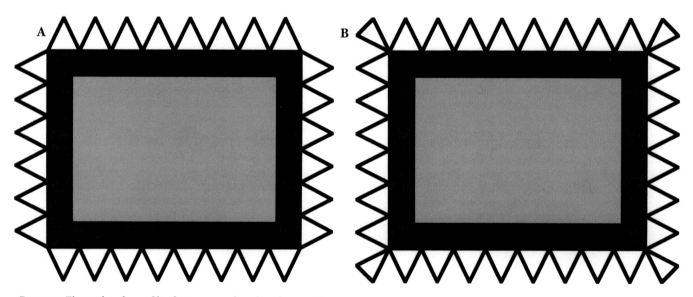

Corners: Zigzag borders of both types can be placed around corners.
(A) shows the inside corner falling exactly at the outside corner of the base braid; stretch the corner slightly to make an elongated angle.
(B) shows a triangle at the corner: see instructions above.

Triple-Cornered Zigzag Border Is Shown Making a Triangular Corner

ZIG ON PICOT BORDER

The Zig on Picot border is composed of 2 previously reviewed borders stacked on top of each other: the triple picot border in the first row, and double-cornered zigzag border for the second row. The curve of the picot braid softens the triangular geometry of the spaces in the zigzag.

See instructions for both borders in prior sections.

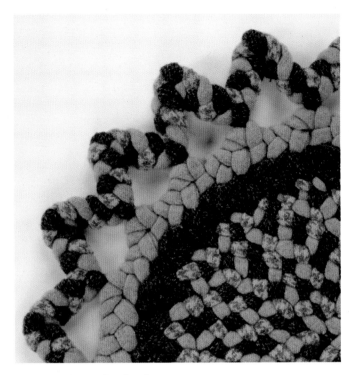

Detail of Zig on Picot border

Sage and Shadow, Christine Manges. 16" diameter. 2010. Zig on Picot border.

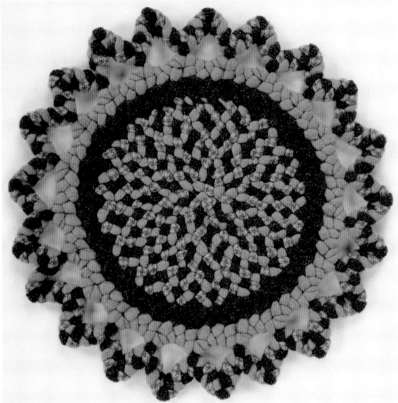

Lacing: Row 1 is laced on as usual for a triple picot, skipping the crossover loops and lacing through 2 loops on the base braid.

When lacing on the double zigzag border, lace the second loop of each inside double to the space between loops 2 & 3 on the triple of Row 1. Carry the lacing thread in the outer loops of the triple picot row until lacing the next zigzag corner.

All other instructions are the same as for the zigzag border.

The next set of 3 borders are in the category of "Solid but Interesting," which means that there is no openwork, but they make interesting turns in rows that are stacked atop each other. One of the similarities of these borders is that they look best when the path of the braid is emphasized, but not the loops within the braid. For this reason, each border row is made with 3 strands that are the same, or very similar, to each other in color; each row, is a different color.

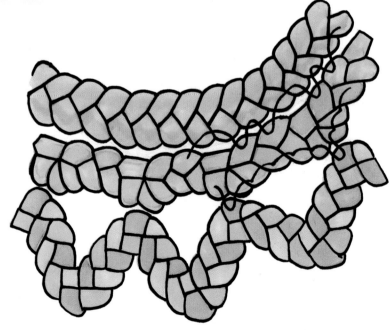

Lacing: The gray base braid is shown on top; Row 1 is the green triple picot border, and Row 2 is the double-cornered zigzag.

STACKED PICOT BORDER

The stacked picot border is just as its name sounds: rows of triple picot borders stacked one on top of the other. The gentle scalloped curves appear as waves around a straight piece, such as a basket; or as pointed flower petals encircling a round hooked or braided center. Although any number of rows could be stacked when making this border, it looks best with at least 3, or more.

This border looks best when attached to a round center or basket. It is possible to place this border around ovals and square-cornered shapes, but it is difficult because the loop count changes for each row and within each row at every corner or curve. Gain experience with placing this border around the easier shapes before attempting the harder ones.

Instructions will be presented first for placing this border around a round center, and then on a basket.

Stacked Picot Border around a Round Center

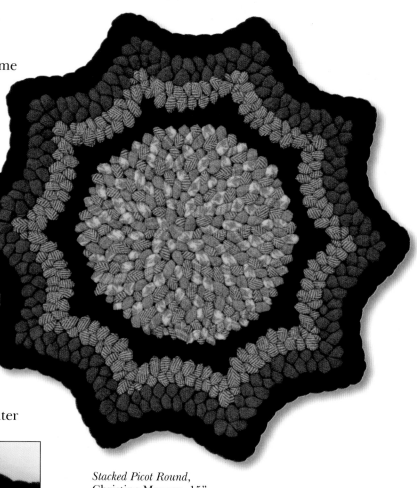

Stacked Picot Round, Christine Manges. 15" diameter. 2010.

Detail of Stacked Picot Border

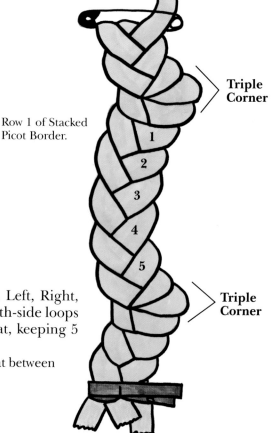

Row 1 of Stacked Picot Border.

Triple Corner

Triple Corner

Make an Enclosed End Butt Start for each row.

Start braiding with the right strand. Braid Right, Left, Right, Left, then make an outside triple corner. Braid 5 smooth-side loops of straight braid, then an outside triple corner. Repeat, keeping 5 smooth side loops between each triple.

• OR: R, L, R, L, *(RRRL), 5 smooth-side loops*, repeat between **.

Motif size: 5 loops on base braid.

Lace Row 1 onto the base braid with regular lacing. Do not lace the crossover loop.

Note: This row appears quite similar to the Triple Picot border, but it is NOT laced in the same manner. The Triple Picot border skips lacing the crossover loop, but leaves a space for it by going through 2 loops of base braid. For this border, the crossover loop is skipped, but no space is left for it, the next loop is laced to the base braid as if the crossover loop did not exist. Leaving no space makes the triple corner "tight" and forces the triple loops outward prominently, helping to form the design of this border.

Making Rows 2 & 3 (for a round center): Start braiding with the right strand. After 2 smooth-side loops, make an outside triple corner: (RRRL). Braid 8 smooth side loops, then a triple, and repeat.

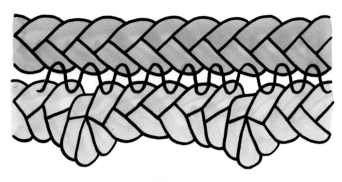

Lacing Row 1 onto Base Braid

Lacing Row 2: lace each loop of Row 2 except the crossover loop. Remember to alternate the location of the B loop with each row: in one row, B should be laced between the base braid's loops 1 & 2; in the next row, between loops 2 & 3.

Comment: Because of the triple corner at the picot, each braided row increases the space between picots by a loop count of 3 (e.g., 5, 8, 11, etc). To prevent ruffling from too many increases, only increase every other row, keeping the alternate rows without increases. When the loop count is kept the same between rows, however, decreases will need to be made while lacing to keep the picots lined up. Decreases are the reverse of increases: 2 loops of base braid are laced to one loop of the border.

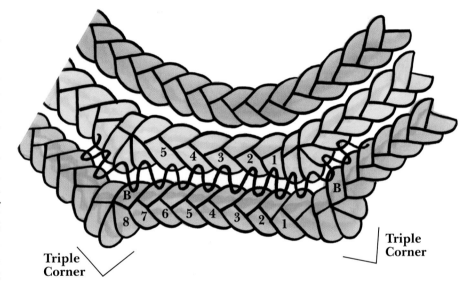

Triple Corner

Triple Corner

Lacing Row 2: Shown in the diagram are the base braid, Row 1, and Row 2. Because there are 5 loops between triples in Row 1, and 8 between triples in Row 2, each loop in Row 2 can be laced.

Lacing Row 3: The base braid and Rows 1, 2, and 3 are shown in this diagram. There are the same number of loops braided between triples in Rows 2 and 3, so 3 decreases are necessary to keep the triple corners centered. The decreases are located at loops 3, 5, and 7; in another row, they may be located at loops 2, 4, and 6. Note that the (**B**) loops of Row 3 are laced between Row 2's triple loops 2 & 3.

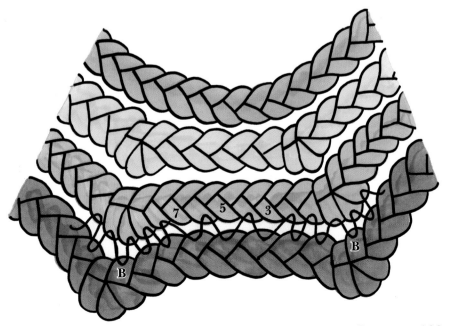

Row 4 and each row afterward: With each row, judgment must be used to determine whether the row should increase its loop count by 3 (in which case, no decreases will be needed when lacing on the new row) or whether it should keep the same loop count as the prior row (3 decreases between triples will be needed). If the piece is starting to ruffle, keep the same loop count as the prior row. If the braid must be stretched to make it to the next triple corner, then increase the loop count.

Why loop counts of 5, 8, 11, 14, etc. between triples? Each row increases by a loop count of 3 between triples because of the prior row's triple corners. The reason that these numbers are chosen (instead of using, for example, 3, 6, 9, etc.) is because they will make the triple corners look the same if 3 different strand colors are used. Seeing that each triple is made of the same strand colors is a good way to check that the loop count is correct between triples. Can different numbers be used between triples? Absolutely.

Butting: Butt each row in the straight braid between triples, using the Enclosed End Butt as described in Chapter 7. Make sure the loop count between triples is correct.

Finishing: Adjust any misshapen loops, hide seams if possible, and steam iron with a pressing cloth. Dry flat.

Stacked Picot Border on the Sides of a Basket

The Stacked Picot Border on a straight-sided piece such as a basket or tote bag is easier, in many respects, than placing this border around a round center. After the first border row, each row is braided and laced identically to a basket. Since there is the same loop count for each round, it is not necessary to judge whether or not to increase the loop count between triples, as is necessary when placing this border on a round center. Instead,

• each row has the same loop count between triples, and

• lacing each row requires 3 decreases spaced between triples.

Braid the oval or round bottom of the basket or tote bag, and taper. Add one row of straight braid, then the rows of the Stacked Triple Picot are added following these instructions:

Make an Enclosed End Butt Start for all rows. Start braiding with the right strand. Braid Right, Left, Right, Left, then make an outside triple corner. Braid 8 smooth-side loops of straight braid. Repeat from the first triple corner.

OR: R, L, R, L, *(RRRL), braid 8 smooth-side loops*, repeat between **.

Motif Size: 8 loops on base braid.

Lacing Row 1: Lace Row 1 onto the base braid with regular lacing; lace every loop except the crossover loop. Note that these are different directions for lacing than found in the triple picot border, which this braid resembles.

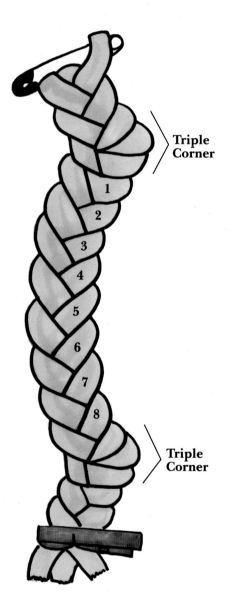

Triple Corner

Triple Corner

Starting the Stacked Triple Picot Border for a Basket.

Lacing Rows 2, 4, 6: Lace the new braid onto the base braid with regular lacing. Do not lace the crossover loop. Place the B loops of the new braid in the space between loops 1 & 2 of the base braid triple. Make 3 decreases between triples. Make the decreases by skipping base braid loops 2, 4, and 6, lacing 2 loops of the prior row to one loop of the new braid.

Lacing Rows 3, 5, 7: Lace the new braid onto the base braid with regular lacing. Do not lace the crossover loop. Place the B loops of the new braid in the space between loops 2 & 3 of the base braid triple. Make 3 decreases between triples. Make the decreases by skipping loops 3, 5, and 7 in the base braid, and lacing 2 loops of the prior row to one loop of the new braid.

Butting: Make an Enclosed End Butt in the straight portion of the braid between triples.

Adding a Handle to this Border on a Basket or Tote: The handle looks best if it takes off from the top row at a picot point, not from in between points. See Chapter 9 for handle instructions.

Finishing: Adjust any misshapen loops, hide seams if possible, and steam iron with a pressing cloth. Dry flat.

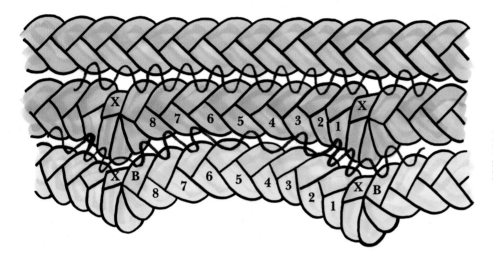

Lacing Row 2 onto Row 1. Note skipped loops in Row 1, making decreases by skipping loops 2, 4, & 6.

SCALLOPED BORDER

The inspiration for this border was the "lamb's tongues" around penny rugs. This border looks different when placed along a curved or a straight edge: the scallops splay outward around a curve, and closely fit together along a straight side. With only 2 rows making the border, there are no adjustments in loop count needed for placing it along a straight or curved edge.

Scalloped Round, Christine Manges. 18" diameter. 2010.

Color Considerations: If the same look of lamb's tongues shown in the photo is desired, then make the straight base braid and Row 2 the same colors, and Row 1 a different color. Keeping the 3 strands the same color emphasizes this look.

Row 1: Make an Enclosed End Butt Start.

Start braiding with the right strand. Braid: Right, Left, Right, inside triple, 2 smooth loops, outside double, outside double, 3 smooth loops, inside triple, 3 smooth loops, and repeat from the first corner.

OR: R, L, R, *(LLLR), L, R, L, R, L (RRL), (RRL), R, L, R, L, R, (LLLR), L, R, L, R, L, R*, and repeat between **.

Motif Size: 6 loops on base braid.

Detail of Scalloped Border

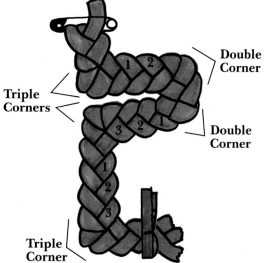
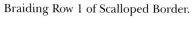

Braiding Row 1 of Scalloped Border.

Lacing: Start lacing Row 1 to the base braid with the loops between inside triple corners. Lace the first two loops of the inside triple, and the base braid loop just after the second loop of the inside triple.

Next, the braid is laced to itself to form the center "spoke" of the scallop. As braids going in 2 different directions will need to be laced to each other, the lacing here is a form of shoe lacing. However, since there is only one piece of lacing thread and one needle, the lacing will go *down to the double corners* first, catching every other loop side to side, then *back up* catching all the remaining loops. Follow the numbered loops in the above diagram closely. See discussion on shoe-lacing in Oval Centers, Chapter 6.

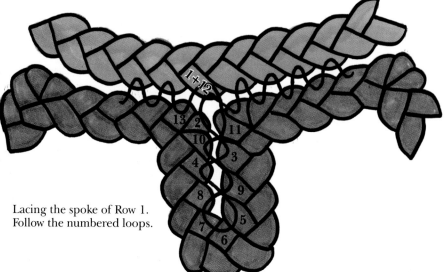

Lacing the spoke of Row 1.
Follow the numbered loops.

Row 2:

Make an Enclosed End Butt Start.

Start braiding with the right strand. Braid: Right, Left, Right, Left, Right, inside triple, inside triple, then braid 10 loops on the smooth side.

• OR: R, L, R, L, R, *(LLLR), (LLLR), then straight braid for 10 smooth side loops*, and repeat between **.

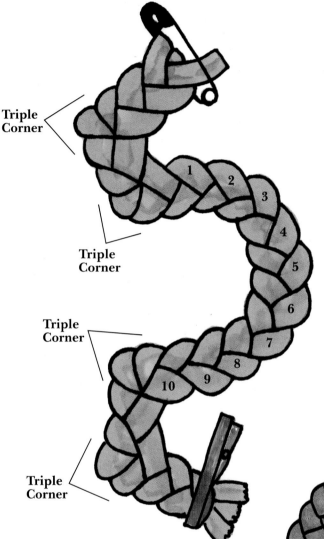

Row 2 of Scalloped Border.

Lacing Row 2: Start by lacing the middle loop of the first triple, then the first loop after the crossover loop in Row 1. Lace regularly, placing the B loop of Row 1's next triple between loops 1 & 2 of Row 2's next triple.

Lacing Row 2 around Row 1's spoke: Lace regularly until reaching the loops of Row 1's two double corners. Make increases at each of the loops of the two double corners, for a total of 4 skipped loops (marked with X's in diagram) when lacing on Row 2.

Lace back down to the straight portion between spokes, making sure that the B loops of the triples in Row 1 fall between Row 2's loops 1 & 2 of the triple corners.

4. Butting: Butt both Rows 1 and 2 in the straight braid portions of the border, following the instructions found in Chapter 7. Make sure the loop count between corners is correct at the butt site.

5. Finishing: Adjust any misshapen loops, hide seams if possible, and steam iron with a pressing cloth. Dry flat.

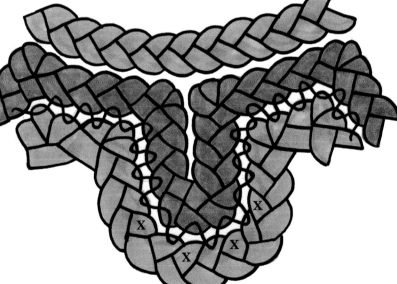

Lacing Row 2 onto Row 1 of Scalloped Border. Note the increases at each of the 4 loops of Row 1's double corners, indicated by skipped loops in Row 2 marked with "X."

CASTLE TOP BORDER

The "crowning" border shown in this book is the Castle Top Border. Created with the battlements at the tops of castles in mind, this border is sharply geometric in its right-angle paths. The border looks best along square-cornered shapes: squares, rectangles. Because the border was designed for a cornered shape, the instructions for corners are incorporated into the basic instructions.

Two rows create the border above the straight base braid. At the corners, a small square opening is necessary to keep the outside edge of the border even.

Detail of Castle Top Border.

Making the Border: Row 1:

Make an Enclosed End Butt Start.

Start braiding with the right strand. Braid: Right, Left, Right, inside triple corner, Left, outside triple corner, outside triple corner, Right, inside triple corner, 3 smooth loops, then repeat from the first inside triple corner.

• OR: R, L, R, *(LLLR), L, (RRRL), (RRRL), R, (LLLR), L, R, L, R, L, R*, and repeat between **.

Making the Corners, Row 1: Make the first 2 loops of the first inside triple corner fall at the edge of the base braid's corner. If the loop count on each side of the base braid is a multiple of 6, then this will come out perfectly.

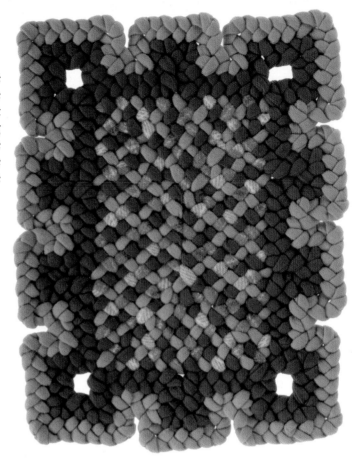

Castle Top Mat, Christine Manges. 11" x 14". 2010.

To add a corner, insert a small stretch of cornered braid into the pattern between the 2 outside triple corners (RRRL), (RRRL), on a spoke. See asterisk for location of where to insert the corner braid into the pattern in diagram below.

• Braid: until asterisk in diagram below.
• Corner Insert: Right, Left, outside triple at corner, Right, Left; (OR: insert R, L, (RRRL), R, L).
• Resume braiding as for sides.

Motif Size: 6 loops on base braid.

Lacing Row 1 onto Base Braid: The inside of each spoke has a braid that doubles back on itself, and must be briefly shoe-laced. The remainder of the lacing is regular lacing.

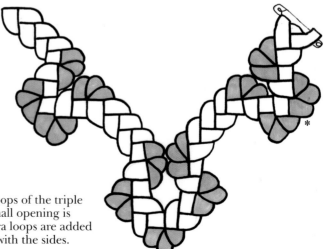

Braiding Row 1. Note that the loops of the triple corners are colored purple. A small opening is formed at each corner when extra loops are added to keep the corner's edges even with the sides.

144 BORDERS

Only the first 2 loops of the first inside triple, and the last loop of the second inside triple, are directly laced to the base braid.

Lacing the Inside of the Spoke: Follow the numbers in the diagram to shoe-lace inside the spoke. From the base braid loop between triples, lace through: left triple's middle loop, right side's B loop for outer triple, 2 crossover loops, 1st loop of left triple, 3rd loop of right triple, and back through the starting loop on the base braid.

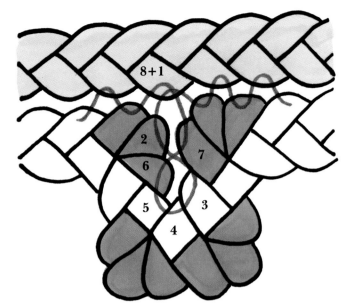

Lacing Row 1's Spoke, and Regular Lacing to Base Braid.

Lacing Row 1 at its Corner: Lace the 1st loop of the right triple, then the base braid's middle triple loop. Lace the 2nd and 3rd loops of the left triple, the 1st and 2nd loops of the right triple, and back through the base braid middle triple loop. To hide the lacing thread, pull it tight.

Lacing Row 1's Corner. The path of the lacing thread through the loops is numbered.

Row 2:

Start: Make an Enclosed End Butt Start.

Start braiding with the right strand. Braid: Right, Left, outside triple, Right, inside triple #1, inside triple #2, Left, outside triple, 3 loops straight braid, and repeat from first outside triple.

• OR: R, L, *(RRRL), R, (LLLR), (LLLR), L, (RRRL), R, L, R, L, R, L*, and repeat between **.

Corners, Row 2: Braid in the border pattern until the first outside triple where the corner starts (shown in gold in the upper right aspect of the diagram below). Braid the outside triple #1, 4 smooth loops, outside triple #2, 4 smooth loops, outside triple #3, and resume border pattern.

• OR: (RRRL), R, L, R, L, R, L, R, L, (RRRL), R, L, R, L, R, L, R, L, (RRRL). Resume the border pattern above.

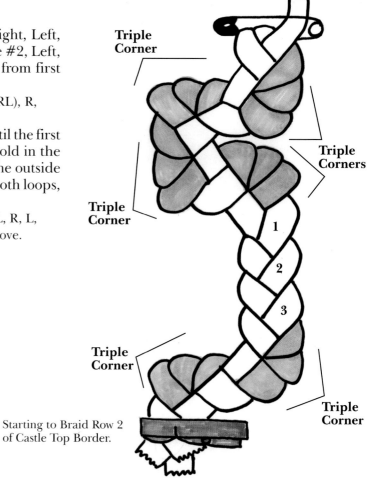

Starting to Braid Row 2
of Castle Top Border.

Lacing Row 2 onto Row 1: the two inside triples of Row 2 fit into the 3-loop spaces in Row 1. Study the diagram carefully to note the location of the B loops and the adjacent triple loops to determine where each loop should be laced.

• The B loops of Row 1's inner triples will be laced into the spaces *between loops 2 & 3* of Row 2's inside triples.

• On the outer portions of the border, where there is an outside triple, 3 smooth loops, and an outside triple, the corners switch. The B loops of Row 2 are laced to the space *between loops 1 & 2* of Row 1's triples.

Butting: The butt sites are placed in straight braid portions of the border. Count loops to make sure there is the correct loop count between corners at the butt site.

Finishing: Adjust any misshapen loops, hide seams if possible, and steam iron with a pressing cloth. Dry flat.

Braiding the corner;
Lacing Row 2.

When joining shapes together to form a rug or other project, shapes can either join completely along sides, e.g., squares to squares, rectangles to rectangles; or with some open spaces, e.g., circle to circle, square to circle. A hall runner of multiple circles, for example, has sharp angles where the circles meet. These can either be filled in completely with hooked shapes or a braided border, as in the pictured multi-circle hall runner, or they can be left open and lacy between the circles and their surrounding border, as in the pictured velvet table runner.

Velvet Table Runner, Dianne Tobias.
38" x 17". 2010.
Made with 1" velvet and thin wool.
Note color of oak table sets off shimmering texture of velvet.

7-Circle Multi-circle Runner, Dianne Tobias. 15' x 36". 2009. *Photographed by Mike Trask*
Beautiful runner, used later as an example of size calculation and design of multi-circle rugs.

Large spaces can even be left deliberately open between irregular shapes, and united by a border of braids, as illustrated in the wall hanging, *Leaves of Grace*.

This section discusses the decisions and challenges of joining and bordering multiple shapes.

CHOOSING TO KEEP OPEN SPACES

Generally floor rugs made from multiple joined shapes are joined completely, without open spaces, because of the danger of tripping. In this rug with joined circles and multiple rows of border, the spaces are deliberately left open for a lacy look. While this rug will have to be carefully situated to avoid any tripping accidents, it appears lovely with the open, unbraided areas.

Leaves of Grace, Kris McDermet. 47" x 43". 2010. *Taken from The Tree of Life painting by Hannah Cohoon (1788-1864). Design used with permission from the Hancock Shaker Village, Pittsfield, Massachusetts.*

Circles, Maryann Hanson. 96" diameter. 2008. *Photographed by K.P. Carr*
Multi-circle round rug. Note open spaces and designs were incorporated into the rug.

Table runners, chair pads, and wall hangings are well-suited for including open spaces in the design. The amount of "space" in the design is personal preference of the hooking or braiding artist. In Kris' heart rug: *Grey Anatomy*, for example, the spaces are deliberately wide and united by a single, dainty border of one row of braid. In contrast, the tiny braid table runner below has small and delicate openings adjacent to the angles. Note the careful, regular spacing of the open areas around *I See Ewe's*, below right.

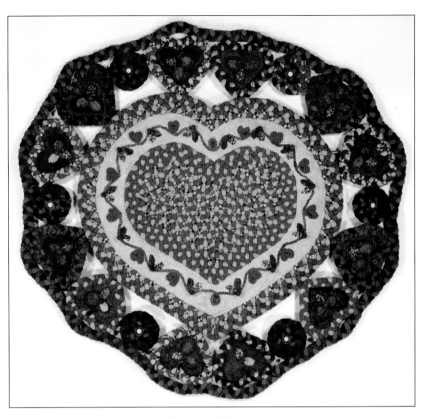

Grey Anatomy, Kris McDermet. 37" x 34". 2010.
Photographed by Laurie Indenbaum
Felted Wool Balls by Jill Cooper.

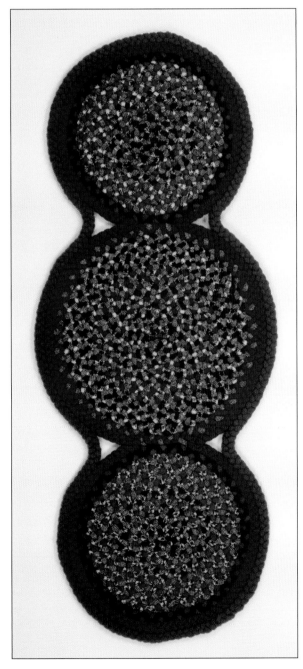

Christmas Runner, Dianne Tobias. 34" x 14.5". 2008. Note open work created by attaching border; last two rows are solid, picking up earlier colors and setting off the piece.

I See Ewe's, Joyce Krueger. 26.5" diameter. 2009.
Hooking pattern designed by Ingrid Hieronimus and used with permission.

CHOOSING TO CLOSE SPACES

There are several options for filling closed spaces when the design calls for joined shapes to be closed.

• Filling in with Hooking: This technique is similar to creating a hooked border. Trace the shape needed, allow a few unpatterned rows at the edges of hooking in case the hooking expands the size slightly; pad and line the shape as usual, and attach with lacing thread to the adjacent braids.

Antique Combination Hooked and Braided Rug. Owned by the Authors. Age and artist unknown. Note how the hooked inserts contrast nicely with braids and add a decorative element.

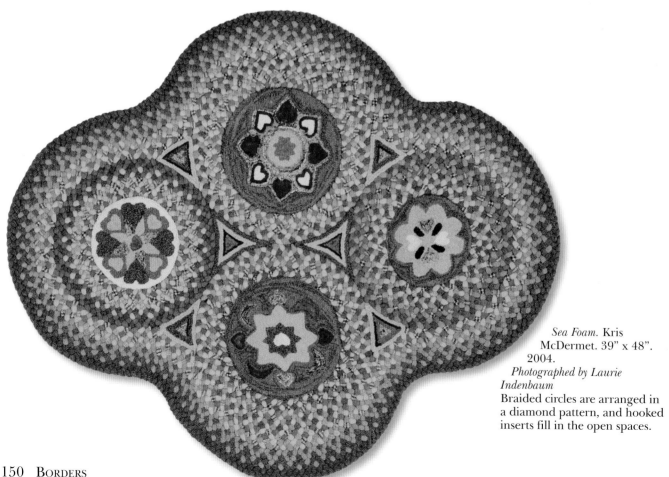

Sea Foam. Kris McDermet. 39" x 48". 2004.
Photographed by Laurie Indenbaum
Braided circles are arranged in a diamond pattern, and hooked inserts fill in the open spaces.

• Filling in with Proddy: Another option is to use prodding to fill the open spaces. See proddy instruction in Chapter 11.

• Filling in with Braiding: Spaces between shapes can either be filled in with a braided shape or with a series of braided border rows.

Fringe Flower, Judy Hartzell. 56" x 35". 2010.
The space between the 4 braided circles was filled in with a crocheted base; strips of wool were prodded through the base.

Another, more complex example of filling in with braids is the gold star in the center of the joined diamonds shown in the photo. When the large pink diamonds were completed, an unexpected narrow star shape was left open. Initially, 2 butted rounds formed the tiny center star. The long points were filled by gold and black braids which were tapered into the sharp points.

• Braided Borders to Fill in Sharp Angles: A series of butted, braided borders can be used to fill in the sharp angles created by joining circles in a line, as for multi-circle runners. See below for a more extensive discussion.

Starburst Lily, Christine Manges. 6' Point to Point. 2010.
An unexpected star-shaped opening between pink diamonds was a challenge to fill with tapering gold and black braids.

MULTI-CIRCLE PIECES

Multiple hooked or braided centers can be joined in a line and surrounded by a series of braids to create a table or hallway runner. Due to the interest in this design, and also to the unexpected challenges inherent in this design, this is discussed more extensively. Note that for these instructions, the hooked or braided centers should both have one row of butted braid attached before proceeding.

Measuring

It is important to take the time to plan the design, size, and shape of this type of complex piece.

• The braided borders add enough width and length to the rug that they must be planned for, before the hooked or braided centers are made. If the piece must fit into a specific space, such as a hallway, measure the length and width. Subtract the amount of floor space that is desired to show around the rug. A decorative rug such as this should not fit tightly against the sides of the hall, but should show at least a few inches of floor space to balance the rug and add color contrast.

• Width of braid: Measure the width of a single braid from the fabric planned for the runner. Each butted border row of braids will add double this measure to the width, and length, of the rug. Multiply the width of a single braid by 2 to get the width of a braided row.

• Estimate border rows: The number of rows that border the rug is a matter of personal preference. General guidelines are to have fewer border rows for a table runner, and more rows, at least 4 or 5, for a rug. With a hallway rug, it is desirable to have a gradual softening of angles with additional border rows, but there should not be so many rows attached that the scallop effect is obliterated.

Multiply the width of a braided row by the number of border rows planned to get the width of the border.

• Estimate circle size and number: Subtract the border width from the planned width of the rug. The result will be the diameter of the center circles. Subtract the border width from the planned length of the rug. Divide this number by the diameter of the circles. The result will give the number of circles that will fit into this length. Generally, an odd number of circles, e.g., 3, 5, 7, etc. is more visually attractive.

The results of the measurement may not be what the artist had planned. Making these measurements ahead of time provides the opportunity to make adjustments in the center number and dimensions.

Example with Dianne's hall runner:
Total width of rug: 36"
Total length: 15'
Width of braid: 1"
Width of one border row: (1" X 2) = 2"
Number of border rows: 5
Width of border: (2" X 5) = 10"
Diameter of centers: Total width (36") minus border width (10") = 26"
Number of centers: Total length (15') minus border width (10") = 14'2"
14'2" (or 170") divided by 26" = 6.5

These calculations result in 6.5 rounds of 26" diameter surrounded by 5 rows of border. Since 6.5 is not a whole number, and the closest "odd" number is 7, she used 7 circles ... but chose to vary the size of the circles artistically to accommodate the space and to make the runner more interesting; the middle and two end circles are larger than the others.

Colors and Fabrics

The planned colors and fabrics for the hooked or braided centers should coordinate with the bordering braids. If the runner is for the floor, wool should be used. If the runner is for the table, there are many options for fabrics. See the table runner of braided velvet above, which has a shimmery appearance.

For braided centers, consider choosing color plans that make matched pairs around the center. For example, with a 5-circle runner, perhaps circles 1, 3, and 5 could appear the same while circles 2 and 4 could be similar, but different. Another option might be to choose hit-or-miss colors for the centers, with borders that are planned in a more solid fashion.

JOINING THE CIRCLES

Nothing could destroy the beauty of this shape more than having the center circles joined irregularly, so that they do not form a perfectly straight line.

To keep the centers perfectly aligned, Nancy Young[7] has described a method of bolting the exact center of each circle to a yardstick or other long piece of wood. The bolt comes up from the wood and is carefully worked through the hooked or braided center before being held by a nut on top. Keep the centers bolted while attaching at least the first few rows of border.

Join adjacent circles tightly with lacing thread. Keep the number of joined loops the same between each set of circles, although the number of loops may differ if the centers are unequal in size.

Braiding and Lacing the First Border Row

The first row of border is the most challenging. How will the deep angles between centers be braided? Will any space be left in the angle?

Options include:

a. Braid a triple, quadruple, or even quintuple corner at the exact point of the angle. If the centers are all the same size, try to keep the type of corner the same at all angles within each row. If the centers are different sizes, the angles where they meet may be different from each other, and would need to be managed differently within each row. The goal is to fill in the sharp angles as completely as possible.

b. Taper the strand widths of the braids when nearing the angles, so that they will fit more easily.

c. Leave a lacy opening, which is equal in appearance at each angle. This was done in the table runners; may not be desirable in a rug.

One or more of these strategies may be chosen for working the braid into the deep corners between centers. Lace firmly at each corner to pull the points into the angles. Some experimentation with lacing the triple, quadruple, or quintuple corners into the angles may be necessary. Typically the rows are laced onto the rug as they are made; butting should occur over one of the curves and not immediately adjacent to an angle. Space the butt sites around the rug in subsequent rows.

Additional Rows

With each added border row, try to soften the angle between centers. If starting with a quadruple corner to fill the angle, try to make the next row use a triple or double corner. Eventually straight braids can be used. Do not eliminate the natural scalloping completely, as this border is attractive.

Consider a fancy border row at the edge of the rows of straight braid if not for the floor.

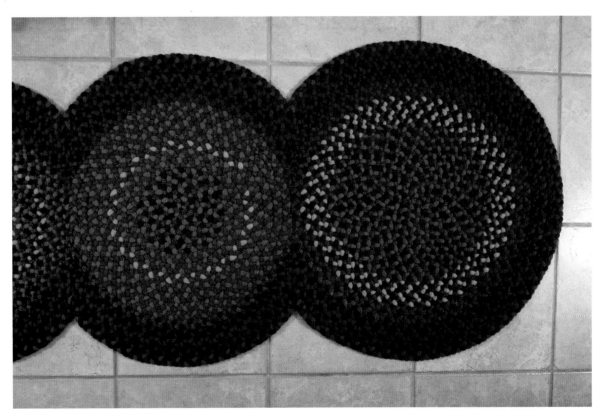

Hall runner, close up
Photographed by Mike Trask
Note attachment of centers, 4 butted rows of border, and sharp angles that required triple corners and manipulation to fill.

1. Gordon, Beverly. *Shaker Textile Arts*. Hanover, New Hampshire: University Press of New England, 1980. P. 107-108.
2. Sturges, Norma. *The Braided Rug Book*. New York City, New York: Lark Books, 1995.
3. Young, Nancy. *Braiding, "Inc," A Newsletter for Braiders*. March 1998, Issue #22, p. 2.
4. McKeever, Donna. *Rug Braiding Ink Newsletter*. July 2007, Issue #3, p. 2-3.
5. Sturges, Norma & Sturges, Elizabeth J. *The Braided Rug Book, Revised Edition*. New York City, New York: Lark Books, 2006. p. 103.
6. Eastwood, Anne. Personal communication, July 20, 2009.
7. Young, Nancy. *Braid On: A Manual for Experienced Rug Braiders Who Want More*. Winthrop, Maine: Self Published, 2007, p. 53.

9 Off the Floor

Off the Floor

Overview

The art forms of braiding and hooking have traditionally been used to make rugs as decorative and utilitarian floor coverings. Recent years, however, have seen an extension of hooking and braiding into areas "off the floor."

Hooked projects have expanded their use to include wall hangings as well as rugs. Braided objects are being made as baskets and table mats or runners. Larger combination hooked and braided pieces, such as those made by Kris McDermet, lend themselves nicely to large wall hangings. Openwork borders offer an interesting dimension as seen in *Peaceful and Quiet Offerings*.

This chapter explores the uses for braided and hooked centers and borders outside of traditional rugs. Baskets, table mats, runners, bags, and wall hangings are discussed, and instructions are given for making a basket, adding a handle, and fringing the ends.

Many of these off the floor items are daintier than floor rugs, and as

Peaceful and Quiet Offerings, Kris McDermet. 34" x 39". 2006.
Photographed by Laurie Indenbaum. Designs used with permission, Chinese Brush Painting Studio by Pauline Cherrett, 1997, Barnes and Noble.
A good example of a combination rug made as a wall hanging. Note openwork created by the addition of small hooked and braided irregular shapes allowing the wall to be part of the piece.

Techniques Discussed in this Chapter

- Tiny Braids
- Baskets, Handles, and Fringe
- Wall Hangings

such deserve the elegance of silk or velvet as fabrics, made into much smaller braids than usual. Before delving into the specifics of making some of these off the floor items, the differences inherent in using tiny braids of finer fabric are presented.

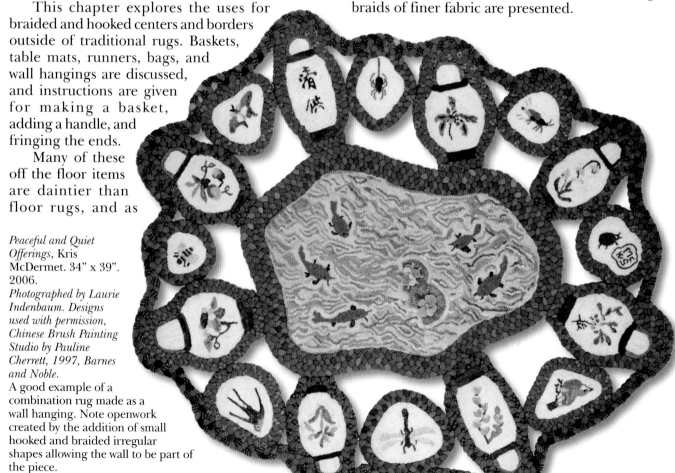

Tiny Braids

Braided rugs and braided borders placed around hooked shapes have traditionally been braided with strips ranging in width from 1.5" to 2", or even wider, to produce a finished braid of at least 1" in width. "Tiny braids," using strips ranging from 1 to 1.5", produce a braid that is smaller and daintier. Tiny braids can be used alone or can be made into borders for a larger braided or hooked center. Smaller, finely hooked pieces can be enhanced with a similarly sized, tiny braided border rather than a larger braid as a border.

Although not sturdy enough to be used for rugs, tiny braids can be used for projects as varied as a mat for under a potted plant, a table centerpiece, a coaster, trivet, basket, or table runner.

Tiny braid projects offer intriguing opportunities for the braiding artist. When planning a tiny braid project, it will almost certainly be a piece designed to be placed off the floor, and freed from utilitarian considerations such as fabric durability. Tiny braids lend themselves to novelty fabrics, the flourishes of openwork braids, elaborate hooked designs set into the piece, and fancy embellishments.

The techniques used in braiding with tiny braids are similar to those for traditional braids: double-folding the fabric in the same manner as braiding, with the goal of folding in raw edges. Depending on the fabric and its thickness, all raw edges may not be hidden on the back of the work with such a narrow strip, and therefore tiny braided projects may not be reversible.

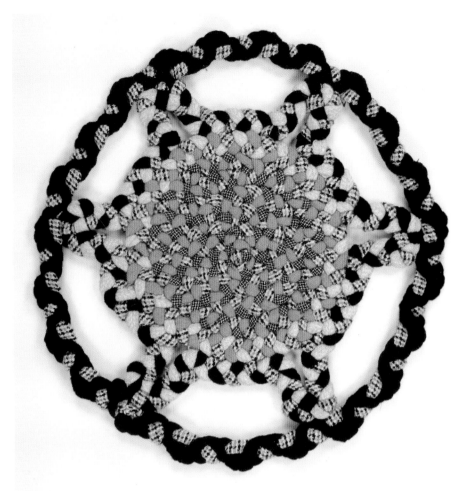

Tiny Braid Starburst, Dianne Tobias. 9.5" diameter. 2009.
Made from non-wool and wool crepe strips cut about 1". Could be used as a small wall hanging or table mat.

Tiny Braided Silk Basket, Dianne Tobias. 4" x 2.5". 2009.
Made from 1" strips of silk fabric.

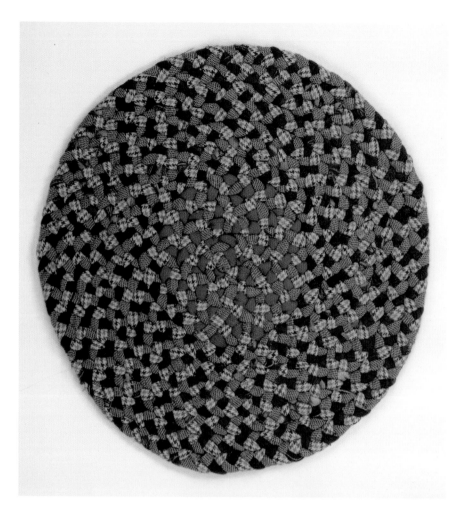

Fabrics for Tiny Braids

Although a thin, shirt-weight or light skirt-weight wool may be used, wool is not as important for tiny braids because durability is not as critical. Other fabrics such as rayon, cotton, velvet, silk, and polyester can be used successfully, and recycled garments are a good source for these fabrics. Although pre-pressing of folds is not necessary, often non-wool fabric is more wrinkled, and pressing the strips flat can make folding easier.

As with wool braiding, the goal is a pleasing braid with equal-size loops, so widths of strips may need to be varied if one fabric is thicker than the other two. New wool fabric is often left unwashed, since thin fabric is the goal, and thickening and felting is not desired.

Small Green Table Mat, Dianne Tobias. 9" diameter. 2008.
Made from twill, polyester, and rayon fabric cut into 1" strips. Used as table mat under potted plant.

Round Table Mat, Dianne Tobias. 15.5" diameter. 2008.
Photographed by Mike Trask
Tiny braids made from fine wool and non-wool cut into 1" strips. Note how the flecks of color complement the richness of the table and bowl.

BRAIDING TINY STRIPS

Most braiding techniques are the same when working with narrower strips and making tiny braids; it is just harder to manipulate the smaller folds. Braid-Aids® and Vari-Folders® do not fold such a narrow strip, so finger folding is necessary. Tapering, increasing, braided designs, and borders are all possible with narrow strips. All shapes discussed in this book can be made with tiny braids.

As stated above, braided narrow strips often have raw edges on the back or reverse side. This is rarely a problem for a table mat or runner; however, for baskets, the raw edges may be visible on the inside. If the raw edges are a problem, the basket may be lined with a complementary fabric to hide the inside braids.

The Enclosed End Start and Enclosed End Butt are successful with most fabrics used for tiny braids, but occasionally a thin fabric frays so much that it is difficult to turn the ends for the Start and Butt without tearing. If this is the case, fold the long edges inward as for the first fold of braiding, then fold the top edge 1/4" down; make the final lengthwise fold and stitch in place with a few whip stitches to secure. Perform all other aspects of the Start and Butt as usual.

SUPPLIES FOR TINY BRAIDS

There are a couple of differences in the supplies used for tiny braids. The larger varieties of lacing thread, such as #7, #8, or #9 cotton splicing thread or linen, are difficult to hide between loops. Sewing thread is too thin and not strong enough to use as lacing thread. A vintage button and carpet thread works best because it is heavier than the current variety of either button or upholstery thread. This thread can be found in some long-forgotten sewing chests or thrift stores. If unavailable, use heavy button thread as it is better than sewing thread. Do not use cotton crochet cording, as it will stretch.

The traditional braidkin lacing needle is too broad to easily slip between the loops of a tiny braid. A blunt-tipped tapestry needle or using the eye end of a broader sewing needle works well for lacing tiny loops. Thread should be laced between loops and pulled snugly, as with traditional braids.

Examples of tiny braided objects are shown in this chapter as well as in the Gallery, Chapter 14.

Table Mats and Table Runners

Braided table mats can add a decorative, interesting touch to a formal dining table or an informal coffee table, or under a potted plant. Although these items may be made with larger, more traditionally sized braids, the larger braids do not give the elegant and delicate look that tiny braids provide in these pieces and do not lay as flat. Although braided rounds are most practical as table mats, any shape may be made for this use; ovals and rectangles are especially attractive. Bordering a table mat with butted and/or fancy borders, especially open, lacy borders as described in Chapter 8, is particularly striking as the table surface shows through the braided border.

Table runners are a variation of mats, longer and often oval, rectangular or multi-circle in shape. The larger size of table runners offers more opportunities for introducing hooking into the design, as either hooked centers with tiny braid borders, or as separate hooked insets that are framed by braids. As with mats, runners can have interesting fancy borders and be made with fabrics usually not used in rugs, e.g., velvet. See Chapter 8, Bordering Challenging Shapes, for a discussion of multi-circle runners.

Colonial Table Runner, Kris McDermet. 11" x 30". 2008. *Photographed by Laurie Indenbaum, hooked rug design by Cherylyn Brubaker.*
Combination piece with hooked center and braided border, used as a rectangular table runner.

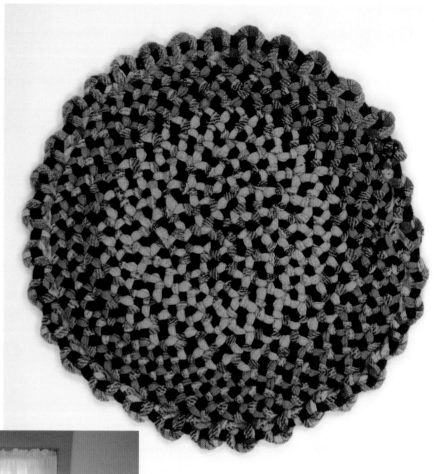

Heathered Tiny Braid Table Mat, Dianne Tobias. 14.5" diameter. 2009.
Note ribbon effect of brown in Fancy Border.

Velvet table runner with openwork fancy border.

Chair Pads

Chair pads are another example of an Off the Floor item that can be braided, hooked, or both. They are especially adaptable to combination pieces made with a hooked center and a braided border. Techniques, described elsewhere in this book for making a round braided center with a hooked border and ending with an additional braided border, can be used to make a finished chair pad of 15" – 17" diameter. There are detailed instructions in Chapter 12 for a Chair Pad composed of a braided center, hooked wreath border, ending with straight braid and fancy border as well as examples of chair pads in the Gallery, Chapter 14.

Bird with Berries Chair Pad, Kris McDermet. 13" diameter. 2006. *Photographed by Laurie Indenbaum* Hooked center, braided border used as chair pad. Note how use of complementary colors integrates the braiding and hooking.

Baskets

Braided baskets are an attractive use of the braided techniques discussed in this book. Baskets may have shapes for their bottoms that are circular, oval, rectangular, or square. They may be made with larger or with tiny braids, and with a variety of fabrics and fabric weights. They may have handles, be smooth-edged, or use fancy borders for the final row on top. Braiding with 2 strands of one fabric and a contrasting strand of another can produce interesting designs. They can be used as true baskets for holding items, or decoratively as for holding a potted plant. If braided larger, the same techniques for baskets can be made and used as tote bags.

Hooking can also be an attractive addition to baskets. Baskets can have hooked shapes inlaid around the sides of the basket, or decorative hooked pockets.

Group of Baskets, Dianne Tobias. 2008, 2009.
Tiny braids, 1-1.5" strips. Note design effect in green basket from using 2 green and 1 tweed strand and baskets show variations in finishing: handle, fancy border and fringed ends.

CONTINUOUS VS. BUTTED BASKETS

Most baskets and bags are made with a continuous braid rather than butted. While continuous braided baskets are easier and faster to complete, there are 2 slight disadvantages:

• Any braided designs that are introduced have a stair-step effect at the row change site; and

• The top row of the basket may appear asymmetric because one side is slightly higher than the other.

Baskets and bags that are butted on the sides take more time, but color changes are easier, design opportunities are unlimited, and the top edge is smooth and even. Additionally, hooked inserts are easier to attach to straight braided rows which have been butted, because the rows are even horizontally.

Black and Tweed Basket, Dianne Tobias. 8" x 4". 2007.
Continuous braided basket with fringed ends. Note designs made by using two strands black and one tweed.

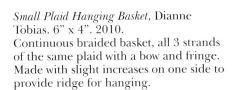

Small Plaid Hanging Basket, Dianne Tobias. 6" x 4". 2010.
Continuous braided basket, all 3 strands of the same plaid with a bow and fringe. Made with slight increases on one side to provide ridge for hanging.

Green Plaid Basket, Dianne Tobias. 6" x 2.5". 2007.
Continuous braided basket with fringed ends.

Butted Basket, Dianne Tobias.
6" x 3". 2010.

Small Oval Basket, Dianne Tobias.
8.5" x 3". 2007.
Continuous braided oval basket
with fringe.

Small Orange/Brown Basket, Dianne
Tobias. 2.5" x 4". 2008.
Small continuous, cylindrical basket
used for pens and pencils.

A nice variation is a continuous braided flat bottom with butted rows on the sides. The continuous braided bottom is tapered on the last row before the sides. The basket's side rows are butted as enclosed rows and then laced onto the basket, or braided and laced onto the basket, then butted. In each case, the number of loops remain the same for each row of braiding, because there are no increases.

Baskets and tote bags use the same basic instructions for braiding and lacing. In Projects, Chapter 12, there are detailed instructions for making a tote bag with an embellished hooked pocket.

Pink and White Basket, Picket Fence Border, Dianne Tobias. 7" x 4". 2009. Continuous braided bottom and butted sides ending with a fancy border.

Brown and Beige Basket, Dianne Tobias. 5" x 3". 2009. Continuous braided bottom and butted sides ending with a fancy border. Note the band of all brown fabric sets off border.

INSTRUCTIONS: MAKING A CONTINUOUS BRAIDED BASKET, WITH FRINGED ENDS, WITH OR WITHOUT A HANDLE

1. Design: Choose the desired shape for the basket, most typically a round or oval, although other shapes can be made into baskets as well. Determine the size for the completed project, both height and width. An oval basket is started by calculating the length of the center braid in the same way as with an oval center, see Chapter 6. Choose the fabrics for the basket.

Bottom of oval basket shown above. Note Enclosed End Start and lacing are as for oval center.

2. Braid the Flat Bottom: Make an Enclosed End Start with the 3 strands of chosen fabric. Braid continuously and lace until the desired size of the bottom for the basket has been braided, increasing as necessary to keep the round or oval center laying flat.

Once the bottom has been completed, flip the bottom over so that the back, reverse side is facing upward, and becomes the inside of the basket. As side rows are added, the front of the braid is on the outside of the basket, and the back, reverse side, is on the inside.

3. Shape the Sides: Until now, increases in the loop count have been made frequently to keep the bottom flat, as with any round or oval center. To shape the sides, no further increases are made. The sides will curve upward sharply with the first row that lacks increases.

For a round basket, the location where increases are stopped and the sides are started does not matter. For an oval, it is best to end the increases and begin the sides at the row change site. Continue to braid with no increases until the desired height of the basket is reached.

Straight Sides vs. Flaring: Straight sides are easy to make; each row simply has the same number of loops for each round because there are no increases. A variation is to make the sides slope gradually outward. This flare is accomplished by making a scant number of increases on the sides every few rows so that the sides slant outward. To create more flare in the sides, make more increases. For a steeper slant, make fewer increases. For a round basket, be careful to increase somewhat evenly around the piece so the slant is even; for an oval basket, keep the increases spaced around the curved ends. Some trial and error may be necessary to get the desired look.

ENDING THE BASKET WITH A FRINGE

A simple continuous braided basket can be finished by pulling the ends of the 3 strands through the loops of the braid below, as a fringe. The ends can be cut decoratively with a slant or into a V-shape. The site where the ends emerge can be hidden by a button embellishment, if desired.

Because the braid is continuous, there is a side of the basket that is slightly higher than the rest. To minimize this asymmetry, try to end the basket, and place the fringe, at the location just prior to this highest point. Choosing this location to end the braid helps to even the top row height.

To finish the basket with fringed ends, mark the desired fringe site with a safety pin. Braid 5" beyond the pin, cut the braid straight across, and secure the braid at the fringe site with the pin. Unbraid back to

Christmas Basket, Dianne Tobias. 8" x 4". 2008.
Continuous braided basket. Note the use of two strands of the same fabric.

Simple fringe on green basket. This soft fabric pulled straight through loops nicely without twisting.

the pin, and use a hemostat or pliers to pull the first strand of the braid through the loop of the braid in the prior row below, as if lacing it. Twist the remaining 2 strands once, and pull them through the next 2 loops adjacent to the first pulled strand. Adjust the strands so that the back of the strands face the basket and the fringe lays flat. Trim the fringe to decorative points or any shape desired: diagonal, "V", etc. Adjust the fringe with pliers or a hemostat to achieve a pleasing look.

An alternate look with thicker fabric is not to twist the 2 strands, but to pull each strand through a loop on the prior row and adjust to make a pleasing end. There is no one way to end with a fringe; experimenting with various combinations is key.

ENDING THE BASKET WITH A TAPER AND BUTTED ROW

An alternative method for ending the braids at the top of the basket is to make a taper, exactly as done for a round or oval braided center, and then attach a single butted row. Choose the taper site where the taper is best hidden, usually on the curved sides of an oval basket; on a round basket, place the taper near where the bottom increases stopped and the braids began to climb up the sides. This planning helps to make the top row more level. Attach a butted row as the last row.

ENDING THE BASKET WITH A HANDLE

Some basket shapes clearly require handles, e.g., carryalls. Other, smaller baskets for holding paper clips, pens, dresser items may not need a handle. Handles for baskets are usually of 3 types:
• an Easter basket type handle, going up over the top from one side to another;
• a tote bag handle, with 2 long loops on either side; or
• a casserole handle, which is small and goes outward from the sides.

Handles can either be attached to a basket as a continuous braid or as a separate, butted row that is laced on. When positioning handles, it is necessary to determine the exact centers of each side. For an oval basket, these center sites fall in the centers of the straight sides. For a round basket, the decision is somewhat arbitrary, but the round must be split into two half-circles of equal loop count. Place 2 pins to mark these center locations.

Easter Basket Handle: To make an Easter Basket Handle, braid the basket continuously to the top row. Turn the braid upward with a right angle for the handle by making a triple corner (LLLR). Straight braid the length that looks pleasing when draped over the basket to the other side, and place a safety pin through the braid at this site. Use a needle and matching thread to secure the ends to each other at the pin, and then to the side of the basket. Unbraid back to where the braid has been stitched, and arrange and cut the ends decoratively. This method places the fringed ends at the bottom of the handle. Lace the triple corner securely to the prior row.

End of a tiny braid basket handle, strands pulled through straight for fringe.

An alternative method for making the Easter Basket Handle moves the fringed ends away from the handle. After starting the handle along the top row with a triple corner (LLLR), straight braid a length that looks pleasing when draped over to the other side, then make another triple corner (RRRL) and a couple throws: R, L, and place a safety pin through the braid at this site. Lace both triples securely to the prior row. Pull the fringe through the loops of the top row to make a pleasing fringe. This method provides a strong attachment at both ends of the handle, and distributes the weight more evenly, so this method is preferred if the basket is used to carry heavy objects. A button or another embellishment can be used to hide the ending attractively, as shown in the photo.

Continuous braided orange basket with Easter Basket Handle, triple corners to secure both ends.

Orange basket, button embellishment to hide triple corner.

Caserole Handle: These can be made two ways depending on the weight of the fabric. Either the entire last row can be straight braided, with the handles made simply by leaving an equal number of loops unlaced to the prior row, on opposite sides of the basket. Alternatively a double or triple corner is made at the beginning and end of the short, straight braided handles. When lacing either kind of casserole handle braid onto the prior row, lace normally up until the handle. Then pass the lacing thread through the loops of the prior row until the handle returns to the basket.

The ending strands are finished as described above for baskets without handles, if continuous braided.

Casserole Handle Basket: Top butted row braided in all orange to set it off from the rest of the basket. Orange wool is fairly heavy weight, which made handles stiffer than would result from softer fabric so corners were not made; straight braids used for handles.

Casserole Handle Basket, from the top. Note the continuous braided base, taper, and butted sides.

Tote Bag Handles: Tote bags usually have 2 handles, one on each straight side; however, as shown in photos, a handle can be diagonal depending on what it will be used for. Fringes are ended as described above for baskets, and may be accentuated as part of the bag's design or hidden with a decorative button or embellishment. See Tote Bag Project, Chapter 12, for specific instructions for making a braided bag with hooked pocket.

Pink Bag with Tiny Braid Embellishment, Dianne Tobias. Note diagonal handle.

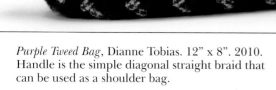

Purple Tweed Bag, Dianne Tobias. 12" x 8". 2010. Handle is the simple diagonal straight braid that can be used as a shoulder bag.

Simple tote bag handles ending with straight braid and pulled strands to make the fringe more prominent and centered on bag.

Embellishments: Baskets and bags can be enhanced by adding embellishments such as buttons or beads. Think of shiny silver buttons studding the outside top row of the basket, or a beaded fringe around the edge. A lining could be added with a complementary color or fabric choice. See Chapter 11, Embellishments, for ideas.

Pink and White Basket, Dianne Tobias.
6" x 3". 2008.
Continuous basket with simple embellishment of beads adds sparkle.

Wall Hangings

Wall hangings are a beautiful and colorful addition to wall art. Over 50% of hooked rugs now are hung instead of being used on the floor. With a braided border attached to the hooked center, these wall hangings can look exotic. If openwork braids are used in the body or the border of the piece, the wall surface color will show through and also become part of the hanging.

The best way to hang a combination rug is to make a pocket on the back of the rug to accommodate a wooden dowel or decorative expandable curtain rod. The ends of the dowel or rod can rest on two nails in the wall. The ends of the dowel should not show, however the decorative ends of the rod can extend out beyond the border of the hanging. The pocket can be made of wool or another strong fabric and sewn to the back of the wall hanging.

If openwork has caused the hanging to be floppy in places, use small brads to anchor the piece to the wall. Place the brads carefully between the loops, so that no fabric is caught. Hammer the brads into the wall, angling downward slightly so that the angle will help hold the braids in place.

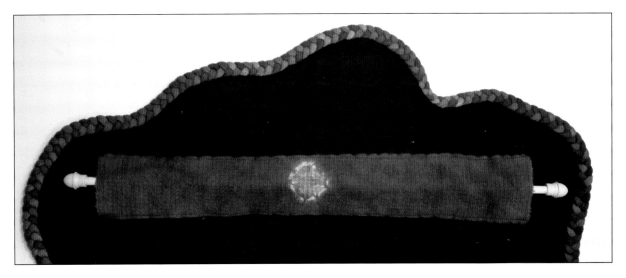

Back of *Making Peace with Snow*, Kris McDermet.
Shows pocket and decorative curtain rod for hanging as wall hanging.

10 Interviews with the Authors

Kris McDermet

Kris McDermet is a hooking and braiding artist, but her talents go beyond thinking of them as two separate arts. She has successfully incorporated hooking and braiding into unique pieces which hang on walls as well as cover floors. She has taught throughout the United States, has presented at a number of shows and was highlighted in the March/April 2009 Rug Hooking magazine. She lives with her husband and two mellow retrievers in Vermont.

Kris was asked by her coauthors to share her perspective of integrating hooking and braiding into art.

Which did you learn first, hooking or braiding?

In 1979, I was new to the Gaithersburg, Maryland, area. I saw an ad for "rug braiding" classes taught by a neighbor, Isabel Clough. I don't think I'd ever seen a braided rug, but was intrigued by the description. I signed up and learned much during the class. I still use many of the techniques Isabel taught in that first class.

Isabel suggested several of us take a rug hooking class from Mary Shepard Burton, but early on I preferred braiding and did not take up hooking seriously for several years. I had first seen hooking in college when my dear friend Vicki's mom gave me a table mat of a hooked starfish made by her mom, Jane Earl.

How do you define a combination piece?

For me, it is combining the two arts of rug braiding and rug hooking, and at times adding embellishments.

What was your first combination rug?

My first try at a combination rug was actually not hooked and braided; it was a needlepoint bargello center with a braided border. The combining of two art forms fascinated me from the beginning, but the bargello center did not hold up well... as my cat at the time thought it was a scratching post. I replaced it with the same simple design, only hooked. I began teaching braiding and didn't take up hooking again until my Mom started hooking and we bought a cutter and a Puritan stand together—quite an investment at the time. Mom loved hooking and inspired me to start again with the result being a wedding celebration rug for my brother Tim and his wife Robin in 2001.

Why do you see braiding and hooking as complementary within a piece?

I think braiding and hooking blend together so well because they are both made of wool, the colors can compliment or provide tension, and the delicacy of the hooking is strengthened visually by the strength of the braid. Both hooking and braiding can be embellished. I like to match the hooking wool with the braiding wool in each rug, often hand dyeing the wool. One or two braids added to the outside border of a hooked piece frame the work and add stability. The same piece of wool looks very different both hooked and braided in the same rug—patterns, plaids, and checks take on interesting visual appeal.

A good technique is to learn a straight braid as a border first and then branch out to going back and forth between hooking and braiding.

A hooked chair pad center is a place to start and then add one row of straight braid and one fancy border. After that, the choices are endless for making all kinds of combinations.

When you design a project, do you decide in advance what will be hooked and what will be braided?

I think of the center first—it can be a braided or hooked center, such as the braided heart in the center of in "Tear of Sadness/Hearts of Peace," or a hooked center as in "Ode to Fibonacci." For me the center is not necessarily the focus but a place to start. I think of the piece as many layers of various borders. I'm always thinking of the next border. What a wonderful challenge this can be!

How did you branch out from using braiding as a simple border around a hooked piece to integration both art forms within the same piece?

My challenge now is to start with both braiding and hooking and switch back and forth between both styles and see what designs develop. My inspiration comes as I am working on a piece and often talking about design and colors with my husband Stewart, my sister Lynn, sister in law Beth, or artist friends Ruth and Karen.

Does your design ever expand as you are completing it?

It almost always expands beyond my original design. I think up my best hooking ideas in the car while looking at nature, listening to the radio, or talking to my husband, Stewart. Then the fun part is deciding how they will be attached with braid.

Which do you prefer doing, braiding or hooking?

I love whichever is the one I'm working on at the time. Hooking is great because it is portable; I use a small frame and can easily hook in the car, on a bus or train, or on an airplane. Braiding is great because of the wool choices and each new row adds such variety and interest due to the colors of the wool and the weave and works up quickly, at least in the beginning rows. It is very satisfying to see a rug grow whether for the floor or wall.

Do you "see" designs in everyday life, e.g., nature, objects, etc.?

Designs are in stories, nature, books, photos, etc. We are surrounded by color combinations, designs, and textures. I need to remind myself to keep looking and paying attention to my surroundings and then write my ideas down.

What is your favorite part of the process of completing a combination piece?

After the center is finished, I love thinking about all the possibilities for various borders and at times make myself stop and not add more!

Do you find your recent pieces are more appropriate for the wall rather than the floor?

We have 2 beautiful cats, Honey and Scooter. They don't use the braid for anything other than sleeping, but do scratch the hooking, so most rugs now go on the wall. Also I think I can see them better when they are higher.

What is the story behind "Making Peace with Snow?"

Vermont is snowy, and cold, and wet, and beautiful. I was trying to appreciate the beauty of winter. My first thought was of falling snowflakes and Snowflake Bently—a Vermonter who documented the differences in flake designs in nature with a special photographic process. I knew they could be both braided and hooked, as I had seen a pattern for a snowflake braided border designed by my friend and coauthor, Christine Manges. I started making snowflakes and stars and, though not jointly present visually in a snowy sky, they are together in my imagination.

At first I thought they would hang like a mobile, or be surrounded by a window and curtain valance, and finally settled on the finished design as the first two were not practical and too heavy. I learned the dyeing technique from Karen Schellinger for the blue wool piece behind the snowflakes—small rocks wrapped inside the wool and tied closed with wire. The nature scene was easy as it is just tree trunks with 9 loop centers inserted. What fun it was to make the rug sparkle with old glass buttons and pearls from a choker bought at a yard sale.

The addition of the deer was last—our house is surrounded by deer though we don't often see them because of our barking dogs. The hardest part was deciding on the background color for the nature scene and my sister-in-law, Beth, found the perfect color dyed by Linda Spear. It was a lesson for me about being open to non-traditional colors, as who has heard of a blue forest?

How do you see the two communities of hooking and braiding? Are there similarities, differences?

So many similarities—we are mainly women who love the art/craft we have chosen, the look of the colors, the feel of the fabric, the designs that are from our hearts or from others, the touch on our feet, the look on the wall, the gathering together or working alone, the process, and the finished work. The differences are in the finished piece, but by combining the two, it is for me the best of both worlds.

What's next?

Like all people who hook and braid, my mind is spinning with new combinations, using more proddy techniques, other types of fabrics, and embellishments. I'd like to hook and braid with silk and have been inspired by the work of Michiko Shin in Japan. It would be interesting to make a rug with the 13 moons of the year, in braid, and hook the stories of each moon. I'm thinking of painting dye on a braided circle and re-dyeing it as the blue moon.

Other ideas are: braid a labyrinth and hook the paths; design a wall rug around Mother Nature's wind; and design hooked and braided tote pockets for my friend and co author, Dianne Tobias, who makes great totes, bags, and baskets.

Christine Manges is a braiding artist who loves experimenting with variations in basic braiding techniques to obtain new designs. She has created many of the borders and designs seen in this book. Christine is the founding president of the Valley Forge Rug Braiding Guild and has coordinated a number of Braid Ins sponsored by the Guild as well as teaching beginning and advanced braiding. She lives with her husband, two children, and 2 rambunctious dogs in Pennsylvania.

Christine was asked by her coauthors to share her perspectives on experimentation within braiding.

How did you first begin to incorporate designs into your rugs?

When I was making my first rug, I saw that the play of light and dark loops could create patterns. I was intrigued by the braided designs. In my second rug, I deliberately put in a diamond pattern at the edge and had a lot of fun doing it.

Do you always plan for designs in your rugs, your projects?

Almost always. I love playing with patterned designs.

How did the idea of borders first interest you?

When I was a kid I went through a phase where I liked crocheting doilies. My favorite part was always the lacy border of the doily. I think I've just always liked putting lacy edges on my projects.

Do you use all the borders you have created? Do they work best on the floor or on the wall?

Some of the borders are clearly too lacy and open to be safe on the floor—a heel could catch. I've used the openwork borders more for chair pads, table top pieces, and for trivets. Some of the other borders are fine for rugs: the solid borders, and the simple picot, for example.

Dianne Tobias' experimentation with bags and baskets has inspired me to plan braiding a tote bag next. I'm thinking of one that has several borders stacked on top of each other to make the sides of the bag. In some of the border instruction, we've tried to show how a "border" can be used not just at the edge of a project, but throughout. I think a tote bag would be a good place to display the inter-linked fancy borders—maybe with a black lining showing through the openwork braids.

What is the difference between an open and a solid border?

An open border has open spaces. A solid border is still "fancy," but maneuvers the braid with double and triple corners to create an interesting, but tightly packed, braid—no open spaces.

How do you make use of contrasting colors in a border?

I like to use contrasting colors. Lights and darks make a rug more visually exciting than a series of medium tones. Contrasting colors can bring out a braided design, or be used to emphasize certain aspects of a fancy border.

Is wool the easiest to use for a braided border; can other fabrics be used?

Certainly you can use other fabrics. Wool is best for its durability, slight elasticity, and stain resistance, but if the project will not end up on the floor, those qualities are less important. It's fun to throw in a little shimmer and sparkle with silks, satins, and even tulle. But, the more twists and turns the braided border has, the more important using wool is to make the project lay flat. Some of the borders require a fair amount of pressing to get them flat. Wool is the easiest fabric to convince—with some steam and a pressing cloth—to become flat.

Can you braid an entire rug with multi-strands?

Multi-strand braids spiral beautifully. If making a multi-strand circle, you might have to start with only 3 strands to make the tight spiral in the first few rows, but you can add strands quickly to make as wide a multi-strand as you'd like. At the end, tapering is just the slow elimination of strands, then a normal taper and butted row.

Why do you love braiding?

Most people who do some sort of textile art also enjoy many other techniques. My Mom was a Home Ec teacher, so I learned to sew, crochet, knit, embroider, and quilt at a young age. There were beautiful braided "rag rugs" around the house from my grandmother, but I never learned to braid rugs while she was alive. It wasn't until I had to repair one of the rugs that I learned to braid. I think the early exposure to many forms of textile creativity made me enjoy just about all crafts to some extent.

But, braiding seems to satisfy me in ways that other arts/crafts don't. I love the geometry of the patterns, the possibility of a dozen more border designs, and

I am endlessly challenged by new shapes and ideas. I like the usefulness of the pieces I make, and the quiet repetition of the task in moments when I need to sit and think. Luckily, I have a very tolerant and supportive husband who doesn't seem to mind my obsession with braiding!

How do you see braiding and hooking in the same rug?

They're fascinating together. I like how the same fabric can be used to create such different effects within the same piece. I want to figure out how to put multi-strand braids around a variety of hooked shapes—maybe with the multi-strand getting thicker and thinner in areas by adding or removing strands. I really enjoyed making the octagonal piece with Fritz Mitnick—she designed and hooked the center, and I made the multi-strand border. It was fun to collaborate like that.

Could you make other combination rugs—could they go on the floor?

I have a few designs with wool embroidery and braiding or multi-strands that I am thinking about. They probably are not suitable for the floor simply because of the wool embroidery. Like penny rugs, that sort of texture is more suitable for table tops or dresser scarves.

Kris McDermet and I have talked about a rug of hooked and braided squares, perhaps united by multi-strand braids as the sashing and frame. I have a lot of fun with multi-strand braiding, and the patterns created are a lot of fun as well.

How did you start braiding?

In 2006 my mother's dog Max ate the edge of a rug my grandmother had braided in about the 1930s or '40s. I had grown up with these rugs around the house, and loved them in the way I loved scrap quilts—all the colors arranged in repeating patterns. I went to thrift stores to find wool that sort of matched, and braided a new outer row for the rug. I had such a fun time doing it, I started my own first rug immediately afterward.

In late 2006 I went to my first braiding conference, which was tremendous fun. I learned so much, too. I met Dianne there, and Kris at a later braid gathering. I encourage everyone to consider a weekend braiding event—you'll be amazed at how much you can learn, and there are wonderfully friendly and entertaining people who are similarly interested in fiber arts. The exchange of ideas at these gatherings really encourages creativity.

Do you feel there is room for being very creative in rug braiding?

Yes! The colors, the contrast, the designs one can incorporate, the shapes, the borders…. And that's just for 2-dimensional designs. Designs with different layers and 3-D shapes (think of a 3-D stargazer lily made out of braids…) haven't been explored much. And then there's all the possibility of mixing techniques (penny rugs, hooking, etc.) that I haven't tried enough of yet.

What part(s) of the braiding process do you like best?

Different things at different times—sometimes I like to just sit quietly and braid, and sometimes I lay awake at night trying to figure out how to make interlocking spirals fit together. I do especially like the challenge of figuring out new shapes and designs.

What is your favorite rug that you have made?

My rug of moss and mauve that reminds me of violets in the woods. It's a simple braided oval, with no border. I made it as a demonstration piece for teaching patterns in classes, and I just love the colors. It contains a lot of recycled wool from my mother's old sewing projects, and it's made with big, comfortable braids.

Do you color plan the entire rug before starting?

No, what an awful idea! I think that would be terribly boring. I start working with a vague idea in mind and just see what happens, what interests me as I go along.

Do you use new or recycled wool?

Both. I started out using exclusively recycled wool, because I liked learning to braid the way my grandmother had, but then I met Loretta Zvarick at her Wool Shop and got lost in the delight of having shelves and shelves of wool to pick from. I still try to use recycled wool in every piece I make: the different weights and extra seams add a little challenge, but it's thrifty and traditional and makes sense.

What is it like to teach a rug braiding class?

It is great fun. I have truly grown so much in my braiding simply from having to organize my thoughts and diagram things out to be able to teach others. When students run into problems, I have to figure out how to handle them. It has been really great to work with such nice people, too—people who are interested in a practical craft like rug making tend to be good folks. Some of my greatest friends are my students. And it's fun to see what they come up with—their ideas often surpass my own, and I find that delightful.

Dianne Tobias

Dianne Tobias is an avid braider and sometimes rug hooker who has been the organizing force behind this book. She has specialized in creating braided baskets, table runners, and tote bags with embellished and decorative flourishes, often using narrower strips to create tiny braids. Her home in California has beautiful braided rugs—a recent 7-circle hallway runner that Dianne created is just stunning. She lives with her husband and an energetic toy fox terrier.

Dianne was asked by her coauthors to share her perspective on braiding and hooking.

Why did you start to braid? Are you self-taught?

I inherited several large oval and round rugs from my great aunt. She was an artist who appreciated fine work and I imagine she had them made. As they began to show wear and I couldn't patch them any longer, I realized how attached I was to them and to their look. I began to search for replacements and quickly found how difficult that would be. My husband then suggested, really challenged, me to learn to braid so that I could replace them. I had always been a knitter and had woven in the past.

I began to look for classes. I live in Northern California and could not find any classes at local universities, art centers, adult education, etc. I started searching the internet and bought a kit from Braid Aid shortly before they went out of business. Without a class or someone to show me what to do, I stumbled along and the rug was somewhat of a disaster. To this day, my husband will not allow me to toss this first effort because it shows how far I have come!

Through the internet I found Loretta Zvarick, a braider from Pennsylvania, who befriended and encouraged me. I visited her for a few hours while back East on a business trip and watched her braid, bought some wool, and she helped me get started on my second rug. She has become a wonderful friend.

Why do you like Braid Ins?

There are fewer braiders in California and on the West Coast. I think braided rugs are less popular out here. Our homes tend to have tile or carpet rather than hardwood floors. Braid Ins offer me the opportunity to share, teach, and learn informally from others. I prefer the less formal get-togethers where there is ample time to work on projects, take a short project-oriented class or two, and bond with others with similar interests. I have made wonderful friends through this type of networking.

Why did you start the National Rugbraiders Database, and what is it?

It was somewhat of a selfish reason, to find more braiders! Several of us thought it would be helpful to network braiders with others in their area. This is especially helpful for new braiders and those who do not live near a guild or Braid In. Braiders send their name, email, city, state, zip and phone (optional) to rugbraidersdatabase@gmail.com and I will enter them into the database and run a query of braiders in their state. I will not share the information with anyone other than braiders looking to network. Currently we have over 250 US and Canadian braiders in the database.

You love tiny braids and making very large rugs—tell us about that?

I enjoy making large round rugs, using the pattern, plaid or color in the wool to create a more random design than with the more traditional, colonial types of rugs. One large 5 foot diameter rug is almost entirely from Pendleton upholstery fabric, which has designs of green and red bears and trees. Of course the strips do not show the design, but since the wool was reversible, I used the two sides of the fabric to bring more red or more green to the rug as it developed. It is one of my favorites.

I prefer not to plan my rugs too carefully, but rather see how they develop and be open to incorporating new fabric and color as I go. I think in this way my rugs might appear more contemporary than the traditional colonial designs. In California we have tile floors which can be warmed literally and figuratively with braided rugs.

I have always preferred narrower strip widths (1.75" or narrower) for my large rugs. I like the finished appearance from the narrower strips. I was at a Braid In in Maine a few years ago where a new braider brought her mother's decade-old unfinished project, fine thin wool in 1-1.25" strips. I was intrigued by the look of the tiny braids. When I returned home, I went to the thrift store and bought some men's wool and polyester trousers and a wrap around skirt in rayon and began what became a potted plant table mat with 1" strips. It was possible to fold and braid this width of strip and lace with carpet thread to produce a handsome, yet utilitarian braided piece and I was "hooked." Since then I have made a number of "tiny braided" objects with narrow strips.

How do you find wool on the West Coast?

I remember the first time I went to a local fabric store and asked for wool. The clerk said, "I think we had one bolt last winter!" We are lucky to have Pendleton Woolen Mills in Oregon, which has been a good source of remnant and bolt wool. I have used the internet and many of the suppliers we list in the book to obtain a good "stash" which I call my palette of fabric. Lately I have been using recycled wool and other fabrics for the tiny braids. My husband maintains "the hunt for wool" is part of my fascination with braiding.

You have learned several butting techniques. Which do you like the best?

After resisting learning any butting technique, I must say I enjoy it now and especially like the finished look it gives to both a large and tiny braid project. I have learned 3 or 4 techniques. My favorite was taught to me by Maryann Hanson, a talented braider from Virginia. She does not like to take credit but since she taught me, I call it hers. It uses a diagonal seam and once you get it, it works every time. I like it because it can easily be done on or off the project. Every time I use it I remember the laughter Maryann, Loretta, and I shared the night she taught us. That might be partly why I like it so much! It does not work for fancy borders as well as the technique we describe in the book, though.

What is your favorite part of braiding?

As I said before, I like making round objects such as rugs, multi-circle runners, baskets more than ovals. One reason is that they are so fluid in the beginning, growing so quickly, and curving in such a flat, pleasing way. So I would say the beginning few rows of a round project are my favorite part, which would include both the braiding and the lacing.

I have been known to slow the braiding when a large project is ending, so as to continue it as long as possible, similar to not wanting a good book to end!

Is rug braiding a creative outlet for you?

Yes, I find it very meditative and creative at the same time. My life has been hectic and braiding and other fiber arts provide a respite for my over-worked left brain. The tactile aspect of the wool is most pleasant for me; that is one reason I do not use Braid-Aids or Vari-Folders; I like the feel of the wool as I fold and braid. My mother was a very talented artist and seamstress. I like to think that my love of braiding has been inherited from her. I am slowly using up her huge inventory of threads in my braiding.

What are your favorite colors and fabrics to use in a rug?

For rugs I prefer wool in a medium weight. My coauthors tease me, but I incorporate black into most of my rugs. I think it adds an elegance to any rug. For other projects, especially in tiny braids, I use wool if it is very fine weight so it is possible to fold and braid when cut into 1" strips, but I have used other fabrics such as rayon and velvet.

Do you use the baskets and bags that you braid? How?

I do use the other braided objects I have made. There are several small and larger baskets around our home and I find baskets make a great gift. I have used smaller tote bags as a sock knitting bag, as they are the perfect size.

You have tried hooking—what do you like about it compared to braiding?

I am a novice at hooking, but I look forward to combining this technique with braiding to achieve interesting results. I have hooked with wool in a combination braided/hooked/braided tiny braid project and have experimented hooking a center for a tiny braided flower, hooking with sock wool, embroidery floss, and synthetic material.

What kind of embellishments do you like to use on bags and baskets?

Continuous braided baskets need to be finished and I have used a variety of techniques to "hide" the ends, with buttons, bows, etc. I have used beads to embellish smaller projects and look forward to experimenting with other forms of embellishment.

Has writing a book about braiding and hooking changed the way you approach a project?

I think more now of exactly what I have done in case I have to document it! I find I am more adventuresome in what I see as possibilities and I enjoy sharing those ideas with my coauthors. I hope our collegial collaboration will continue far into the future.

What's next?

I plan to make a large round hit or miss rug for a new space in my home, using black as the constant strand! I also have plans to hook and braid a combination piece using a classic Arts and Crafts design for my home.

11 Embellishments

Overview

Embellishments are any types of ornamentation that can be added to braided, hooked, or combination pieces to provide dimension, visual interest, height, or sparkle. Embellishments can be added while making a hooked or braided piece, or can be added after the initial work is completed. Since embellishments add height, these pieces are not suitable for the floor but work well for pillows, wall hangings, bags, baskets, and table mats or runners.

This chapter explores the various ways to embellish hooked, braided, and combination pieces.

Techniques Discussed in this Chapter

- Knots
- Proddy
- Stamens
- Felt Balls
- Buttons
- Trinkets and Beads
- Sparkle Fabrics

Grey Anatomy, Kris McDermet. 37" x 34" Wall Hanging. 2010. *Photographed by Laurie Indenbaum* Felted Wool Balls by Jill Cooper. 12 small hearts and six 9-Loop Centers surround the center of the rug that has two borders around the braided heart center. The felted wool balls enhance the designs of the small hooked hearts, forming a berry for the hooked leaves.

Materials that can be used as embellishments: novelty fabric including metals, buttons, sequins, yarn, beads, sewing trims, etc. Shown is a hooked hexagonal center surrounded by a braided border embellished with beads and novelty fabric.

Knots

Knots can be made of any fabric or decorative trim as long as it can be tied. The wider the yarn or wool strip, the larger the knot will be. The knot is added after the hooking has been completed, but before it is padded and backed. It has the look of a French knot but is really a traditional knot, and is quite easy to make and secure to hooking. A small area of exposed rug backing is left unhooked to accommodate the knot.

2. Thread one end of the strip through a tapestry needle or other large-eyed darning needle. After the hooking is finished, pierce the rug backing with the needle at the desired area for the knot, working from front to back.

3. Pull the needle down to the backside and stop pulling when the knot hits the unhooked area on the top. Make sure not to pierce a hooked loop. Tie more knots if a thicker look is desired.

1. Cut 1 or 2 strips of fabric 1/4" x 12" long and tie right over the center, pull tight, then left over center and pull tight in the center of the strip. The knot is now ready to be hooked into the center of a hooked flower, or as another design element used to highlight a hooked area.

4. Take the other end of the knotted strip, on the other side of the knot, and put the needle in the closest hole of the backing to the first hole. Thread the other end of the knotted strip, and drive it down to the back close to where the first strip was sewn through the backing. (not pictured)

5. Turn the hooking over and tie the ends in a knot on the back. Cut the excess tails down to 2". The 2" tails of the two strips will be hidden when the hooking is padded and lined. (not pictured)

Photo shows the completed knot.

Proddy

Prodding wool strips into hooking or braiding adds a three dimensional look by permanently securing extra fabric that appears to sit on top of the flat hooking or braiding. An excellent resource for proddy techniques is by Gene Shepherd[1].

Wreath of Grace, Jan Fruit.
16" x 16" Table Mat.
Photographed by Stephen Jones.
Note 9-Loop Center in the middle of the wreath and prodded leaves surround the flowers.

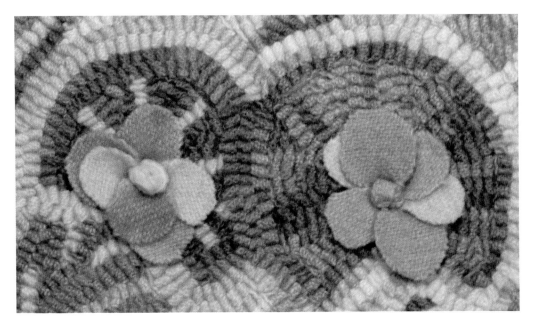

Detail of Prodded Water Lilies in *Peaceful and Quiet Offerings*, Kris McDermet.

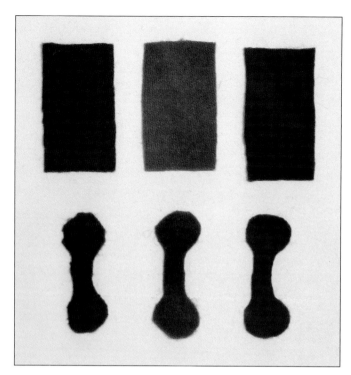

1. Cut 3 pieces of wool 2" x 1". Trim the 3 pieces as pictured. Typically the background leaves—or water or plain background—are hooked first, with a small space left unhooked for the proddy flower. The size of the area left unhooked depends on the size of the proddy flower.

2. With very thin needle nose pliers, a rug hooking hook, or hemostat, pull one short end of the cut piece of wool up through a hole on the front of the rug hooking backing, and the other end up through an adjacent hole. These small shapes are easy to pull up through the small holes of the rug backing.

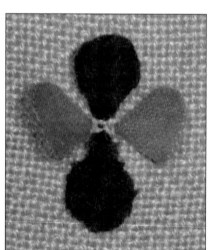

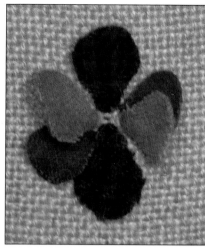

4. Repeat with the third 2" x 1" piece of wool. At this point the proddy ends can be re-trimmed or shortened.

5. The final step for this flower is to make an imitation French knot in the center of the petals using a 1/4" x 12" strip of wool. The petals and French knot can be made of similar or contrasting colors of wool or other fabric. Tie the knot 2 or 3 times depending on the desired thickness. See the instructions for making knots above. Use a hook, pliers, hemostat, tapestry or darning needle to pull the knotted strip ends to the back.

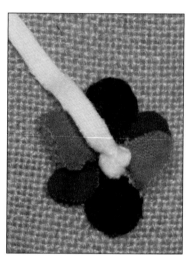

3. Repeat with the second 2" x 1" piece of wool that has been trimmed to look like a petal, but choose slightly different backing holes to pull up the new petal.

6. Tie a square knot on the back with the two ends of the knotted strip. The proddy flower is now finished. This photo shows the flower from the top.

The petals can be trimmed in a variety of shapes to produce different flower designs.

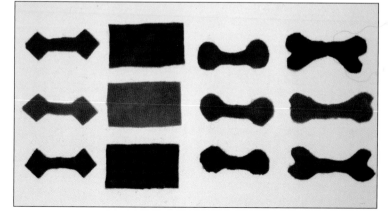

Stamens

Thin strips of wool can be cut like fringe and pulled up through the middle of a 9-Loop Center to look like flower stamens. Instructions to make a 9-Loop Center are described in the Trivet Project in Chapter 12.

Stamens made from
fringed wool

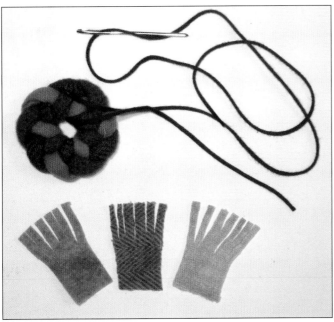

1. Make a 9-Loop Center, lace around the loops, but leave the lacing thread unknotted, with a 1/4" opening in the center. Cut 3 pieces of tightly woven wool into 3/4" x 2" rectangles, then cut the top 3/4" of each piece of wool into 4-6 small fringe strips, as pictured.

3. Finish the back of the 9-Loop Center by cutting a 1.5" square of wool. Trim the ends of the 3 strips on the back, flatten out these ends, and cover them with the square of wool. Whip stitch the wool square to the back of the braided 9-Loop Center.

2. Fold each of the fringed pieces in half lengthwise and pull through the middle of the 9-Loop Center. Pull the lacing thread closed tightly around the fringed wool. The 3/4" strips can be trimmed to the desired length for the stamens.

Felt Balls

Felted Ball Technique[2]: The felted balls are made of wool roving, either dyed or bought pre-dyed. To make approximately 1/2" balls, pull off 7 very small pieces (wisps) of fiber from the roving and make a small pile in your hand. A few fibers of another color can also be added to this pile to make the ball bicolored. Dip your hand holding the fibers in a small bowl of warm soapy water for 10 seconds. Lift out and squeeze slightly, form the fibers into a small ball, and begin rolling from hand to hand, as if making a meatball. The rolling helps the fibers shrink by about half their size. It takes time for the fibers to become firm and each ball can take 5-10 minutes to make. While rolling the ball, it is important to keep both hands moist; dip the ball back in the water for a second if it becomes too dry. Let the balls dry overnight on a protected surface.

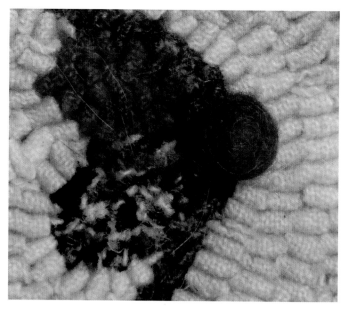

Small Felted Ball on *Grey's Anatomy*, Jill Cooper.

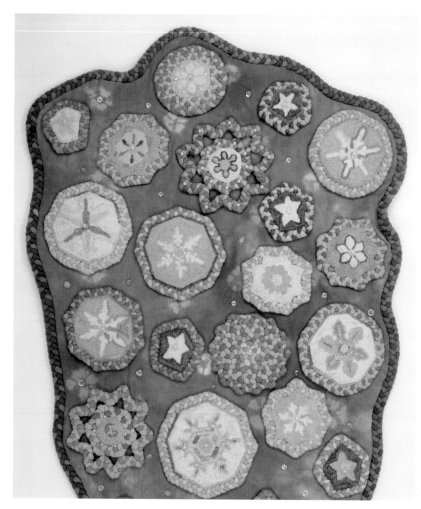

Antique Glass Buttons and Yard Sale Pearls Used as Embellishment on *Making Peace with Snow*

Buttons, Charms and Sequins

Old and new buttons come in all sizes, shapes, and colors. They are made from various types of materials, but usually from plastic, metals, or shells, and can be full of sparkle or quite subtle. Check yard sales, antique stores, and second hand stores for hidden boxes of old buttons, or sewing stores for new buttons.

Buttons must be sewn securely to the hooking or braiding using the braiding lacing, upholstery thread, or clear fishing line. For a hooked piece, the buttons are sewn on after the hooking, but before the piece is padded and lined. With braiding, the button is anchored by sewing through the braids with a sharp needle. A square knot is tied on the underneath side, and the 2" long ends are run through the middle of the braids.

Sequins can be sewn individually to hooking or braiding using clear thread or fishing line. Large beads can be added to baskets and bags. Smaller beads or sequins can be time consuming, however they can set off a finely hooked or tiny braid project. Very small beads can be strung on a wire and interlaced through braided loops.

In hooking, buttons can call attention to interesting features. In braiding, buttons can be used to either hide or accent areas. They can be used to disguise row changes, endings of continuous braided baskets or bags, awkward tapers, or to highlight picot corners or other fancy edges.

Glass Button on
9-Loop Center

Hooking Embellished with Glass Buttons and Pearls in *Making Peace with Snow*, Kris McDermet.

A red plastic poppy button has been sewn in the middle of a 9-Loop Center.

Trinkets and Beads

Trinkets and beads are made of any material and can be sewn onto the completed hooking or braiding. The trinket must have a shank and the bead must have a center hole so that they can be attached with upholstery thread, fishing line, or lacing thread. For hooking, cut 15" of thread and run one end through the shank, or hole, making the ends even. Tie a square knot over the shank or on the bottom of the bead. Taking each end one at a time, thread it through a large-eyed needle, and sew it down through the top of the hooking. Pass the other end downward through a near but not identical hole in the rug backing. Tie the ends in a square knot on the back, and run each end through several inches of the layers of fabric.

An identical technique is used for anchoring a trinket or bead to a braided piece, sewing down through the braid loops with a sharp needle and burying the knotted ends through the braid fabric. Cut off any excess thread.

The small blue trinket heart has a short shank and was sewn to the hooking using fishing line.

Tiny Braid Embellishment for Pink Bag, Dianne Tobias.
Note center flower hooked with small crochet hook and sock yarn, embroidery floss, and novelty yarn. Pink novelty fabric used in braids with wool and beads. Tiny beads threaded on wire and interwoven through a row of braiding.

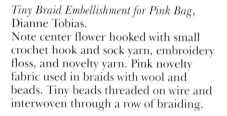

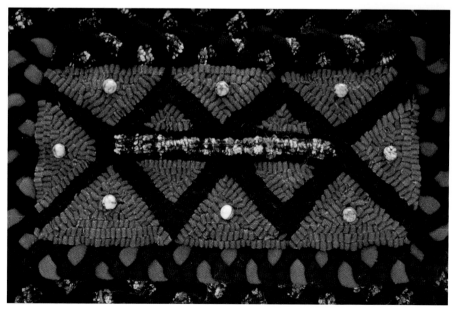

Beads Sewn onto Hooked Pocket.

In the *Calendar Project-Hats*, the artists used a variety of embellishments to enhance the hat designs: ribbon with wire, pearls, beads, bows, fringe, knots, sparkles, and a hat pin. Most of these were added after the squares were hooked but before they were padded and lined.

Artists: Nancy Jewett – January; Kris McDermet – February; Linda Pitkin – March; Fran Oken – April; Hilary Farquhar – May; Karen Kale – June; Dayle Young – July; Bonnie Capowski – August; Dolores Park – September; Lory Doolittle – October; Cheryl Connor – November; Shirley Chaiken – December.

Sparkle Fabrics

Sparkle fabric is usually made with stretch fabric that has been decorated at the mill with small metallic disks resembling sequins. This fabric can be hooked or braided. Because sparkle fabric tends to be thin, it may need a filler piece to make the strip heavy enough to braid. If the braiding strip is 1 3/4" wide then cut or tear the filler wool fabric 3/4" to 1" wide. Some hooking artists only hook with sparkle fabric, which gives a shimmering quality to the entire piece.

Sparkle fabric can add glitter to a hooked and braided table mat.

Roving

Wool roving can provide a shimmering addition for "off the floor" pieces such as wall hangings. Adding roving to a strand while braiding, or a strip when hooking, gives an added color line and added texture

The reader is encouraged to try several embellishments to add spice and sparkle to a project. While most of these embellishments are unsuitable for floor pieces, they can be applied to many other useful and beautiful pieces. Experiment!

[1]Shepherd, Gene. *Prodded Hooking for a Three-Dimensional Effect.* Mechanicsburg, Pennsylvania: Stackpole Books, 2008
[2]Jill Cooper of Atlanta, Georgia, made the 26 half-inch felted balls used as berries for the leaves in *Grey Anatomy.* Jill has given permission to share her instructions.

White roving used in hooked center—note also the use of the beads.

1 2 *Projects*

9-Loop Center Trivet

OVERVIEW

The decorative and functional trivet described in this section can be used under a hot dish or potted plant to protect a dining table. The trivet has been designed to include openwork borders. The item placed on top of the trivet should be small enough to allow the open spaces of the trivet to show. The hanging loop allows the trivet to be hung on a wall hook, adding another way to show the beauty of the braiding with the wall surface showing through the open spaces.

The trivet is made of 5 separate butted rows of braiding, beginning with the 9-Loop Center. If using 1 5/8" strips, the completed trivet will be 11 1/4" point to point.

This trivet was made with instructions given in this chapter.

Techniques Discussed in this Section

• 9-Loop Center

This trivet was made with instructions given in this chapter. Note color choice and using 2 strands of one fabric give this a more dramatic effect.

Prior Techniques Needed for this Project

- Enclosed End Butt
- Triple Corners and Double Corners
- Hand Sewing Techniques

Trio of 9-Loop Centers, Kris McDermet.
Note the variation in design depending on the choice of fabric and colors.

All Butted Basket made with 9-Loop Center, Dianne Tobias.
Note contrast of center design because one strand was different. Also, note rim row was made with complementary but patterned strands of straight braids for a decorative border.

Center of *The Greeting*,
Kris McDermet.

INSTRUCTIONS

The first row of the trivet is an all butted center. The 9-Loop Center, adapted from instructions by Nancy Young[1], is a useful technique for other braided and hooked projects. It may be used as the center for an all butted rug or project, such as the first row of an all butted basket; or as a decorative braided flower or snowflake set into rug hooking. When set into hooking, the 9-Loop Center creates textural contrast between the braiding and hooking.

Note the use of a 9-Loop Center in *The Greeting* as the center of the hooked turtle. Other examples of 9-Loop Centers, either set into hooking or with a second row of added braid, can be seen in photos in the Gallery chapter: *Starburst Lily, The Greeting, Grey Anatomy, Making Peace with Snow.*

9-Loop Center. The color choices of strips for the 9-Loop Center can create a 3-pointed star design if a contrasting color and two background colors are chosen for the 3 strands. The star is created with the contrast strand.

1. Cut 3 strips of wool 1 1/2" x 10". This photo shows one of the 1 1/2" x 10" strips right side up. Cut the other 2 strips identically.

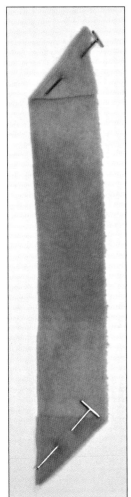

2. Next place the first strip on a flat surface vertically, as shown. Fold the upper left hand corner down and lower right corner up as pictured to make 45 degree angles. Pin the folds.

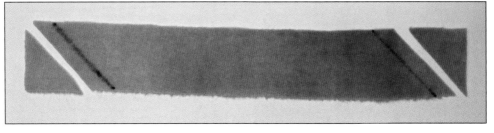

3. Cut along the fold line. Repeat the 45 degree folds and cuts with the 2 other strips. The strips are right side up. Next measure 1/2" down from the diagonal cuts on the right side of each strip, and draw a line here parallel to the cut edge, on both ends of the strip. Use a black or silver waterproof marking pen to mark the diagonal lines, which should all be slanting the same way, as pictured.
Remember that these lines are on the right side of the wool.

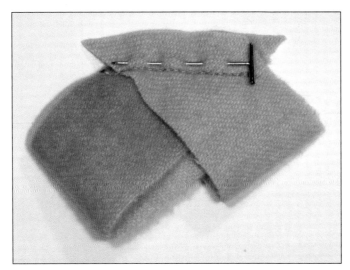

4. Sewing Strips 1 and 2. Put the opposite short ends right sides together and pin along the marked lines, which are on the inside of the joined ends. Using a sewing machine or a hand-sewn backstitch, sew each seam twice 1/8" from the pinned line towards the circle of wool, to secure. Cut off the seam allowances on the marker line. Two strips are sewn using this technique, and the 3rd strip is left not sewn.

5. Fold strips 1 and 2 as for braiding, and hand sew the folds closed with an invisible stitch. The stitches can be 1/2" apart. End the hand stitching with a knot. The two joined, folded, and sewn strips are referred to as "bracelets."

6. Arranging 3 Strips on Start Pin. There are now two bracelets and one long strip. Fold the long strip, with the marking pen line on the right side and facing out, as in regular braiding with the folded edges to the left. Put the long strip on the safety pin first, down two inches from the high point of the diagonal cut. Next put on the 2 bracelets, also with folded and sewn edges facing to the left.

Do not put the pin through either of the two seams. Stagger the diagonal seam lines so they will be distributed around the 9-Loop Center.

8. Sewing the Third Strip. Pull on the ends of the third strip to make them longer, and open out the folds. Put the opposite short ends right sides together and pin along the marked lines which are on the inside of the 2 ends, shown in the photo above.

Using a sewing machine or a hand-sewn backstitch, sew each seam twice 1/8" from the pinned line towards the 9-Loop Center to secure. Cut off the seam allowances on the marker line.

Refold the strip as for braiding, and hand sew the folds closed over the seam using a blind stitch and matching thread.

9. The third strip has been sewn together, folded and hand sewn shut. The center is ready for adjusting.

7. Braid the two bracelets and one long strip, starting with the long strip over the center bracelet, then left over center. Continue braiding until the Start and Finish Ends of the long strip meet to form what will be the ninth loop.

Counting the smooth side of the loops, there are 8 loops plus one set of ends, "coming out" on same side of the ring.

10. Carefully pull the strands back in place, using a hemostat or pliers, so that all the loops are equal in size.

11. Lacing the Center. Cut about 20" of lacing thread, and thread through the eye of a darning needle. Leave a 5" tail of thread unknotted. To begin lacing, run the thread under any loop on the inside of the 9-Loop Center, leading with the eye of the darning needle. Now run the eye of the darning needle under the other eight loops on the inside until back around to the start.

12. Both the start end and the finish end of the lacing thread come out from adjacent loops.

13. Closing the Center: Pull tightly on the two ends of the lacing thread to close the center hole. If the hole does not close completely, run the thread around the 9 inside loops a second time and pull tightly. The re-laced ends should again come out from under adjacent loops.

14. Knotting: Tie a square knot and run the ends of the lacing thread under four loops, hiding the knot and cutting off any excess. (not pictured)

15. Adjust the loops with a hemostat or pliers so that the seams are hidden under loops. The 9-Loop Center is completed.

16. Row 2: Make an Enclosed End Butt Start and braid 24 loops. Only 18 loops are laced around the 9-Loop Center, but the extra 6 loops give room to complete the butt. Complete the butt with an Enclosed End Butt. Lace the second row around the 9-Loop Center, skipping every other loop on Row 2 while lacing, making 9 increases.

17. Row 3: Start with the Enclosed End Butt Start. Braid right, then left, followed by *a triple corner (RRRL), then R, L, R, L* and repeat between ** eight more times. There should be 9 triple picots. Straight braid for another 2" to allow room to complete the butt.
Lace the third row onto the second row, remembering not to lace the crossover loops. For this row all loops are laced onto the base braid. This row can be butted "on" or "off" the piece, meaning that it can be laced on first and then butted, or it can be butted before it is laced onto the base braid.

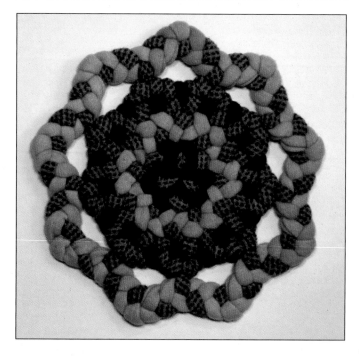

18. Row 4: Enclose the ends for the Enclosed End Butt Start. Make a row of Zigzag braid as follows: braid right, left followed by *a double corner (RRL), then R, L, R, then another double corner (LLR), then L, R, L* and repeat between ** 8 more times. Straight braid 2" beyond the last set of double corners to allow room to complete the butt. Complete the butt and lace onto Row 3 of the trivet. Row 4 creates small open spaces, in the shape of lopsided diamonds, by lacing the second loop of Row 4's inner double corner between the 2nd and 3rd loops of Row 3's triple corners. Then lace through the smooth side loops on Row 3 until reaching the next triple picot, where the next double corner of row 4 is laced between the second and third loops of the triple corner.

19. Row 5 and the final row: Make an Enclosed End Butt Start. If a hanging loop is desired, see the directions below before starting to braid. Braid 3 smooth side loops: R, L, R, L, R, L, followed by a *triple corner (RRRL), and 7 smooth side loops.* Repeat between ** eight more times. End with 5 straight braids plus an extra 2", to allow room to complete the Enclosed End Butt. When identifying the Butt site, be sure to count 7 smooth loops between the 9th triple corner and the first triple corner. The Enclosed End Butt is made on the straight part of the braid.

20. Hanging Loop: Make the hanging loop on the second (middle) loop of one of the triple corners in row 5. Braid the first loop of the triple, identify which strand will make the second loop, and place a clothespin across the braid. Blind stitch about 4 inches of the identified loop strip with matching thread so that the folds are closed, and make the loop. Tack the beginning and ending of the loop together so that it will not untwist. Resume braiding, keeping the loop free until ready to finish.

21. The Finished Hanging Loop: The front of the loop can be embellished with a button or bead, if desired.

1. Young, Nancy. "The Killer Chair Pad." *Braiding INK Newsletter,* Issue #12, July 1995, 7-8.

OVERVIEW

This bag was adapted from a 2008 pattern by Lois Stauffer.

This 16 1/2" by 12" tote bag is braided continuously, including the bottom, sides, and handles. The "briefcase" handles are slanted diagonally to give a unique look, but the option of braiding a more traditional handle is presented. A hooked pocket pattern is given, with instructions for finishing and attaching the pocket. The top of the bag is finished by fringing the ends of the braid through the row below.

Although the dimensions of the bag are given above, if a wider, smaller or higher shape is desired, this is an easy pattern to adapt to different sizes by altering the start instructions and/or altering the fabric weight.

In planning the tote bag design, determine the desired length, width, and height of the bag. The length of the first row of the oval base determines the length of the bag, similar to an oval rug. Note that the finished dimensions and appearance may vary depending on the weight of the wool fabric and how tightly it is braided. Using equal weights of wool is preferred to limit tweaking, and coat weight wool is ideal since it has body and will produce a stiffer braid, however it adds weight that might not be desired in a bag. Thinner fabric can be used with good results; any tendency to tweak on the backside can be hidden with a lining.

Varying colors in the design, introducing new colors or putting patterned designs into the braids can offer interesting variations. In this bag, 2 strands of black are used with one of tweed, a band of solid black is integrated into the body of the bag, and a hooked pocket is added as a functional embellishment and a way of combining both art forms.

> **Prior Techniques Needed for this Project**
>
> - Basic Braiding
> - Basic Hooking
> - Oval Center and Start
> - Shoe-Lacing
> - Finishing a Hooked Edge
> - Hand Sewing Techniques
> - Enclosed End Butt
> - Attaching a Braid to a Hooked Border
> - Triple Picot Border
> - Embellishment

Turquoise Bag with Hooked Pocket, Dianne Tobias and Kris McDermet. 16.5" x 12". 2010. Two colors enhance the wool bag's boldness with briefcase style handles and a hooked pocket with picot border, embellished with beads.

BAG INSTRUCTIONS

1. Start: Using equal weight wool strips, start a center braid as if braiding an oval center, using the Enclosed End Start. Braid for approximately 4" shorter than the desired length of the finished bag, then braid two double corners back-to-back once (RRL, RRL). The length of this first row determines the size of the bag's base. The pictured bag was braided with 2" strips of coat weight wool for 12" before making double corners.

2. First Row: Continue braiding until the number of loops is equal on both sides of the center line. Braid a double corner (RRL), a right and left, another double corner (RRL), then braid approximately 6" beyond the length of the Start. Lace the center braid with the shoe-lacing method, and then around the Enclosed End Start as for an oval center.

3. Bottom of Bag: Braid and lace 4 rows, or as many rows as needed to reach desired final width of bag. The pictured bag was braided for 4 rows. Make increases on the curved ends as for an oval center; suggested increases: 5 increases on end opposite enclosed end start; 6 increases on second curve; 3 on each of next two curves.

4. Up the Sides: Starting at the row change curve after the 4th row near the 2 o'clock location, begin to lace every loop of new braid to the bag base braid, e.g., no more increases are made. Without any increases on the curve, the braid curls upward and creates the straight sides of the bag. Make sure that lacing the straight sides occurs on the outside of the bag, and that the back/reverse side of the braid is the "inside" of the bag.

Make use of the opportunities for incorporating braiding designs on the bag. Using 2 strands of the same color can result in a dramatic look as in the pictured bag, where 2 strands of black are braided with one contrasting strand of tweed.

Continue braiding and lacing. If color changes are made on the straight sides, make them at the same 2 o'clock location where they are made on an oval rug, but carried upward on the straight sides. Because there are no increases, it is relatively easy to match the loops as they are laced.

5. Handles: When the sides have reached 1" short of the desired height of the bag, begin the handle row. Measure side to side along the top edge of the bag and count the loops. Find the center of the last row on both sides of the bag. Count an equal number of loops from the center outward to determine the beginning and ending of the handle, and pin these two loops on both sides of the bag. The pictured bag handles' start and end sites are pinned 7 loops from the center.

This bag has a flat, slightly angled handle, resembling a briefcase handle.

Braid the handle row by straight braiding until the first pin, braid a double corner (LLR), straight braid for 4 smooth loops, make a double corner (RRL), straight braid for 2 smooth loops (RRL), straight braid for 4 smooth loops, double corner (LLR) and continue straight braiding around to the opposite side where the handle positions have been pinned. Repeat the above instructions to make a handle on the second side.

Lace up to first double corner, and reinforce the double by pulling it tight and adjusting any distortion with a hemostat or pliers. Carry the lacing thread through the smooth loops of the top row until the end pin is reached. Lace the ending double of the handle to this site. Lace the braid around to the other handle and repeat.

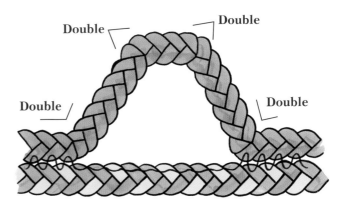

Diagram of Briefcase Handle

To end the braid, each strand may be pulled under loops of the previous row and long tails either cut on the diagonal, snipped in a inverted "V," or tapered. Experiment with several placements of the ending to obtain the desired effect. Depending on color choice and design, accentuate the ending by pulling the tails through on the side of the bag, at the bottom of the second handle, or minimize the ending by pulling the tails at the curved edge of the row at the 2 o'clock location. The ending may be embellished with a button or appliqué if desired.

In this case, because the bag is embellished with a hooked pocket, the top row is braided with all black, and the ending and fringe are minimized so as not to draw attention away from the hooked pocket.

A more rounded handle could be substituted by braiding the handle as described above but omitting the double corners, and making the straight braid of the handle longer. A sharper cornered handle could be made with triple corners instead of double corners, either at the first corner of the handle and/or at the top of the handle.

Note the pictures of other bags in the Gallery chapter, 14, and the Off the Floor chapter, 9, for more ideas of bag designs and handles.

Close Up of Fringe

HOOKED POCKET

A hooked pocket can be placed on the outside of a braided bag to provide extra storage space for a small note pad, comb, or other small flat objects. Take the time to consider the pocket design. Should the pocket be large or small, square or curved; should the colors complement or contrast with the braided bag; what embellishments would be fun to use?

This pocket's geometric design complements the design of the bag, yet stands out due to its different texture. In this example, the pocket is outlined in coordinating braid, with a decorative picot edge border across the top. The tricolored beads pick up the colors in both the bag and the pocket. Other embellishments, such as buttons, could also be used.

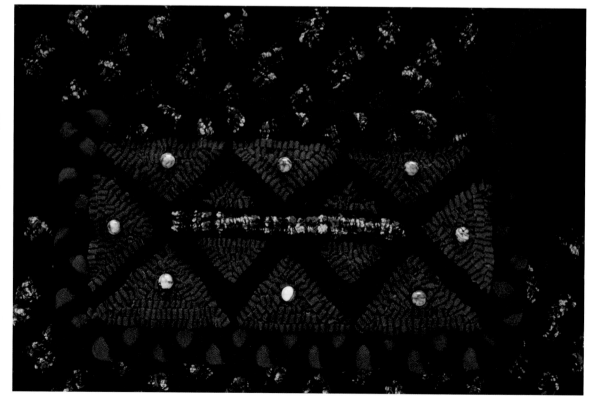

Turquoise bag, hooked pocket detail, Kris McDermet.

POCKET INSTRUCTIONS

1. Hooking: Copy and enlarge the pattern below to the desired size. Transfer it onto rug hooking backing and hook the pattern. Remember that the braided border will enlarge the overall pocket size. The finished pocket on the pictured bag measures 3.5" by 7". The example pocket has been hooked with 3 of the colors that are found in the braided portion of the bag.

Block the hooking if needed and pad and line the hooked pocket.

Bead embellishments are sewn to the padded and lined hooked pocket with clear fishing line used as thread. Tie a square knot on the back and run the ends of the fishing line through several inches in the middle of the layers of the hooked pocket. See Embellishments, Chapter 11 for more specific instructions.

2. Braiding: Choose 3 colors for the braid that will surround the hooked pocket. Enclose the ends as for the Enclosed End Butt Start and begin braiding. Start to sew and lace the braid to the middle of the bottom long side of the pocket.

The braid is sewn and laced up to the first corner, a triple corner is braided (RRRL), then the triple laced to that corner of the hooking. Continue braiding, lacing, and sewing up the side of the pocket, and lace another triple (RRRL) to the upper left corner of the hooked center.

Now braid a picot edge across the top of the pocket. Approximately 4 to 5 picots should fit across the top of the pocket between the left and right triple corners, depending on fabric weight.

At the end of the picots along the top of the pocket, braid and lace another triple (RRRL), resume straight braiding along the side, make and lace another triple (RRRL), and braid until there is a 4" overlap of the Start End. Butt the braid, following the directions for the Enclosed End Butt. Complete lacing the braid around the pocket.

3. Sewing: The pocket is now ready to be sewn onto the front of the bag. Determine the desired position, and pin it on with large safety pins to secure before sewing it in place. Thread a large eyed tapestry needle with a 1 1/2 yard piece of upholstery thread; double the thread and knot the ends. Hide the knot under one loop of the braid, and begin hand sewing the pocket to the bag at one of the upper corners. Sew back and forth between the bag and pocket, by driving the needle through the fabric of the braids with 1/4" hidden stitches, securing them firmly. Sew around the sides and bottom to the other upper corner of the pocket, and tie a very secure final knot. Run the excess thread through several inches of the braid.

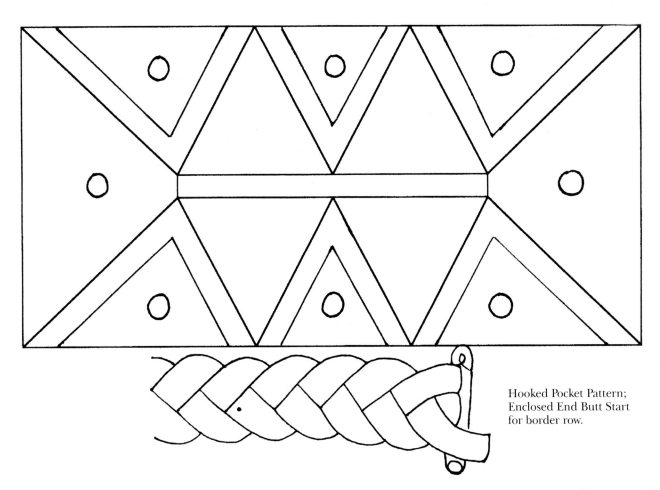

Hooked Pocket Pattern;
Enclosed End Butt Start
for border row.

Many other embellishments and designs are possible. The bag in this photo was embellished with a tiny hooked center, surrounded by tiny braids and beads.

Pink Bag with Tiny Braid Embellishment, Dianne Tobias. 15" x 10". 2010.
Continuous braided bag, 3 stands of same fabric set off the center hooked and braided flower embellishment; simple diagonal handle.

Chair Pad Wreath
Pattern designed by Kris McDermet

OVERVIEW

This project integrates many of the techniques described in this book to create a combination piece that could be used as a chair pad or table mat. Several borders are layered: a hooked wreath is used to border a braided center, followed by a butted straight braided border row and one picot border row. This style of a chair pad or table mat can be enlarged and made into an attractive and functional floor rug, however it should not be in a high traffic area due to the picot border.

INSTRUCTION

Many of the steps described below are pictured in Chapter 4, Hooked Centers.

Prior Techniques Needed for this Project

- Hooking Basics
- Braiding Basics
- Braided Round Center Start
- Lacing
- Tapering
- Enclosed End Butt
- Finishing the Hooked Center
- Attaching a Hooked Border to a Braided Center
- Attaching a Braid to a Hooked Border
- Triple Picot Border
- Tiny Braids
- Hand Sewing Techniques

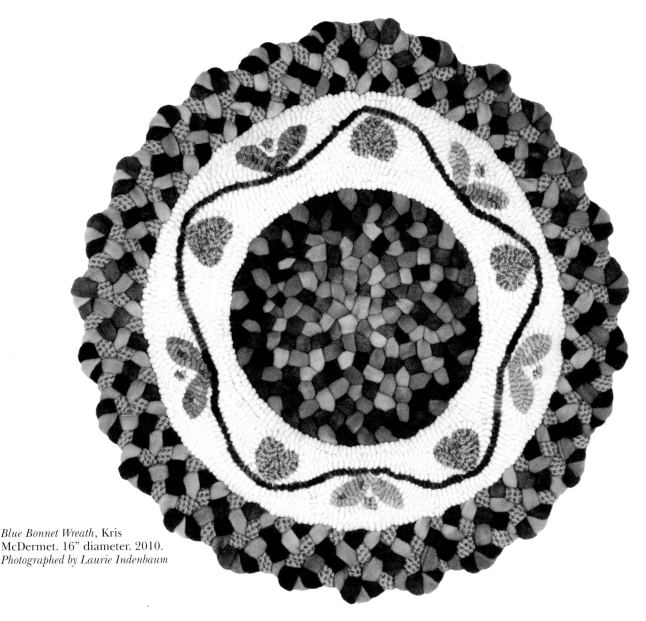

Blue Bonnet Wreath, Kris McDermet. 16" diameter. 2010. *Photographed by Laurie Indenbaum*

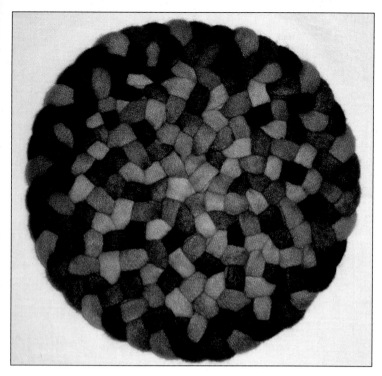

1. Center Round: Prepare 3 strands using the Enclosed End Start. Braid two complete rows and taper on the third row of braid, making sure that the center circle is evenly round. Finish with one butted row using the Enclosed End Butt Start and the Enclosed End Butt to finish the row. The braided center has a total of 4 rows.

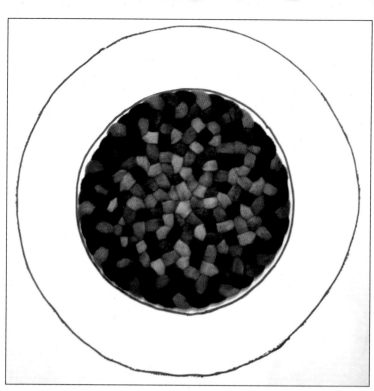

3. Draw the outer border on the newsprint wreath pattern by adding 2", or more depending on the desired hooked wreath size, to the first traced line.

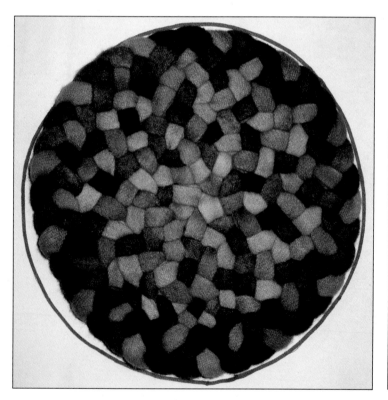

2. To make the hooking pattern, trace the outside border of the finished braided center onto a piece of newsprint paper, making the traced circle line 1/8" larger than the braided center. This extra 1/8" gives some room for attaching the hooked border, as the hooking often expands slightly in size as it is worked.

4. Draw your wreath design to be hooked onto newsprint paper. Transfer the hooked pattern onto the rug backing, by laying a piece of inexpensive netting, e.g., the kind used in bridal gowns, on top of the pattern. Trace the pattern with a waterproof marking pen. The pattern will appear lightly on the netting. Make sure to tape the paper pattern to a hard surface and tape the netting on top so that it does not shift when tracing.

5. Place the netting, with the traced design, on top of the rug backing. Tape it securely to avoid shifting, and retrace the design. The marking pen ink goes through the holes in the netting and transfers the design to the rug backing. Take off the netting and darken the design on the rug backing if the lines are too light.

6. Hook the design and background in the desired colors. It is important that the hooking along the inside border be left free of design. The inner 2 to 3 rows of hooking should be made in circles that outline the inner border in the background color. Block if needed.

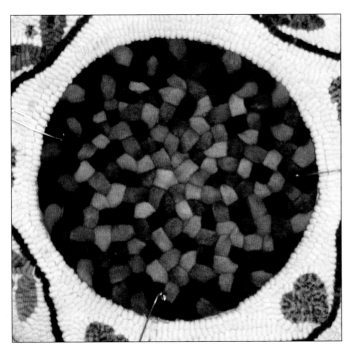

7. Before cutting off the excess rug backing 1-1 1/4" larger than the outside border of the hooking, make sure that the braided center fits inside of the hooked wreath. Adjust the size of the hooking, if needed, by pulling out an extra row of hooked background strips or by adding a row or two on the inner border. Use 3-5 safety pins to hold in place if needed to turn the piece over to check the fit on the back.

8. Cut off the excess rug backing 1-1 1/4" beyond the outside row of hooking. (not pictured)

9. Put the thin wool lining on a table surface, and place the hooked wreath right side down on top of the lining. Cut out the lining the same size as the rug backing. (not pictured)

10. Place the padding on top of the wrong side of the hooked wreath and carefully cut out the padding so that it is 1/8" smaller than the inner and outer border of the hooked wreath. (not pictured)

11. Make the 3 layers in the following order: lining, padding, and hooked wreath right side facing up.

12.(not pictured) Pin the 3 layers together using large safety pins but do not pin close to the outer border, as room is needed to fold the lining over the edge of the padding and to fold the rug backing to the wrong side. The lining and the rug backing that are on the inner part of the wreath will be cut out after sewing the outer border of the wreath. (not pictured)

13.The outer border of the wreath is ready to be sewn before the inner border. Use a whip stitch and matching lining thread. First, finger press a 2" area of the rug backing to the wrong side of the outer border of the hooked wreath. (not pictured)

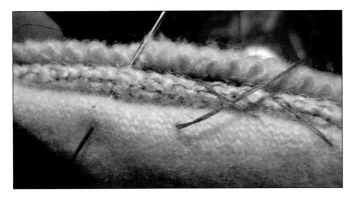

14. Fold the lining around the padding that is opposite the finger pressed 2" area of rug backing, and sew the wool lining to the thin rim of folded rug backing. The lining is pale blue. Fold the next 2" area. Sew and repeat this technique around the outer border. End by tying a knot. These stitches will stabilize the piece before cutting out the inner edges of the 3 layers.

15.(not pictured) When looking at the side of the finished padded and lined hooked piece, three layers are apparent: hooked rug loops standing straight, thin rim of rug backing, and the thin wool lining. The padding should not be seen as the thin wool lining covers it. The braid will cover the 3 layers.

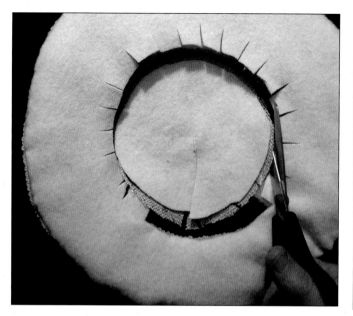

16. Cut out the inner border of the lining and rug backing 1 - 1 1/2" from the inner last row of hooking. The padding has been cut to size and is in place. Make "ease" cuts to within 1/8" to 1/4" of the rug backing, at one inch intervals, around the inner border of the wreath.

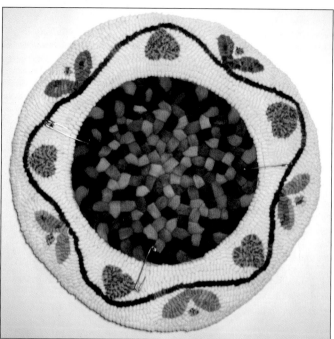

18. Make sure the braided center fits nicely into the wreath space. Use 3 large safety pins to attach the braided center to the inside border of the wreath. This is to stabilize the piece before sewing and lacing them together.

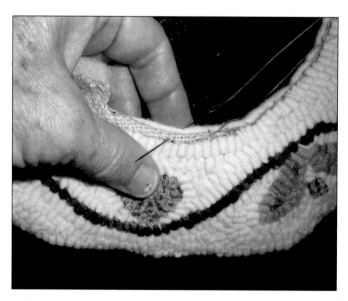

17. Fold and sew this inner border using matching lining thread.

19. Thread a tapestry needle with lacing thread, leaving a 5" tail of thread free when starting to lace, with the eye end of the needle, and lace into any loop on the braided center.

20. Sew 1/2" stitches through the thin rim of the rug backing that is visible on the inner hooked border, alternating with lacing the outer edge of the braided center. Lace only every other braided loop. When the hooked border is fully sewn and laced around the braided center, tie the start end of the lacing to the finish end of the lacing in a square knot. Hide several inches of the lacing thread under loops on the braided center and cut off excess.

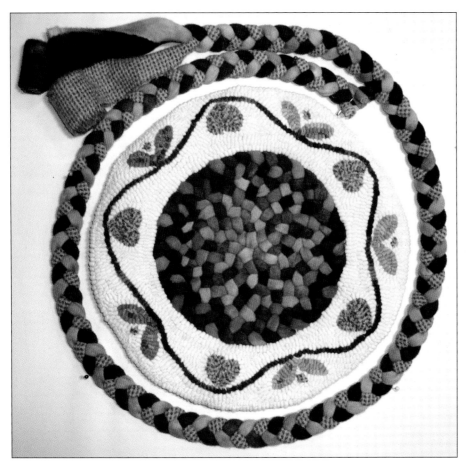

21. Straight Braid Border: Make an Enclosed End Butt Start and braid a length of straight braid that will go around the outside of the hooked wreath approximately 1 1/8 to 1 1/4 times. Begin sewing and lacing this row of braid to the outer edge of the hooked wreath, leaving a 5" tail of lacing thread and 4" tail of braid at the start. Remember to ease in some fullness in the braid so that the entire piece lies flat. If the hooking or braiding cups or buckles, take off the braid and add more fullness by re-sewing and lacing again.

22.(not pictured) Complete the Enclosed End Butt when the braid is sewn and laced around to the start. Finish lacing and sewing the braid to the hooked wreath, tie the start and finish ends of the lacing thread in a square knot, and hide about 4" of the lacing ends under several loops of braid. Cut off the excess.

23. The final braided row in this piece is a Triple Picot braided border, which gives the piece a decorative look. After choosing the colors for this row, make an Enclosed End Butt Start and start braiding using the instructions for the Triple Picot border in Chapter 8. This row will take more fabric because of the triple picot corners. Braid enough to go around the outside of the piece 1 1/4 times. More braiding may be needed as this row is laced onto the straight braid row. (not pictured)

24. Leave a 4" tail of braid and 5" tail of lacing thread and begin to lace the triple picot row to the straight braid row. When laced around to the beginning, choose the butt site carefully. Press the Start and Finish Ends of the braid against the loops where they will be laced, choosing a butt site on the Finish End that will allow enough loops for even lacing after the butt. Complete the Enclosed End Butt. (not pictured)

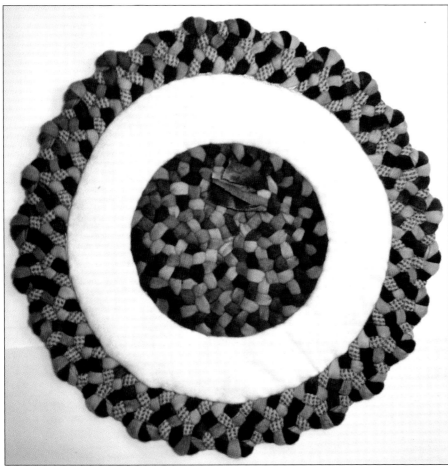

25. Finish lacing and tie the start end and the finish end in a square knot. Hide the ends in the braid before cutting off the excess. Block the two rows of outside braided border, if needed, and dry flat. Turn the chair pad over to observe the neat lining on the back.

13 Hooking and Braiding Tips

Overview

This section includes miscellaneous information and tips on hooking and braiding. It is organized in a Question and Answer format.

Hooking Tips

Can I use different cuts of strips in the same piece?

Yes, different cuts can be used, but be careful about the over-all height if the piece is to be walked on.

Should the hooked loops be of equal height and how high?

Depending on fabric, cut/width of strips, and height of loops, there are several possibilities for different, distinct looks. Some hooking artists prefer even loops and others like a more nubby look; both are "right." More uniformity in loop height is better if the hooked piece will be a rug or chair pad, as it will wear more evenly. It is not as important if the piece is to be hung on the wall. Even loops come with practice.

Can any fabric be used for hooking?

All types of fabric can be used for hooking, but wool is used most frequently. Others include yarn, silk, threads, polyester, fleece, sparkle fabric, plastic, and tee shirts. If it can be cut in strips, it can be hooked! It is best to use fabric of approximately equal thickness and weight in one area of the design, although different weights can be used successfully in the entire piece, especially if it not intended as a rug. Generally more tightly woven fabric is better for hooking.

Do I need a cloth cutter?

Fabric may be cut by hand with scissors, with a rotary cutter, or with a cloth cutter. A cloth cutter is not absolutely necessary, although it does make the cutting process easier and faster.

What hook should I use?

It is best to use a hook appropriate to the weight of the fabric and one that is comfortable to hold. Hooks with large shanks open up the holes in the rug backing to allow for the wider strips to be pulled as loops.

The last loop keeps unhooking, coming out of the backing. What do I do?

Pull loops towards the last hooked loop to avoid pulling out this last loop.

Can I twist the wool underneath the rug backing to hook in a different direction?

Try not to twist the wool strips under the rug backing as these areas will wear differently. This is especially important if the piece will be on the floor.

Can I add braid to a hooked rug or wall hanging that has finished edges? Or add braid to an antique rug?

Yes, a braided border can be added to most any rug, if the outside finished border of the hooked rug/piece is in good condition and if there is an edge that the braid can be attached to. See Chapter 8.

Do I have to braid triple corners at the corners of my first row of braid on a square or rectangle-shaped hooked center?

You can attach a straight braid without corners to a square or rectangular piece, but it will not have the sharp angles of the hooked square corners. The corners will be more rounded, which might be the look that is desired.

Does the piece have to be padded and lined if I have braided tiny braids or if it is a rug that has finished edges?

If the tiny braids are thin and match the thickness of the hooked center, then the center doesn't need to be padded and lined.

Can a rug that has been embellished go on the floor?

Yes it can … if it is in a "no" traffic area or under a table that is free of footsteps and cat claws.

Is it hard to repair a hooked rug?

Yes it can be hard, but most rugs can be repaired, though it can be quite tedious. Good materials, patience, and skills are required.

Is there a right side and a wrong side to the wool strips used in hooking?

This is a matter of personal choice.

Can I combine hand dyed wool and "As Is" wool in the same piece?

These two types of wool can be combined beautifully. Important considerations are color, texture, weight, and desired look.

How many times can I pull out a wool strip and re-use it?

The wool strip can be re-used many times if it is in good condition, e.g., not frayed and retains its linear shape.

My hands and body hurt after rug hooking or braiding for a length of time.

It is very important to take breaks from holding a hook and hooking for hours on end. These hints also apply to braiding. Some things to do, combined with frequent breaks: use good lighting, sit as straight as possible, sit in a comfortable chair, relax, get out of the chair and walk every hour, flex and extend fingers on both hands, lift arm towards the sky and stretch, eat good food, and have good conversations.

Can anyone hook?

YES! Some special equipment is needed but we all have the ability.

But I can't hold onto those thin hooks that look like pencils.

Find a hook with a built up handle. Try as many hooks as possible before purchasing.

Can I attach a row of braid around a hooked center if I don't butt?

The authors suggest The Enclosed End Butt or any of the other butting techniques described in Resources. However, there has been an article written in an older Pearl McGowan newsletter that suggests starting with a taper, attaching the braid to the hooked piece, and ending with a taper parallel to the first taper. The authors have tried this and it does work, but does not look as finished as the butted method. We encourage you to experiment!

Braiding Tips

Can I use wool blends? What are the fabric blends that work best/worst with wool?

• Try to use a blend of at least 70% wool/alpaca/cashmere.

• Beware of spandex. It is very difficult to keep your "tension" on a stretchy wool, ending up with uneven braids.

• Nylon is excellent and blended with wool, it will last forever. But, wool blended with rayon, silk, cotton, etc. will not hold up as well, nor resist stains. Silk with wool, e.g. men's suiting, can produce interesting fabric when washed; some surprises that may or may not be what you want!

Help! Some of the wool I was given has moth holes.

• Moth damage: wash the wool in hot water or dry clean, and do not use the "eaten" areas. Hold up the fabric up to the light to find the holes. You can use everywhere that is not eaten.

• Moth prevention: put moth balls or cedar balls in amongst wool stored in sealed containers or bags; use cedar chests; put cedar chips, from hamster bedding, in sachets.

• **Mold: Can I use moldy wool?** Yes: wash in hot water and dry thoroughly on a heated setting. Often the color will be "off" where the mold was.

Should I tear or cut the wool?

Generally wool tears well and tearing is especially useful when working with plaids, as you will get a true edge.

• You can tear more than one strip by grabbing every other "start" of the strip and tearing all at once. This works for light to medium weight wool. If the wool won't tear or shreds when tearing, use a quilting rotary cutter, strip rotary cutter, or scissors to make strips.

• For bias cut skirts, do not cut on the bias as the strips will stretch too much as you braid them, making your loops uneven.

Do I have to cut the wool perfectly on the straight grain?

No, you can cut the strips a bit off from the straight grain, and still work with them nicely. Just don't cut them too far off the straight or they'll start to stretch.

Are there any tips for preparing fabric for tiny braids?

Thin wool used for tiny braids can often be torn successfully, but non-wool will not. The lengths of fabric needed are less for tiny braid projects so scissors and a ruler are often fine for cutting strips. Non-wool fabric can dull cloth cutter blades more than wool. Most velvets fray excessively when torn. Using a cutter and placing the velvet right side down on the cutter plate seems to work best.

One side of my wool is fuzzy, and the other is crisply woven. Which side should be the "right" side?

Although the fuzzy side has a slight tendency to pill, it is your choice for which side to use.

How do I know if my remaining wool will make it around my rug?

If you can lay the strand around your rug 1 1/2 times, then you have enough wool.

The braidkin is catching on the fabric when I lace.

Every once in awhile a new lacing needle has a rough edge that catches fabric. Use an emery board to file the rough edges.

My oval rugs are egg-shaped. What am I doing wrong?

When making a continuous oval rug, one of the risks is ending up with more increases on one side than the other, creating an "egg" shape. Mark the end with your first double corner with 1 safety pin, and put 2 safety pins on the end with the Enclosed End Start. The first increases per row start with the single pin side. Make as many increases as needed to make this first curve lay flat, marking with flat pins if you want, and keeping the number of increases equal for both quarters of the curve. The second curve with 2 pins should have the same number of increases as the first curve.

A friend and I want to make a continuous rug. How do we join my braid to her braid?

Butt them. You can join group rugs together, especially if they are hit-or-miss, at any place. If you want to put the new braids on "invisibly," then lace the rug until the usual place for a color change, and butt at that site. You may be butting three strands to three completely unmatched strands, but it will work.

How can I hide my seams when I am joining strips?

Seams that show are a wear point and detract from the beauty of your piece. If you hide them, you can use the same thread throughout the project without having to change it for every different colored strip.

• If you want to hide all seams, sew seams as you braid: Lay a straight pin diagonally against the emerging strand on the outer edge, as for a color change, catching one thickness, then cut along the pin, from the 2 o'clock location to the 8 o'clock location for left-opening braiders. Sew on the new strand with a 1/4" seam and trim 1/8".

• If you are braiding from a roll of seamed strips and want to hide your seams, examine where your seam is appearing: If the seam falls at the "top" of your loop, unbraid about 6 - 9 loops and try to braid that strand a bit more loosely. If the seam falls at the "bottom" of your loop, unbraid about 6 - 9 loops and try to braid that strand a bit tighter.

I am increasing correctly. Why is my rug humping up in the center?

• As your rug gets larger and larger, try NOT to fold or roll the rug up. The roll in the rug decreases the tension created by having the rug lay flat while lacing, and can lead to an inadequate number of increases. Instead let it drape over the side of the table. You will be glad you did when you end up with a flat rug. This is especially helpful with large round rugs.

• Resist the temptation to pull your braids after braiding.

I end up with crazy seams that don't make straight strips when I sew on a new wool that's a different strip width.

Center the start of the new strip of wool on top of the end of the old strip; both are right side up. Cut both strands on the diagonal, 2 o'clock to 8 o'clock when the strands are held vertically. Flip the new strip over and match diagonal seams, centering the narrower strip, right sides together. Your sewn strip will be straight!

Can I lace 2 loops at once?

Lacing two loops at once saves time, but it is your preference. Start by lacing a rug-side loop, twist the braidkin to be able to go under the next braid-side loop. As you pull the lacing thread through, use your fingers to guide it into the right valley between loops so that it will be hidden.

Why does my lacing thread show?

• Pull it tighter between your loops.

• Use your fingers to guide your thread in the valleys between loops as you pull the lacing thread. Pull forward, then firmly back. Every 5-8 loops, pull tightly.

• Use darker lacing thread or a smaller thread size. Size 7 is smaller diameter than size 9 in splicing thread.

My strips are not exactly the same width when I use the ruler to cut them. My straight cuts angle a little.

Make a cutting guide with clear plastic laminate found at a fabric store. They usually have the kind with 1/4" ruling and thicker 1" lines. If you usually cut your strips 2", then cut a 2" x 6" piece. Make a 1 1/2" straight cut along the 2" and 4" lines, and then a cut just to the right of it (for right-handed people) that comes to a point at the 1 1/2" mark. You are making skinny right-triangle cut-outs. You can place this guide along the edge of the fabric, and make 3 cuts using the 2, 4, and 6 inch edges, then tear as usual. You can make the cutting guide longer or in different widths if desired.

My braids have tweaks, they are uneven, with one strand skinny and lumpy.

• If using a heavy coat-weight wool, consider cutting or tearing narrower and only folding over once. If the wool is heavy with a good edge, it works fine for one strand.

• Identify the thinner strand, the one that is tweaking more. Wash this fabric in hot water with plenty of agitation. If you have a front load washer, consider washing with jeans or taking to a laundromat since front loading washers don't have an agitator.

• Over-fold your strands, so that you end up with 5 fabric thicknesses instead of the usual 4-fold. See Chapter 5 Braiding Basics for instructions on over-folding.

• Try cutting your thicker wool narrower than the thinner fabric.

• If you've already cut all your strips, use waste wool, e.g., selvedges and narrow cuttings to "fill" the inside of your strip. Lay the waste inside your folded strand, no need to stitch closed. Some prefer to use the same wool in case of wear. See Chapter 5.

• When braiding, concentrate on the "twist" step, using slightly more fabric of the tweaking strand as you bring the strand over the other in the braiding. Try to ease in the extra, plumping up the tweaking strand in the braid so it lays flat.

• Look on the other side to see how you are doing and what works best. We obsess about tweaks, but others *really don't see them!*

The folded edges always show on the 2nd and 3rd loop of my triple corners.

Braid a little beyond your triple corner and adjust the loop with pliers or hemostat to hide the folded edges. DO NOT walk away from your rug and start doing something else before you have made this adjustment: even within 24 hours, wool will "set" into position and be harder to adjust.

My color change several rows back is one (or 2) loops beyond where it should be. How do I fix it without unbraiding all that work?

One or two loops can be covered over with a scrap of the correct color of wool. Cut a piece of wool about the size of a loop plus 1/4" all the way around. Place the wool over the loop and stuff the edges into the crevasses all the way around. Tack in place in several sites to secure. Look on the back to see if any raw edges need to be trimmed.

When I went to butt, somehow I couldn't find where the strands would match correctly. The colors on the sides are in a different order.

You put in an odd number of double corners, or did something similar that changed the strand order.

You can still "miss-butt" the strands, butting strands of different colors together; it usually is not apparent once done. See instructions under "Snowflake Border," Chapter 8.

How do I wash my braided rug?

Wool and especially the way the strips are folded make a braided rug resistant to soil. Most are reversible, which can double the life of the rug. If a small spill has made it dirty, use a spot cleaner. Do not ever use bleach on wool: it will damage the fabric.

If you are desperate and are willing to sacrifice the rug, try washing in the machine or steam clean. Often it will come out fine, but the texture may be altered and there is the chance of bleeding colors, especially reds.

I'm left handed. What techniques will I have to modify?

Braiding is neither left-handed nor right-handed; braid as usual. Whether you have your openings to the left (as in this book) or to the right is irrelevant to your handedness, and purely a matter of preference and who taught you.

Lacing is a little different. For left-handers, you will want to do your lacing left to right. You can either lace by reaching across the rug to where the new braid is being added left to right, or you can flip the rug over and lace on the back and close to you.

I'm a right-opening braider. How can I use this book?

Right-opening braiders use the same techniques, of course, but there are a few differences:

• New strips are added with seams that are 4 o'clock to 10 o'clock, when the strips are held vertically.

• Braiding is the same, but the rug will need to spiral counter-clockwise to hide the folds. The double and triple corners at the first turn of an oval or rectangular rug will need to turn "LLR" or "LLLR."

• Because of the change in spiraling direction, the row-change site, color change site, and taper region will flip from 2 o'clock to 10 o'clock.

• Lacing is usually done on the back, where the spiral will switch directions and become clockwise, so that lacing can occur right to left. NOTE: it is best to lace fancy borders from the front; double and triple corners are tricky when laced on the back.

• If you're having trouble adapting the diagrams for right-opening braids, either hold a mirror to the page and look at the reflected image, or scan the page and hit "mirror image" when you print it.

14 Gallery of Photographs

This gallery of photographs is intended to inspire the reader with "what is possible." Pieces have been chosen that illustrate the beauty of combining hooking and braiding and explore ways of using these techniques for pieces other than rugs. To this end we have included photos showing some of the pieces in their intended settings, along with close-up photos of the pieces themselves.

The authors asked several hooking and braiding artists to contribute photographs of their works that fulfill the objectives of this book. We are grateful for their willingness to share their work with our readers. We sincerely thank each one for the enthusiasm they provided us in our efforts to produce this book for the rug hooking and braiding communities.

Liz Bankowski	Judy Hartzell	Fran Oken
Ken Carpenter	Helen Jeffery	Dolores Park
Bonnie Capowski	Nancy Jewett	Linda Pitkin
Cheryl Connor	Arline Keeling	Lois Stauffer
Shirley Chaiken	Joyce Krueger	Jill Temple
Sue Davies	Jane LeBaron	Debra Weinhold
Anne Eastwood	Sandy Luckery	Leah Wentworth
Hilary Farquhar	Bobbie Mahler	Anna Wilks
Janet Fruit	Donna Mickewich	Nancy Young
Val Galvin	Fritz Mitnick	Dayle Young
Maryann Hanson	Myra Jane Ober	Loretta Zvarick

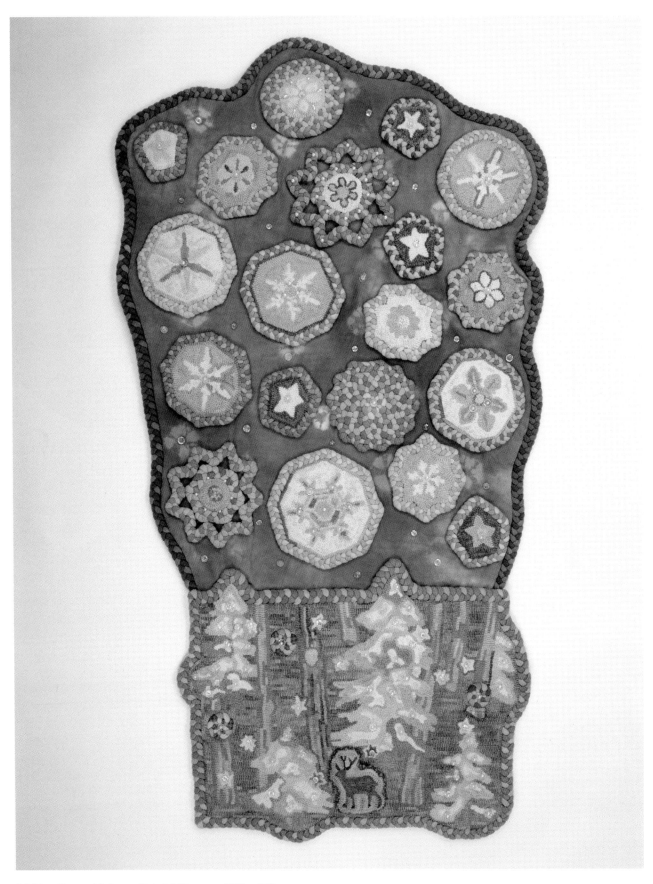

Making Peace with Snow, Kris McDermet. 5'3" x 34"
Combination hooked and braided snowflakes using many braided borders sewn to a dyed piece of wool
sits on top of a snowy scene. 9-Loop Centers, pearls, and glass buttons are used as embellishments.

Crow with Berries, Kris McDermet. 35"
x 39". 2006.
Photographed by Laurie Indenbaum
Hooked pattern inside green line by
Jeanne
Benjamin
Hooked center with braided border.
Note designs in border and how
colors in hooking are complementary
with the braiding.

Starburst Lily, Christine Manges. 6'
point to point. 2010.
Note striking use of design and color,
set off initially with a 9-Loop Center
and ended with a solid black border.

Appliqué Hearts, Kris McDermet. 13" diameter. 2003.
Photographed by Laurie Indenbaum
Hooked center with multiple shapes bordered by braids.

Basket and Mat,
Dianne Tobias.

*7-Circle Multi-circle
Runner*, Dianne
Tobias. 15' x 36".
2009.
*Photographed by Mike
Trask*

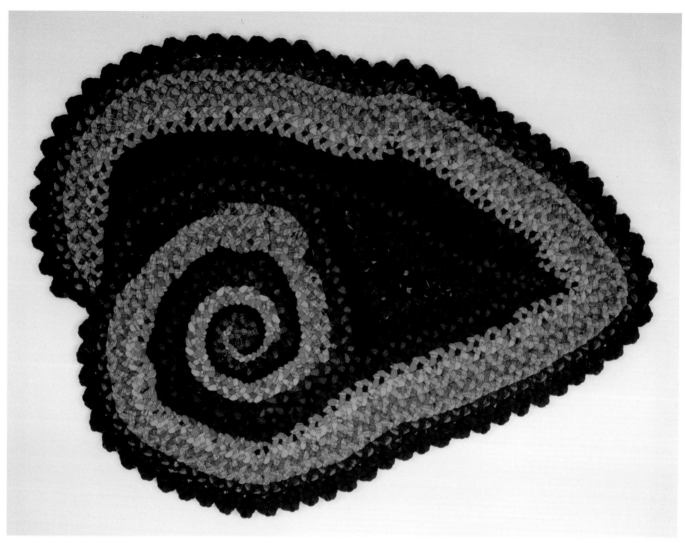

Rex Begonia, Judy Hartzell. 54" x 35". 2008.
All braided in an interesting shape with a fancy border.
Note complementary use of colors.

Poppies, Janet W. Fruit. 8 x 8". 2010.
Photographed by Stephen Jones

Swirl, Anna Wilks. 45"
diameter.
Photographed by Bryon Fair
"Design from a 1936
woman's magazine."
Note use of multi-strand
technique throughout rug.

Reds and Greens, Kris McDermet, wall hanging; Christine Manges, sofa mats; Dianne Tobias, table runner.

Grapes, Maryann Hanson. 36" x 72". 2009.
Photographed by K.P. Carr
Rectangular hooked center with 2 rows
of braided border. "Commercial pattern
antique/unknown, circa 1940."

"Tribute" Quilt Designs, Arline Keeling.
27" x 37". 2008.
Photographed by Tyler Davis
Note integration of braiding and
hooking. Over-dyed with onion skins.

Purples Galore! Lois Stauffer, Heart Rug; Kris McDermet, Chair Pad

BOTHA 1979, Val Galvin.
24" x 44". 2010.
Hooked rectangular center
with braided border set on
top of hooking to give a
framed effect.

Blooms in Braids, Fritz Mitnick,
Hooking; Christine Manges,
Multi-strand Border. 32" point
to point. 2010. Hooking design
adapted from *Three Padulas* by
Laura Pierce.
Combination rug, note
beautifully matched reds in
hooking and braiding.

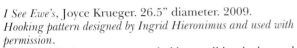

Detail of I See Ewe's, Joyce Krueger.
Detail of round hooked center
and wavy hooked background to
simulate the sheep wool.

I See Ewe's, Joyce Krueger. 26.5" diameter. 2009.
Hooking pattern designed by Ingrid Hieronimus and used with permission.
Large hooked center surrounded by small hooked rounds
attached with braided borders.

Fringe Flower, Judy Hartzell. 56" x 35". 2010.
Braided circles, proddy center, back and forth triple border, and fringe.

Christmas Rug, Bobbi Mahler. 30" diameter. 2008.
Braided center with designs in borders, ending with multi-strand border. Note use of color to set off designs.

Small Braided Bag,
Dianne Tobias.

Turquoise Table Mat, Dianne Tobias.

Hopscotch Wall Hanging, Kris McDermet;
Large and small orange baskets, Dianne
Tobias.

Poinsettia, Val Galvin.
24.5" x 34.5". 2009.
Oval hooked center,
bordered by braids.

Radiant Sun, Christine Manges.
Multiple fancy borders show nicely against a rock wall.

The Greeting, Kris McDermet. 4'11" x 6'2". 2009.
Photographed by Laurie Indenbaum
Aboriginal Morning Greeting; turtle is braided as center with layers of
hooked and braided borders.

Chair Pad, Kris McDermet;
Heart Rug, Lois Stauffer;
Table Mat, Dianne Tobias.

Flower Fringe Rug, Judy
Hartzell; Chair pad,
Christine Manges.

Rust & Teal Tribute, Christine Manges. 31" point to point. 2007. Note 9-Loop Center, all butted octagon allows sharp demarcation of colors.

Multistrand Heart Rug, Christine Manges; Turquoise Chair Pad and Table Mat, Dianne Tobias.

Multicolor Bag with Buttons, Jill Temple. 2009. Note button embellishment, handles, and use of color.

Multicolor Bag with Designs, Donna Mickewich. 15.5" x 10". 2010. Note all butted bag allows for bold designs in bag and sharp color demarcations.

Purple and Green Bag, Debra
Weinhold. 15" x 10". 2010.
Note use of color and
designs.

Group of Braided Bags, Dianne Tobias and Jill Temple.

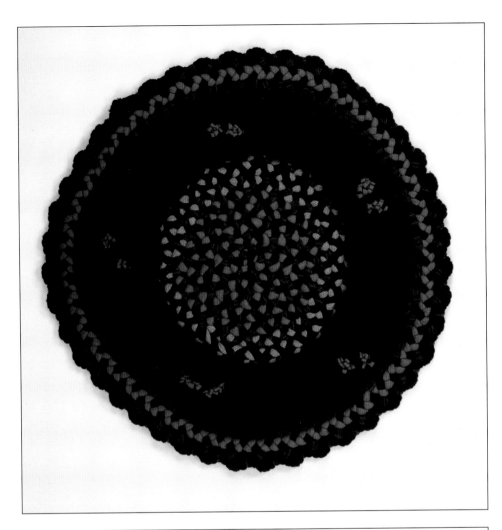

Turquoise Tiny Braid Wreath, Dianne Tobias. 16" diameter. 2009. Tiny braid center with butted end rows, hooked wreath border and final picot fancy border. Use of 1 strand turquoise in straight braid border results in design motif.

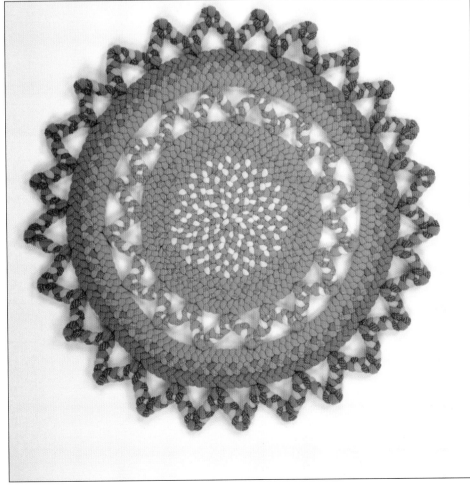

Radiant Sun, Christine Manges. 20" diameter. 2009. Note multiple borders and use of openwork.

Duo of Trivets, Kris McDermet, left; Dianne Tobias, right. 10" diameter. 2010. Note solid color 9-Loop Centers, standard and extended picots, and openwork on last row of braids, tinier braids on right.

Butted Basket with 9-Loop Center, Dianne Tobias.

Blossoms to Fruit, Loretta Zvarick. 33" diameter. 2010.
A rug for the table, wall, or floor. Note use of light colors to set off white.

Wall Hangings, Kris McDermet; Small Table Mat, Dianne Tobias; Larger Mat on Shelf,
Christine Manges.
Note Off the Floor uses for braided and hooked pieces.

Radiant Sun Mat/Chair Pad, Christine Manges; Basket, Dianne Tobias.
Note use of openwork fancy borders.

Bed for Boo, Kris McDermet. 26" x 50". 2004.
Photographed by Laurie Indenbaum
Example of combination rug that uses the pale yellow dots in the outside braid to mimic the stars in the hooked center.

Sage and Shadow, Christine Manges.
16" diameter. 2010.
Striking solid dark and solid pale
picot rows with last row triple/triple
with straight braid in between. Note
3 colors in entire piece.

Chair Pad, Christine
Manges; Small Mat,
Dianne Tobias.

Multistrand Heart, Lois Stauffer.
36" x 29". 2005.
Multistrand border creates
design.

Dos Gallos, Sue Davies. 19" x 19".
2010.
*Photographed by Neil Davies
Commercial pattern designed by Oralia
Crisantes, Las Rancheritas Gonzales,
Mexico. The Rug Hook Project of Agustin
Gonzales, Mexico.*
Note how braided border picks up
colors in hooking.

Lace 11, Kris McDermet. 38" x 37". 2006.
Photographed by Laurie Indenbaum
Use of openwork showing the wall behind.

Table Mat/Chair Pad,
Christine Manges.
Note use of fancy
borders.

Pink Basket, butted sides and Table Mat/Trivet, Dianne Tobias.

Christmas Runner, Dianne Tobias. 34" x 14.5". 2008.
Tiny braids multi-circle.

Tulips, Janet W. Fruit. 10" diameter. 2010.
Photographed by Stephen Jones
Note fancy border and complementary
color design.

Snowmen Wreath, Jane LeBaron. 14.5"
diameter. 2009.
Photographed by Veronica Shelford
Note red in single picot border highlights the
braided center and the red hooked berries.

Shaker Garden, Hilary Farquhar.
23" Octagon. 2010.
Based on detail from a Shaker
Gift drawing.

Blooms in Braids, Fritz
Mitnick, hooking;
Christine Manges, multi-
strand border. Hooking
design adapted from *Three
Padulas* by Laura Pierce.

Blue Wreath Chair Pad, Kris McDermet. 17" diameter. 2009.
Photographed by Laurie Indenbaum

Red Wreath Chair Pad, Kris McDermet. 17" diameter. 2007.
Photographed by Laurie Indenbaum

Lamb Chair Pad, Kris McDermet. 15" diameter. 2006.
Photographed by Laurie Indenbaum

Bird with Berries Chair Pad, Kris McDermet. 13" diameter. 2006.

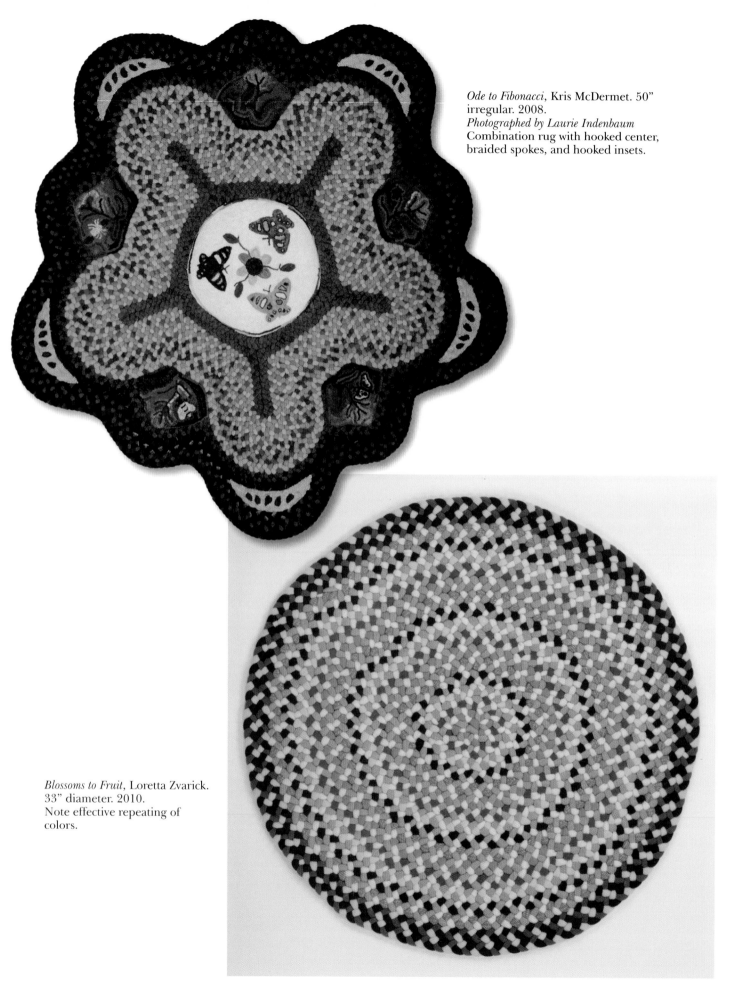

Ode to Fibonacci, Kris McDermet. 50"
irregular. 2008.
Photographed by Laurie Indenbaum
Combination rug with hooked center,
braided spokes, and hooked insets.

Blossoms to Fruit, Loretta Zvarick.
33" diameter. 2010.
Note effective repeating of
colors.

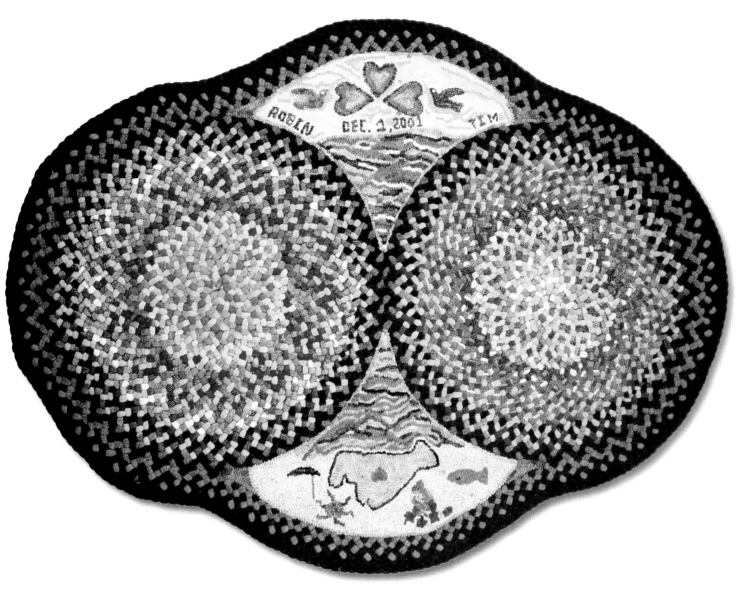

For Robin and Tim Mathiesen, Kris McDermet. 37" x 39". 2001.
Photographed by Laurie Indenbaum
Note how hooked pieces have been used to fill in spaces created by joining braided rounds.

Circle of Rounds, Christine Manges and Dianne Tobias.
Note Chair Pads/Table Mats with a variety of borders.

Grey Anatomy, Kris McDermet. 37" x 34" Wall Hanging. 2010.
Photographed by Laurie Indenbaum
Felted Wool Balls by Jill Cooper. Note 9-Loop Centers and integration of hooking and braiding.

Bittersweet, Kris McDermet. 30" diameter. 2009.
Photographed by Laurie Indenbaum
Painting by Lynn Hoeft.

Rug, Loretta Zvarick; Hooked Footstool,
Beth McDermet; Chair Pad, Christine Manges.

Rex Begonia, Judy Hartzell.

Sock Rug with Knitted Border, Nancy Young.
21" diameter. 2010.
Center braided with dyed tube socks;
knitted border.

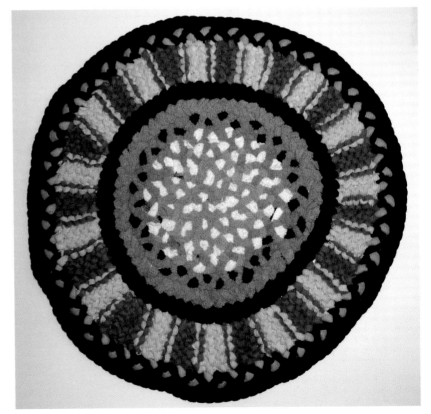

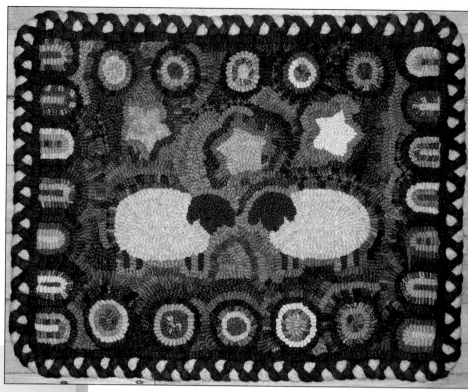

Ewe and Me, Leah Wentworth. 15" x 20".
2009.
Photographed by Ken Carpenter
Hooked rectangular center, braided
border with rounded corners.

Chair Pad, Christine Manges;
Basket, Dianne Tobias.

Pansy Chair Pad, Ken Carpenter. 14" diameter. 2009.
Note how colors complement in hooking and braiding.

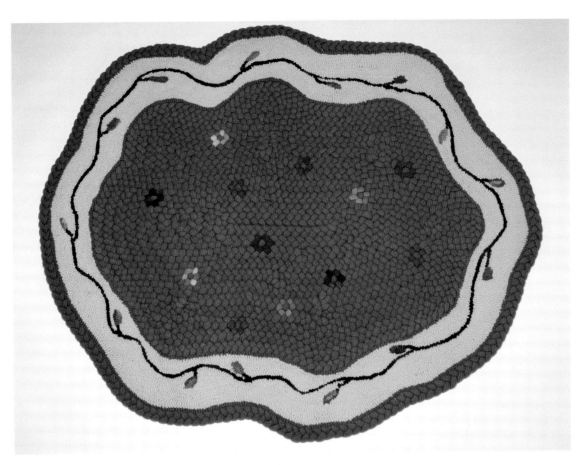

Field of Flowers, Anne Eastwood. 30" x 35.5". 2010.
Photographed by David L. Sutton
Integrated combination piece with braided center and border surrounded by hooking.

Velvet Table Runner, Dianne Tobias. 38" x 17". 2010.
Tiny braids, made with 1" velvet and thin wool.

The Calendar Project-Hats, Nancy Jewett – January; Kris McDermet – February; Linda Pitkin – March; Fran Oken – April; Hilary Farquhar – May; Karen Kale – June; Dayle Young – July; Bonnie Capowski – August; Dolores Park – September; Lory Doolittle – October; Cheryl Connor – November; Shirley Chaiken – December.
Hats are the theme of the 12 months – one row of braid in the same color borders for each square. The squares show a variety of embellishments.

Wreath of Grace, Janet W. Fruit. 16" x 16". 2010.
Photographed by Stephen Jones
Note 9-Loop Center, embellished with rolled wool pink flowers surrounded by green prodded leaves and 2 rows of braid.

Heart with Tulips, Helen Jeffrey. 26" x 27". 2005.
Photographed by Penelope Athey
Hooked heart center with braided border.

Rose Log Cabin, Arline Keeling. 33.5" x 45.5". 2010.
Photographed by Tyler Davis

Pinecones and Needles, Sandy Luckery.
36" diameter. 2007.
Hooking pattern designed by Joan Moshimer
Hooked center, braided borders.

Circles, Maryann Hanson. 96". 2008.
Photographed by K. P. Carr
Many outside borders with designs, open spaces, and connected circles.

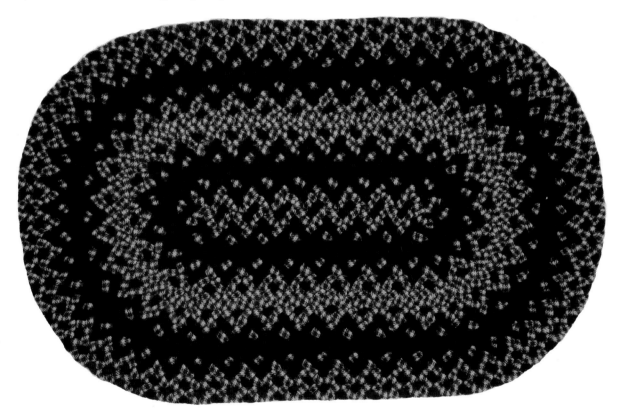

Ric Rac Magic, Myra Jane Ober. 28" x 44". 2010.
Note creation of designs with just 2 fabrics, which are recycled blankets.

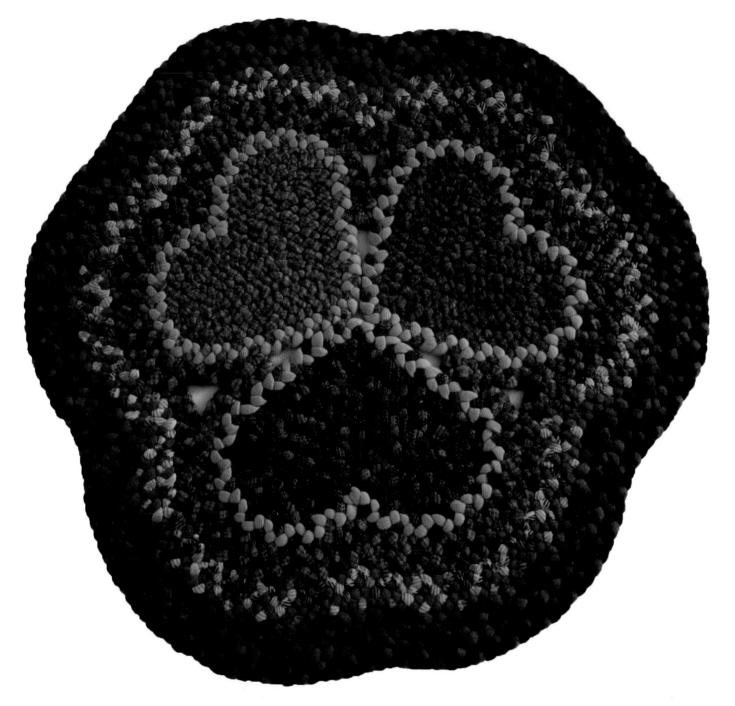

Heart Rug, Bobbie Mahler. 30" diameter. 2006.

Sarah and the River, Elizabeth Bankowski: Hooking; Kris McDermet: Braiding. 27" x 65". 2008.
Photographed by Laurie Indenbaum
Liz hooked the story of her daughter's love of the Connecticut River.

Braided bag with Hooked Pocket, Dianne Tobias/Kris McDermet; Multi-strand Heart Rug, Christine Manges.

Combination Rug
and Chair Pad on sofa
back, Kris McDermet;
Chair Pads on sofa seat,
Christine Manges.

Christmas Basket, Dianne Tobias.
8" x 4". 2008.

Leaves of Grace, Kris McDermet. 47" x 43". 2010.
Taken from The Tree of Life painting by Hannah Cohoon (1788-1864). *Design used with permission from the Hancock Shaker Village, Pittsfield, Massachusetts.*
Note use of 9-Loop Centers as the fruits and flowers on the Tree of Life.

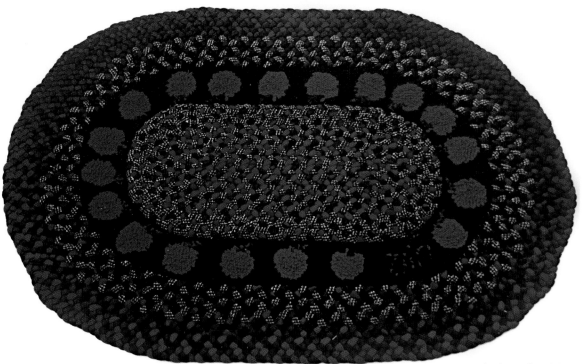

Apples, Val Galvin. 33" x 46". 2010. Note oval shape and complementary colors.

Bed for Boo, Kris McDermet.
26" x 50". 2004.
Photographed by Laurie Indenbaum

20th Anniversary Fireplace Rug, Kris McDermet. 2004.
Photographed by Laurie Indenbaum
Note butted granny square border.

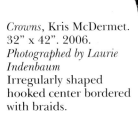

Crowns, Kris McDermet.
32" x 42". 2006.
Photographed by Laurie Indenbaum
Irregularly shaped hooked center bordered with braids.

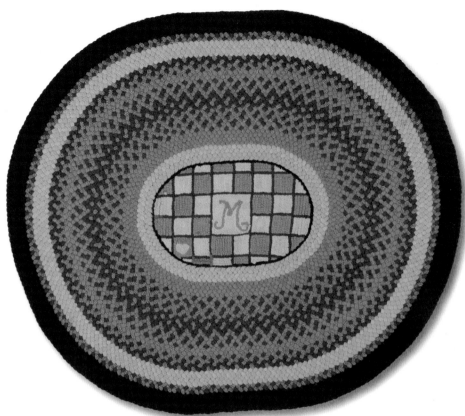

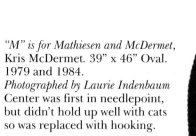

"M" is for Mathiesen and McDermet,
Kris McDermet. 39" x 46" Oval.
1979 and 1984.
Photographed by Laurie Indenbaum
Center was first in needlepoint,
but didn't hold up well with cats
so was replaced with hooking.

Las Esquinas, Kris McDermet. 4'10" x 6'. 2007.
Photographed by Laurie Indenbaum
Note use of hooked and braided borders and pattern in braids. "Las Esquinas" means "corners" in Spanish.

Musical Chairs, Kris McDermet.
24" x 27". 2005.
Photographed by Laurie Indenbaum
Note braided key board.

Combination Rug,
Christine Manges and
Fritz Mitnick; *Baskets,*
Dianne Tobias.

A COLLABORATION BETWEEN FRIENDS

In March of 2009 our friend Beth Bolster organized the Second Annual Thetis Island Braid-In on a small island off the coast of British Columbia. Fourteen of us gathered to talk and work on braiding and hooking, see each other's work, enjoy the atmosphere and beauty of the island. Kris and Dianne heard Beth tell the "dumpster rug" story, below.

Beth gave Kris and Dianne precious pieces cut from The Dumpster Rug. After the pieces hung in the semi-sunny breezes of Vermont and California respectively, they were smelling fresh and clean, and ready to start their new rug life.

Kris decided to make a combination rug, using the old wool hooking as the center, and adding 14 small hooked pieces with a braid connecting them. The result combines several shapes—rectangles, squares, and circles—and was an experiment in old fashioned and contemporary designs, using old and new wool. There are open spaces in the old-and-new rug, four of which have been filled in with braid.

Not only has the beautiful old hooking been resurrected, it has been made more stunning with the additions of braiding and hooking.

Piece of "dumpster rug" before renewal.

A Collaboration Between Friends, Kris McDermet. Unknown date and artist for hooked center. 54" x 37". 2010.
Photographed by Laurie Indenbaum

THE STORY OF THE "DUMPSTER RUG" AS WRITTEN BY BETH BOLSTER OF THETIS ISLAND, CANADA

"My husband and I were traveling with friends in a motorhome across the U.S.A. about thirty years ago. We enjoyed stopping at the antique shops along the way, especially in the Eastern States. It was either in Maine or Vermont, I believe, that we stopped at a little shop, set back from the roadway, a building all by itself. There was a dumpster parked in front by the roadway, obviously used by the shop as it was the only building nearby. As we came out of the shop I glanced at the dumpster and saw a long item spilling out of the dumpster, almost to the ground. It appeared to be some sort of runner carpet and since, even at that time, I was interested in braided and hooked rugs, I "zinged" right in on it. While the others proceeded to our vehicle, I walked over to the dumpster to have a closer look.

The dumpster contained a hand-hooked long runner for a hall or stairway that had obviously been pulled off a floor. There were large holes where the nails or tacks had ripped into the rug, but it had a pretty pattern and was nicely done. I don't think the others were impressed when I actually started pulling it out from its resting place. I could hear my husband saying, "Oh no...we don't have room for THAT...what do you want with THAT...etc. etc."

You can imagine this scene, I'm sure. Over MUCH protesting, we hauled the rug up the ladder in the back of the motorhome and into the pod on top it went.

We hauled that rug, torn up as it was, from the East Coast to the West and hence from the motorhome to our car and then home to Thetis Island. It sat forlornly in a box all these past years, until two years ago, I decided to either put it in another dumpster ... which I couldn't bear to do ... or get it out and somehow revive at least part of it. When I finally got to working with it, I cut out and discarded the badly torn apart sections, saving those pieces I felt could somehow be mended and used.

When we had the Braid-In, I was so happy to share some pieces of it with those who were interested. I mended one of the best of the small rug pieces I had cut, padded and bound the edges, and am using it on the floor as it was intended and enjoy it every time I step on it. I think about the person who put all that labor and hundreds of hours into it, and I wonder, why was it ripped up and not treasured? However, if it hadn't landed in the dumpster, I wouldn't have been able to rescue it, would I?"

Thank you to Beth and her husband Ken, for rescuing a lovely old rug and sharing it with friends far and wide.

15 Appendix

Hand Sewing Techniques

Rug braiding and attaching a braided border to hooking require basic sewing skills. A sewing machine makes sewing faster and can replace most, but not all, tasks that call for hand sewing. This section is designed to provide the reader with several basic hand sewing stitches, but does not replace a more detailed sewing reference.

STITCHES

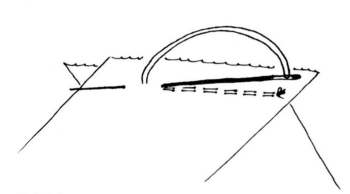

Backstitch.
Insert the needle where the last stitch ended, and come up a half stitch beyond the thread. Sew each seam twice to secure. Cut off the seam allowance, usually 1/8".

Invisible Stitch.
The invisible, or blind, stitch is used to stitch folds shut so that the stitches are not seen. Moving from side to side, catch the upper inner aspect of each fold. Some uses include: Knotted Arches Border, in which a strand has to be sewn then knotted; and closing the bracelets for the 9-Loop Center.

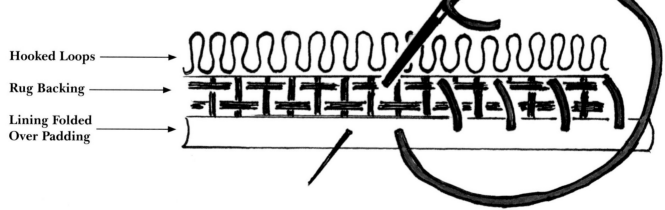

Hooked Loops

Rug Backing

Lining Folded Over Padding

Whip Stitch.
The whip stitch is most commonly used when finishing the edge of hooking, where the rug backing is whip stitched to the lining. Catch a small amount of both fabrics in each stitch.

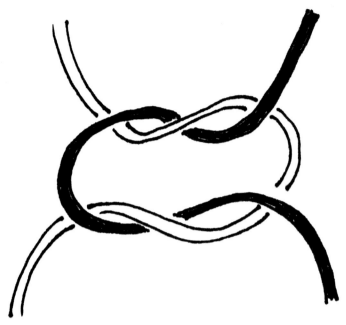

Square Knot.
The sequence for this knot is: right over left and pull tight, then left over right and pull tight. Some uses include: tying the ends of the lacing thread together after lacing a butted braid to a hooked piece, and when tightening the lacing thread around a 9-Loop Center.

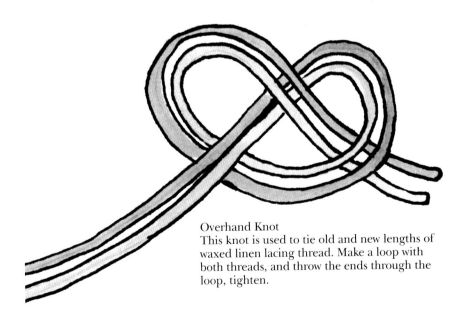

Overhand Knot
This knot is used to tie old and new lengths of waxed linen lacing thread. Make a loop with both threads, and throw the ends through the loop, tighten.

OVERVIEW

The following is a list of suppliers for rug hooking and braiding materials that are familiar to the authors. It is by no means an exhaustive list or necessarily a current list at the time the reader may be reading this. The authors suggest identifying other sources by searching the internet, web auctions, asking guilds and teachers, etc.

Unless otherwise noted, these are suppliers for rug hooking and/or rug braiding supplies and wool fabric.

B. Black and Sons
Los Angeles, CA
800-433-1546
www.bblackandsons.com

Cheapsheep
4709 El Salvador Ct.
Arlington, TX 76017
682-478-3150
www.cheapsheep.com

Country Braid House
Tilton, NH 03276
603-286-4511
www.countrybraidhouse.com

Dorr Mill
PO Box 88
22 Hale St.
Guild, NH 03754
800-846-3677
www.dorrmillstore.com

Anne Eastwood
320 Greenwood Lake Dr.
Venice FL 34292
941-408-9315
Email: idyewool2@comcast.net

Green Mountain Hooked Rugs
2838 Country Rd.
Montpelier, VT 05602
802-223-1333
www.greenmountainhookedrugs.com

Halcyon Yarn
12 School St.
Bath, ME 04530
800-341-0282
www.halcyonyarn.com

Harry M. Fraser Co.
PO Box 939
Stoneville, NC 27048
336-573-9830
www.fraserrugs.com

Heavens to Betsy
46 Route 23
Claverack, NY 12513
518-851-2149
www.heavens-to-betsy.com

Hooked Treasures
6 Iroquois Circle
Brunswick, ME 04011
207-729-1380
www.hookedtreasures.com

In the Wool
P.O. Box 1126
Croix Falls, WI 54024
715-483-1433
www.inthewool.com

Linda Spear
PO Box 313
Madison, NH 03849
603-367-8063

Loretta's Wool Room
271 Eighth Ave.
Collegeville, PA 19426
610-489-6044
www.rugbraidingfabric.com

Donna McKeever
1823 44th ST CT NW
Gig Harbor, WA 98335
253-853-4583
www.rugbraiders.com

Maine Hooked Rugs
6 Naskeag Road
Brooklin, ME 04616-0030
207-359-2822
www.mainehookedrugs.com

Mary Flannigan Woolens
470 7th Ave. #406
NYC, NY 10123
920-589-2221
www.mfwoolens.com

Nancy Jewett Fluff & Peachy Bean Designs
595 Maple St.
Salisbury, VT 05769
802-352-4722
www.fluffpeachybeandesigns.com

The Needleworks
22 Bee Mountain Rd.
New Hartford, CT 06057
860-626-1518
csfitz@snet.net
Hooking Frames

The Oxford Company
445 Swamp Rd.
Cornwall, VT 05753
802-462-2011
www.amyoxford.com
Punch Needle Supplies

Oxford Mill End Store
971 Main St.
Oxford, ME
207-539-4451
www.oxfordmillendstore.com

Ruckman Mill Farm
Susan Feller Designs and Jim's Art

PO Box 409
Augusta, WV 26704
304-496-8073
www.ruckmanmillfarm.com

Rug Art and Supply
The Rug Hook Project, Las Rancheritas
www.rugartsupply.com

Searsport Rug Hooking
11 West Side Dr.
Verona Island, ME 04416
207-249-0891
www.searsportrughooking.com

The Wool Connection
1326 Lincoln Ave.
Pompton Lakes, NJ 07442
973-248-6525
www.thewoolconnection.com

The Wool Studio
Rebecca Erb
328 Tulpehocken Ave.
W. Reading, PA 19611
610-678-5448
www.thewoolstudio.com

Woolrich's Woolen Mill
PO Box 138
Woolrich, PA 17779
800-995-1299 x2327
www.woolrichfabrics.com

Beeline-Townsend Fabric Cutter
Beeline-Townsend
P.O. Box 130
Bettendorf, IA 52722
866-218-1590
www.beeline-townsend.com

OVERVIEW

Networking is a way to find other rug braiding and rug hooking artists, to identify teachers, and to find information about hooking and braiding events. The authors have found that the enjoyment of both art forms is enriched when shared with others who have the same interests. Indeed, that is how we became friends and coauthors. Networking can increase your skills, either by learning from others or by teaching others, which sharpens the teacher's skills. Finding others with like interests can identify new suppliers and patterns. More formal groups can increase the awareness of both art forms by demonstrating at fairs and museums, or working on a group project, perhaps for a charity. The following suggestions are those that are most familiar to the authors based on personal experiences.

BRAID-INS AND HOOK-INS

Braid-Ins and Hook-Ins are happening around the country and are often connected to a braiding or hooking guild. They are usually 2-3 days in length and vary in structure from formal classes and workshops to informal gatherings for working on projects and sharing skills with each other. The following is a partial list of guilds or individuals who currently sponsor these yearly or biyearly gatherings. For more current information, search the internet for Braid-Ins, Hook-Ins, Rug Braiding Guilds, Rug Hooking Guilds, etc.

• Green Mountain Rug Hooking Guild: Hook-In early August in Rutland, Vermont, that is open to guild members. Membership in the guild is open to all. Visit www.gmrhg.org for information on joining.
• Valley Forge Rug Braiding Guild: Braid-In mid-May in eastern Pennsylvania. Visit www.valleyforgerugbraidingguild.com for more information.
• Rocky Mountain Rug Braiding Guild: Braid-In late July in Salida, Colorado. www.RockyMountainRug BraidersGuild.com
• New England Braids: Braid-In held in October in Methuen, Massachusetts. Contact Carol Broadbent at bobbo2@metrocast.net for information. She also hosts smaller gatherings during winter/spring in Alfred, Maine.
• Hunterdon County Rug Artisans Guild: Located in New Jersey and serves surrounding states. Hook-Ins, rug camps, exhibits, and hooking demonstrations. Visit www.hcrag.com.

RUG CAMPS AND CONFERENCES

There are a number of rug camps and schools around the country. Rug camps or schools range from two to nine days, and offer an extensive variety of classes in braiding and hooking. Some provide housing and meals, while others offer classes only and let the student provide their own housing and meals. It is wonderful to gather together with like-minded friends, both old and new. The camps listed below are those that the authors have taught at, attended, or heard about from friends. This is by no means a complete list! Our suggestion is to search the internet for "rug braiding camps" or "rug hooking camps or schools" for more information.

• Hooked in the Mountains Workshops: Vermont www.hookedinthemountainsworkshops.com
• Green Mountain Rug School: Vermont www.greenmountainhookedrugs.com
• Cambria Pines Rug Camp: California www.geneshepherd.com
• Nancy Young's Rug Camps: Maine www.rugbraidingcamp.com
• Sauder Village is an annual rug hooking show with workshops: Ohio www.saudervillage.org
• National Rug Braiders Conference: has been alternating years in Washington www.rugbraiders.com

LOCAL CLASSES

Many communities offer rug hooking and braiding classes as part of city adult education, art centers, and Senior Centers. Some universities also offer classes to community members as part of a college craft center. Other possibilities are private classes and teachers that may be identified through suppliers or word of mouth.

INTERNET SOURCES

The ability to find information about rug hooking and rug braiding has increased over the last 15 years thanks in part to the internet. We suggest using search engines such as Google™ or Bing™ and search for rug hooking and/or rug braiding. You will be amazed at how many sites there are that provide interesting information about these 2 art forms. Also take a look at eBay® for braided and hooked rugs that are antiques, slightly used, or new.

RUGBRAIDERS DATABASE

The Rugbraiders Database lists basic contact information for rug braiders in the US and Canada. Those who sign up can obtain the same information for other braiders in their state or neighboring states to promote networking. Information is not shared outside the database. For more information contact Dianne Tobias at rugbraidersdatabase@gmail.com.

PUBLICATIONS

• *Rug Hooking Magazine* is a wonderful magazine, published 5 times a year and including articles on all aspects of rug hooking and occasionally rug braiding. A free monthly pattern is included, along with informative articles, dyeing instructions, and extensive lists of suppliers, camps, teachers, and guilds. For subscription information visit: www.rughookingonline.com

• Stackpole Publishing (publishers of *Rug Hooking Magazine*) publishes many rug hooking books. Visit www.rughookingonline.com and click on "Books."

• *Rug Braiding INK Newsletter* currently comes out twice annually, and features patterns and techniques in rug braiding. For more information, contact Donna McKeever at donna@rugbraiders.com

INTERNATIONAL ORGANIZATIONS

• The Association of Traditional Hooking Artists (ATHA) is an international Rug Hooking Association to promote the growth of rug hooking. The ATHA newsletter is printed six times a year to inform and educate members. Biennial meetings held every other year in the U.S. in the fall. Visit www.atharugs.com

• The International Group of Rug Hooking Artists (TIGHR) promotes the art, international interaction, exploration of tradition, culture, history of rug making techniques, and education. Visit www.tighr.net

STARTING YOUR OWN GROUP

Talk to rug hooking or rug braiding friends about starting an informal group that can meet at a member's home, a church, an Inn, or at a senior center. Often charging a nominal fee will cover the cost of coffee, heat, and lights. Some groups meet weekly, others bimonthly, or monthly and may range from two hours to all day. Starting groups for rug hookers or rug braiders is a delightful way to share skills within a friendly community. As combination rugs become better known, groups that include all kinds of rug makers will be more popular.

So You Want to Teach?

Teaching can be rewarding and is a good way to promote our art and work. It is important to write your own directions, as copying another teacher's instructions without permission is against copyright laws. Contact senior centers, community centers, and churches if you are interested in teaching a single class, or contact some of the rug hooking or braiding schools or camps if you are interested in teaching in one of those environments.

Write a proposal for a class and be sure to present it with good text and photos so that the school/camp director has a good understanding of your goals. You may decide to sell a kit and other rug hooking or rug braiding supplies or have your students come with their own supplies. As a teacher with a tax I.D. number, you may be able to purchase supplies and receive a teacher discount from your suppliers.

Shows

Rug shows are a way for hooking and braiding artists to gather and show their work for a specific period of time. Shows may be juried or sponsored by a guild or museum. Juried shows require that the rug be submitted for review and meet certain requirements. Open guild shows are often for members only, with some requirements regarding size or when the rug was made.

Smaller shows take place around the country at museums, libraries, and galleries. Some may be juried; others are not. Participating in these shows is a way to display your work and meet other artists who enjoy working with wool and other fibers.

OVERVIEW

As stated, the authors have chosen certain techniques for instruction in this book because they are adaptable to the overall theme of borders and centers. The following resources provide more exhaustive discussions and instructions on various rug hooking and braiding techniques.

RUG HOOKING

Black, Elizabeth. *Hooked on the Wild Side Everything You Need to Know to Hook Realistic Animals.* Mechanicsburg, Pennsylvania: Stackpole Books, 2008.

Halliwell Green, Jane. *Pictorial Hooked Rugs.* Mechanicsburg, Pennsylvania: Stackpole Books, 2009.

Littenberg, Anne-Marie. *Hooked Rug Landscapes.* Mechanicsburg, Pennsylvania: Stackpole Books, 2009.

Oxford, Amy. *Hooked Rugs Today.* Atglen, Pennsylvania: Schiffer Publishing Ltd., 2005

Shepherd, Gene. *The Rug Hooker's Bible The Best from 30 Year's of Jane Olson's Rugger's Roundtable.* Mechanicsburg, Pennsylvania: Stackpole Books, 2005.

RUG BRAIDING

Cox, Verna and Cox, Ken. *Rug Hooking & Braiding Made Easy.* Verona Island, Maine: Cox Enterprises, 2003.

Fisher, Barbara A. and Fitzgerald, Janet. *Braiding with Barbara*tm/Wool Rug Braiding: With a Contemporary Flair.* Atglen, Pennsylvania: Schiffer Publishing Ltd., 2010.

Sturges, Norma, Sturges, Elizabeth J.. *The Braided Rug Book: Creating your Own American Folk Art.* Asheville, North Carolina: Lark Books, 2006.

Young, Nancy. *Braid On: A Manual for Experienced Rug Braiders Who Want More.* Winthrop, Maine: Self Published, 2007

DYEING

Heath, Laurice. *Beautiful Wool-A Hand-Dyer's Guide.* Fredericksburg, Texas: Cabin Ridge Press, 2002.

Lincoln, Maryanne. *Recipes from the dye Kitchen.* Mechanicsburg, Pennsylvania: Stackpole Books, 1999.

Schellinger, Karen. *Dyeing Wool.* Atglen, Pennsylvania: Schiffer Publishing Ltd., 2010.

Index